I0605640

Praise for *The Hypothesis of the Gospels*

How can there be one gospel and yet four Gospels? As Ian N. Mills demonstrates in this engaging survey of the ancient evidence, both Christian and non-Christian, early Christians reacted to the plurality of the Gospels using the intellectual resources available to them. Mills focuses on the ancient literary concept of a *hypothesis*, which straddles the space between story and subject matter, and provocatively claims that gospel literature was to be perceived as competitive. Wide-ranging, thoroughly researched, and utterly up-to-date, *The Hypothesis of the Gospels* is a stimulating entry into the world of ancient gospel production within their Jewish, Greek, and Roman contexts, suitable for students and teachers alike.

—Stephen C. Carlson, associate professor of biblical and early Christian studies, Institute for Religion and Critical Enquiry, Australian Catholic University, and author of *The Gospel Hoax* and *Papias of Hierapolis*

You can read hundreds of books on the Gospels and find little new and nothing groundbreaking. This book is groundbreaking. In a learned, broad-ranging, and compelling study, Mills uncovers the earliest understanding of the Gospels that is, remarkably, unknown to the scholarly world at large.

—Bart D. Ehrman, James A. Gray Distinguished Professor, University of North Carolina at Chapel Hill

Mills's hypothesis about gospel multiplicity is compelling and innovative. This book is as engaging and fun to read as it is learned and thorough. It reframes how we ought to think about the Gospels' relationships to one another, continuing the work of situating Jesus traditions within Hellenistic book culture.

—Nicholas A. Elder, associate professor of New Testament, University of Dubuque Theological Seminary, and author of *Gospel Media: Reading, Writing, and Circulating Jesus Traditions*

In this robust and impressive study, Ian Mills reinvigorates the study of the gospels by revealing how the earliest Christians made sense of their many accounts of the life of Jesus. Canvassing a wide range of ancient evidence, he argues that Christians conceptualized these works as rival and competing texts, all developing and improving upon a common "hypothesis." Smart, deeply researched, and crisply written, this book suggests new ways of integrating classics and early Christian studies. It also cements Mills as one of the most dynamic emerging voices in gospel scholarship today.

—Hugo Méndez, associate professor of religious studies,
University of North Carolina at Chapel Hill

The Hypothesis of the Gospels presents a case so compelling that it will leave readers wondering how they have never seen this before. Ian Mills writes with clarity and force, calmly laying out an argument that is destined to make a major impact on the field. Compulsory reading for scholars and students of Christian origins.

—Mark Goodacre, professor of religious studies,
Duke University

THE HYPOTHESIS OF THE GOSPELS

THE HYPOTHESIS OF THE GOSPELS

NARRATIVE TRADITIONS IN HELLENISTIC READING CULTURE

IAN N. MILLS

FORTRESS PRESS
Minneapolis

THE HYPOTHESIS OF THE GOSPELS
Narrative Traditions in Hellenistic Reading Culture

31 30 29 28 27 26 25 2 3 4 5 6 7 8 9

Library of Congress Control Number: 2024060283 (print)

Cover image: Panel Painting with the Crowned Nursing Virgin and the Twelve Apostles; Ethiopian, second half of the 15th century, National Museum of African Art, Smithsonian Institution, Washington, DC, Gift of Joseph and Patricia Brumit; Conservation of this work supported by the Smithsonian Institution Women's Committee (2004-7-1).
Cover design: Josh Eller

Print ISBN: 978-1-5064-9706-8
eBook ISBN: 978-1-5064-9707-5

To Winona Olive

CONTENTS

ACKNOWLEDGMENTS

This book owes so much to so many. It began as a long text message to Jeremiah Coogan. It became a book at the encouragement of Nathan Tilley. And Laura Robinson has been my constant conversation partner.

I started writing while finishing my doctorate at Duke University. Although they are very different works, many of the ideas in this book appeared first in the opening chapter of that unruly (and probably unpublishable) dissertation. Thank you to Mark Goodacre, a generous advisor and a model of charitable scholarship. Bart D. Ehrman, Jennifer W. Knust, and Joel Marcus each shaped this work with critical feedback. Thank you to my colleagues at Duke University, University of North Carolina at Chapel Hill, and Hamilton College for your friendship, support, and many kindnesses. Thank you to Carey Newman at Fortress Press for helping to shape my voice.

My daughter, Winona Olive, was born on April 23, 2021. I wrote much of this book with her sleeping on my lap, crawling over my shoulders, or clinging to my leg. She is a constant reminder of what really matters, and I do not regret a single minute I spent reading *Paddington* to her, instead of another book on the gospels.

Finally, Jodi Mills, my best friend and wife, has sacrificed more for the writing of this book than I had any right to ask. She hiked alone in Lake Tahoe, the Adirondacks, and Cascade National Park, while I sat in a camper and wrote. Jodi offered only encouragement as I spent evening after evening reading and writing at home. Thank you for all the love and joy you bring to my life.

Please direct any theological concerns to my former youth pastor, David Scrabeck.

Introduction

Sometime in the late first century, someone opened a gospel book and read the story of Jesus sending his disciples into the surrounding villages. In this gospel, Jesus prohibits his disciples from taking any money or provisions on their journey. The disciples are permitted only a staff and sandals (Mark 6:7–13).

This gospel reader, then, turned to a still mostly blank parchment and began to write.[1] At first, he carefully followed the wording of the text in front of him.[2] When he reached Jesus's instructions, however, he made a few changes. He wrote that Jesus had pointedly prohibited his disciples from bringing a staff or any footwear (Matthew 10:10). The very items permitted in the gospel he was reading, he now wrote, Jesus forbade.

Why the change? There is an entire subfield of New Testament scholarship preoccupied with explaining the authorial motivations behind differences between the gospels.[3] A study of this sort might explore the significance of footwear for itinerant preachers or speculate

1. Both the act of reading and writing might have involved the labor of enslaved persons. The composition of literary texts both by hand and dictation are well attested for the period. So too, first-century readers might read to themselves or employ a(n often-enslaved) reader. See Nicholas A. Elder, *Gospel Media: Reading, Writing, and Circulating Jesus Traditions* (Eerdmans, 2024), 125–171; Candida Moss, *God's Ghostwriters: Enslaved Christians and the Making of the Bible* (Little, Brown, 2024), 9–49.

2. The author of Matthew copies Mark's introduction to the pericope (6:7) and then reproduces the description of the disciple's activity from the end of Mark's version (6:12–13) before rewriting Jesus's instructions about provisions (6:8–9).

3. For a dated but still serviceable introduction to redaction criticism, see Norman Perrin, *What Is Redaction Criticism?* (Fortress Press, 1969).

about a community of barefoot Christians. But those are the preoccupations of modern scholars, and modern scholars were hardly the first to notice differences between the gospels. How did ancient readers make sense of these different versions of the same story?

Once the four gospels had been accepted as canonical, only certain kinds of explanations became imaginable.[4] Saint Augustine noticed the difference between Jesus's instructions to his disciples in Matthew and Mark.[5] And like modern scholars, Augustine recognized that—apart from the staff and sandals—the language, content, and context of Matthew and Mark are so similar that the two gospels had to be describing the same event.[6] But Augustine could not admit the contradiction. So, according to Augustine, Jesus must have said something like, "Do not bring . . . two coats, shoes, or a staff—except a staff."[7] There is no problem of translation involved here. The word *staff* is the same in both instances. Augustine concluded that Jesus must have given two instructions about the "staff," once in a literal sense and once with a figurative meaning.

Augustine's explanation is only conceivable in a context where the harmony of the gospels was already taken for granted. Because he is working with canonical assumptions, Augustine can imagine a divine author coordinating human scribes to write ostensibly contradictory accounts of a perfectly coherent story. But the Christian canon and its hermeneutics of inspiration took time to develop. Christians were writing and reading gospels before they could presuppose a harmonious New Testament. How did readers in the first and second centuries understand the multiplicity of gospels?

---

4. On the interpretive assumptions that Christians came to share with Jewish readers of scripture, see James L. Kugel, *The Bible As It Was* (Belknap Press of Harvard University Press, 1999).

5. Augustine, *On the Harmony of the Gospels*, 30.71.

6. Augustine reversed the direction of dependence but, like modern scholarship, recognized a literary relationship between the gospels (*On the Harmony of the Gospels*, 1.2).

7. Augustine, *On the Harmony of the Gospels*, 30.73.

Christianity never existed in a vacuum. And while Jesus was an Aramaic-speaking Jew, the gospels were written by and for Greek-speaking inhabitants of the Roman Empire.[8] This Hellenized culture was well acquainted with rewritten stories. Narrative traditions, like the Oedipus and Homeric cycles, were already classics in the first century. Greeks and Romans read Homer, performed Sophocles, and rewrote these stories into their own tragedies, comedies, histories, and epics. As such, the earliest readers of the gospels belonged to a culture that had already given a great deal of thought to narrative pluriformity—i.e., the existence of stories in more than one version.

The way that early Christians thought about the multiplicity of gospels was shaped by this culture of reading. As soon as Christians began reflecting on the relationship between different gospels, they drew on the conceptual categories and vocabulary of Hellenistic literary criticism to describe, organize, and regulate gospel literature. This book traces how one such concept—a narrative *hypothesis*—shaped the imagination of gospel literature in the first few centuries of Christian interpretation.

The first chapter surveys the use of the term *hypothesis* to describe and evaluate pluriform literature in the two centuries on either side of the millennium. Special attention is given to the Homeric and dramatic scholia as evidence of how readers applied this category in their interpretation of narrative traditions. Across genres, Hellenistic and Roman readers conceptualized stories that existed in more than one version as distinct instantiations of a common substrate. That notional substrate, called a *hypothesis*, served as a standard of comparison, limiting (if only in the minds of readers) the kind and degree of acceptable variation in the retelling of a story.

8. The claim that gospels were written or read as Hellenistic literature implies nothing about the ethnicity of their authors or readers. On the adoption of Greek literary conventions by ethnically Jewish authors and their participation in Hellenistic reading cultures, see Sean A. Adams, *Greek Genres and Jewish Authors: Negotiating Literary Culture in the Greco-Roman Era* (Baylor University Press, 2020).

The earliest reader to offer any sustained reflection on the multiplicity of the gospels was Irenaeus of Lyon. The idea of a narrative *hypothesis* pervades his description of gospel literature. Chapter 2 of this book argues that Irenaeus used the concept of a *hypothesis* to both legitimize and limit the pluriformity of the gospel tradition. It provided, also, a notional standard to be used in the interpretation of the gospels. Although the idea of a *hypothesis* is thoroughly integrated into Irenaeus's thinking about narrative traditions, there is a tension between his use of this concept to interpret the gospels and the protocanonical fourfold gospel that he is most famous for advocating.

Irenaeus's use of a narrative *hypothesis* to organize the gospels is hardly unique in the history of interpretation. Chapter 3 considers five additional authors—Clement, Origen, Eusebius, Epiphanius, and Cosmas—who also imagined the gospels as distinct books on a common *hypothesis*. These authors invoke the *hypothesis* of the gospels to defend the variety of gospel literature and exclude other versions of the life of Jesus. The application of this concept to the gospels in different rhetorical contexts by different authors across several centuries suggests that the idea of a narrative *hypothesis* was just part of the way Hellenistic readers thought about pluriform literature like the gospels. At the same time, allegorical interpreters and critics of allegorical interpretation both point out a tension between thinking of the gospels as varied instantiations of a common *hypothesis* and the assumptions that make allegorical reading possible. The hermeneutics of inspiration—like Irenaeus's fourfold gospel—rendered the idea of a narrative *hypothesis* obsolete.

While Irenaeus was the first gospel reader to use *hypothesis* language, he was not the first to use multiple gospels. Other second-century authors offer passing insights into the reception of gospel literature among its earliest readers. Chapter 4 reviews three authors—Papias, Justin, and Serapion—who knew more than one gospel. While there is no trace of Irenaeus's fourfold gospel in the first half of the second century, these early readers discussed the gospels in ways that reflected the same basic conception of these books as conventional works of

Hellenistic literature. Fleeting allusions to the pluriformity of gospels, moreover, suggest that readers before Irenaeus thought about gospels as discrete works on a common *hypothesis*.

The earliest known gospel readers were themselves authors of gospels and other gospel-type books. Chapter 5 surveys the limited evidence for the reception of gospel literature by this very first generation of readers. These texts do not contain any extended reflection on the multiplicity of gospels. In fact, they make only scant reference to the existence of other gospels. Nevertheless, these late first- and second-century authors reveal certain assumptions about the literary character of gospel books in their self-presentation and passing remarks on other gospels. Not every gospel describes itself as an authored and published work of Hellenistic literature on an established narrative tradition, but all the component parts of Irenaeus's picture of gospel literature are attested among these earliest gospel readers.

Readers assumed that narratives written on the same *hypothesis* reflect a rivalry between their authors. Likewise, ancient authors describe their own works as superseding earlier books on the same *hypothesis*. Chapter 6 shows that gospel readers and writers in the second century thought about gospel literature in the same way. At the same time, however, Hellenistic readers used the idea of a *hypothesis* to excuse or justify the differences between overlapping narratives. Early readers of the gospels, likewise, used the idea of a *hypothesis* to resist the competitive implications of this way of thinking about narrative traditions.

Before there were four *and only four* canonical gospels written by one divine author, readers thought about these books as different works by different authors on a shared narrative *hypothesis*. Each author's retelling might be said to preserve, endanger, harm, or destroy that *hypothesis*. As such, the idea of a *hypothesis* was used both to describe and evaluate different versions of the same story. Early Christian readers used this concept to legitimize and limit the pluriformity of the gospels. Different readers reached different conclusions about whether these books, written on the same *hypothesis*, were inherently competitive.

Over time, a new set of assumptions about Christian scripture made the notion of a narrative *hypothesis* obsolete.

The idea of a *hypothesis* is a largely overlooked piece of the conceptual apparatus that ancient readers used to make sense of their stories. By reconstructing the contours of this idea, we can better understand the assumptions and expectations that the gospels' first readers brought to their books.

CHAPTER ONE

The Literary *Hypothesis* in Hellenistic Book Culture

> "For each person has the authority to make each part happen as they wish, unless they harm the whole *hypothesis*."
>
> —Scholion to Sophocles's *Electra*

Introduction

GOSPELS WERE NOT the only books in antiquity to retell the same stories. Poems, plays, and histories tread and retread the same narrative ground. Hellenistic book culture had its own language for describing such narrative traditions. This chapter identifies a key piece of vocabulary that ancient readers used to understand the relationship between individual works and wider narrative traditions: a literary *hypothesis* (ὑπόθεσις).[1]

1. I have elected to transliterate, rather than translate, the term *hypothesis* throughout. This term had several distinct uses in antiquity (see below). In discourse around narratives, *hypothesis* might be translated with the Latinate "substrate" or "substance." This translation would roughly preserve the spatial metaphor, woodenly rendering ὑπό (meaning "under") and θέσις (meaning "placement"). Using "substrate" as a translation would have the advantage of avoiding a misleading similarity between the Greek *hypothesis* and the derived English term, hypothesis. The literary use of *hypothesis* does not refer to a "guess" or "theory," and an alternative translation would avoid such confusion. On the downside, the English "substrate" lacks any of the evaluative connotations evident in the use of *hypothesis* by ancient literary critics. I follow the practice of most scholars today in leaving the term untranslated. See, for example, George Alexander Kennedy, *Progymnasmata: Greek Textbooks of Prose Composition and Rhetoric* (Leiden, 2003), xiv.

Hellenistic readers and writers used the term *hypothesis* to refer to the essential elements of a story.[2] These elements typically included key characters, settings, and events. This notional *hypothesis*, often abstracted from multiple versions of a story, is what constituted a narrative tradition in the minds of ancient readers. Readers used this language to describe the relationship between different instantiations of the same story, between a specific work and a narrative tradition, and between creative authorship and the prescriptive force of readerly expectations. At the same time, readers appealed to a *hypothesis* to evaluate differences between versions of a story. A survey of this term's uses across several literary genres in the centuries before and after the composition of the gospels will highlight the conventions and conceptual categories available to readers and writers of gospel literature.

"The Same *Hypothesis*"

Dio Chrysostom on the Athenian *Philoctetes*

One morning in the late first century, Dio Chrysostom awoke in ill-health. Perhaps to put his misery into perspective, Dio took up reading Greek tragedies. He selected three works with the same title: *Philoctetes.* Three Athenian playwrights, Aeschylus, Euripides, and Sophocles, each wrote a tragedy by this name. All three plays feature the Homeric heroes Odysseus and Philoctetes.[3] All three are set on the isle of Lemnos in

2. There are no essences, and yet speakers use essentializing language to say meaningful things about the world. D. Holwerda calls this the "szenisch-technische" use of *hypothesis,* defined as "der angenommene Verlauf der Geschichte (der Sage)" or "sagengeschichtlicher Inhalt einer Tragödie." Holwerda, Zur szenisch-technischen Bedeutung des Wortes ΥΠΟΘΕΣΙΣ" in *Miscellanea Tragica in Honorem J.C. Kamerbeek* (Hakkert, 1976): 178, 181, 184.

3. Although Philoctetes is not a major character in the Homeric poems, he appears at *Il.* 2.716–728, *Od.* 3.190; 8.219–20. Philoctetes's story was also known to the Athenian poets from the *Little Iliad* and *Sack of Troy.* On Sophocles's use of Homer, see John Davidson, "Homer and Sophocles' Philoctetes," *Bulletin of the Institute of Classical Studies* 40, supplement 66 (1995): 25–35. On Sophocles's use of the *Epic Cycle,* see Andreas Schnebele, "Die epischen Quellen des Sophokleischen Philoktet:

the final year of the Trojan war. All three depict a dispute over the bow of Heracles.

In his fifty-second *Oration*, Dio describes his experience reading these plays side-by-side-by-side. Dio carefully notes their differences, speculates on the motivation of each playwright, and defends the particular merits of each play. To cite an example: only Euripides's version of the story includes the goddess Athena. In Euripides's *Philoctetes*, Athena transforms Odysseus's appearance so that Ithaca's famous king will not be recognized by the marooned Philoctetes. Dio approves of Euripides's addition to the story as an homage to a similar transformation in the thirteenth book of Homer's *Odyssey*. At the same time, Dio insists that Aeschylus (and, by implication, Sophocles) did not err in omitting that scene. Athena does not need to disguise Odysseus, according to Dio, since Philoctetes spent a decade stranded on Lemnos and the passage of time would have rendered Odysseus unrecognizable.

Dio's comparison reveals overarching similarities between the three *Philoctetes*: The same things happen to the same people in the same places. The remains of Aeschylus's and Euripides's *Philoctetes* suggest that the Athenian playwrights occasionally drew upon the very wording of their predecessors.[4] Moreover, all three playwrights made the same changes to the received story. In *The Little Iliad*, Diomedes alone retrieved Heracles's bow from Philoctetes.[5] But all three Athenian

---

die Postiliaca im frühgriechischen Epos" (PhD diss., Universität Tübingen, 1988), 108–119, 133–154.

4. S. Douglas Olson notes Euripides's "virtually word-for-word" dependence on Aeschylus (Eur. fr. 792 N²; Aesch. fr. 253 R). S. Douglas Olson, "Politics and the Lost Euripidean Philoctetes," *Hesperia: Journal of the American School of Classical Studies at Athens* 60, no. 2 (1991): 269–283. Likewise, Sophocles at *Philoctetes* 797–798 adapts a famous line preserved in a fragment of Aeschylus's *Philoctetes* (fr. 255). Hans Joachim Mette, *Die Fragmente Der Tragödien Des Aischylos* (Akademie-Verlag, 1959); William M. Calder III, "Aeschylus' 'Philoctetes,'" *Greek, Roman, and Byzantine Studies* 11, no. 3 (1970): 171–179.

5. This information about *The Little Iliad*, a lost work of the Epic Cycle, is found in Proclus's summary (*Chrestomathia* ii). Ps-Apollonius (*Epitome* 5.8) and Quintus Smyrnaeus (*Posthomerica* 9) describe Odysseus and Diomedes working in tandem.

plays depict Odysseus leading the expedition to Lemnos. Probably Aeschylus, the eldest of the three playwrights, reassigned Diomedes's role to Odysseus; Sophocles and Euripides then imitated Aeschylus's retelling of the story.[6] These three Athenian *Philoctetes* clearly constitute what modern readers call a literary or narrative "tradition."

At the same time, the three *Philoctetes* are distinct works of creative authorship: Only Aeschylus depicted Philoctetes retelling the story of his marooning to the island's inhabitants. Only Sophocles features Neoptolemus, the son of Achilles, accompanying Odysseus to the island. Only Euripides reintroduces Diomedes alongside Odysseus, conforming his version of the story to the Epic Cycle. Although these three playwrights retold the same set of traditional scenes, each exercised significant creative freedom.

The Athenian tragedies might be described colloquially as three versions of the same "story." One contemporary critic, for instance, writes of the Arthurian legends as a singular "story" retold by the likes of Sir Thomas Malory and T. H. White.[7] Narrative criticism, as an academic discipline, has developed more sophisticated taxonomies of storytelling. The Russian formalists distinguish between fabula, syuzhet, and text.[8] The term *fabula* refers to the elements of a narrative, including their diegetic sequence. The *syuzhet* is an author's arrangement of those elements in a particular presentation of the *fabula*. Finally, the *text* is an author's lexical expression. Following this taxonomy, all three *Philoctetes* share a *fabula*, their syuzhets are closely related but not identical, and their texts are markedly different. The colloquial *story* and the academic *fabula* are modern categories. But readers in antiquity were no less sophisticated.

---

6. Calder, "Aeschylus' 'Philoctetes.'"

7. Constance Grady, "Why the Once and Future King Is Still the Best King Arthur Story Out There," *Vox*, May 18 2017, https://www.vox.com/culture/2017/5/18/15649214/once-and-future-king-th-white-king-arthur.

8. For an introduction to narratology, see Mieke Bal, *Narratology: Introduction to the Theory of Narrative* (University of Toronto Press, 2009).

Hellenistic literary criticism had its own vocabulary for describing distinct but closely related works of literature. Dio Chrysostom used this vocabulary to describe the *Philoctetes* tradition.

> They were the works of nearly the best of men: Aeschylus, Sophocles, and Euripides—all of them concerning the same *hypothesis* (τὴν αὐτὴν ὑπόθεσιν). For it was the theft—or should it be called a 'robbery'?—of the bow of Philoctetes.[9]

Dio recognized the three *Philoctetes* as three distinct works by three different authors.[10] What these plays have in common—the story of how Philoctetes lost his bow—Dio calls a *hypothesis*.

Tensions between tradition and originality, between a story and the work of its telling, and between a text and its artefactual *realia* are abiding concerns of literary criticism.[11] The same puzzles of language and reference intrigued ancient commentators.[12] Nevertheless, first-century readers, like Dio Chrysostom, were more than capable of holding such ideas together. From his analysis of authorial motivations, it is clear that Dio understood the three *Philoctetes* as three different works composed by identifiable authors with discernable literary agendas. Likewise, despite their many differences, Dio understood the

9. *Oration* 52.2. Text from H. Lamar Crosby, *Dio Chrysostom. Discourses 37–60*. Loeb Classical Library 376, ed. Jeffrey Henderson (Harvard University Press, 1946), 338.

10. Despite some suggestions to the contrary, notions of authorship were already commonplace in the first and second centuries. For a sampling of relevant evidence, see Katharina de la Durantaye, "The Origins of the Protection of Literary Authorship in Ancient Rome," *Boston University International Law Journal* 25, no. 37 (2008): 37–111.

11. For a particularly helpful treatment of novelty and tradition in Greek tragedy, see Armand D'Angour, *The Greeks and the New: Novelty in Ancient Greek Imagination and Experience* (Cambridge University Press, 2011).

12. Seneca the Younger, for instance, finds irony in the distinction between an author's literary ownership and owning a physical copy of a book (*On Benefits* 7.6). Similarly, Martial exploits this equivocation for comedic effect (*Epigrams* 1.66, 72). See additional examples in the discussion of Philodemus later in this chapter.

three *Philoctetes* to be three versions of one basic thing. The term he used to pick out what united these three works was *hypothesis*. And Dio was hardly the only author of this age to use the idea of a *hypothesis* to organize a pluriform literary tradition in this way.

The Content of a Narrative *Hypothesis*

The work of ancient literary critics, commentators, and editors are mostly lost to us. Much of what survives is preserved through indirect transmission as quotations, excerpts, or paraphrases in other works. An especially rich store of these materials are the *scholia*, excerpts from older works of commentary preserved in the margins of literary manuscripts.[13] These excerpts are often difficult to contextualize or date with precision.[14] Nevertheless, they provide an opportunity to glance over the shoulders of ancient readers.[15] In particular, scholia on the

13. For introductions to the scholia, see Eleanor Dickey, *Ancient Greek Scholarship: A Guide to Finding, Reading, and Understanding Scholia, Commentaries, Lexica, and Grammatical Treatises, from Their Beginnings to the Byzantine Period*, annotated ed. (Oxford University Press, 2007); René Nünlist, *The Ancient Critic at Work: Terms and Concepts of Literary Criticism in Greek Scholia* (Cambridge University Press, 2009), 1–20.

14. I share René Nünlist's skepticism toward the usefulness (at least, for projects of this kind) of identifying sources for individual scholia. Nünlist, *The Ancient Critic at Work*, 17–19. There is sufficient continuity in the use of the term *hypothesis* between different corpora of scholia (e.g., Homer, Sophocles, Euripides, Pindar, and Thucydides) and known authors of the late Hellenistic and Roman Imperial periods to justify studying a conventional use of the term in the literary criticism of narrative works. On the inevitability of unconventional uses of technical vocabulary, see note 31. Holwerda argues that some of the dramatic scholia featuring *hypothesis* language originate with Aristophanes of Byzantium (d. 180 BCE). D. Holwerda, "Bedeutung des Wortes ΥΠΟΘΕΣΙΣ," 196–198. But these only survive because they were cited in Roman era scholarship (e.g. the lost work of Didymus in the late first century BCE) and then copied into subsequent manuscripts as scholia.

15. For an eloquent defense of studying Hellenistic scholarship alongside the reception of biblical literature, see Maren Niehoff, "Why Compare Homer's Readers to Biblical Readers?" in *Homer and the Bible in the Eyes of Ancient Interpreters* (Academic Publishers, 2012), 3–7.

Homeric epics and dramatic adaptations of classical myths are snapshots of readerly encounters with narrative traditions in the late Hellenistic and Roman periods. Many of these readers used *hypothesis* language to describe and evaluate these pluriform stories.[16]

A scholion appended to the opening lines of Sophocles's *Ajax* illustrates the content of a narrative *hypothesis.* Sophocles begins this tragedy with a speech by Athena, introducing the main characters (i.e., Odysseus and Ajax), the setting (i.e., a camp near the Greek ships), and the main events of the story (i.e., a conflict between heroes). Next to the very first lines of Athena's speech, one late antique reader copied the following excerpt from some earlier commentator:

> [Sophocles] shows all the constitutive-parts of the *hypothesis* in his prelude: Whom the story is about, where is the scene, and what Odysseus does.[17]

Athena's speech, according to this reader's note, functions as a prelude to the *Ajax.* In this speech, says our ancient reader, Sophocles presented "all the constitutive-parts" (πάντα . . . συνεκτικὰ) of the *hypothesis.* This

16. Nünlist cautions against studying the scholia on the basis of terminology alone since parallel arguments often appear in the scholia with different vocabulary. René Nünlist, "Narratological Concepts in Greek Scholia," in *Narratology and Interpretation*, ed. Jonas Grethlein and Antonios Rengakos (Walter de Gruyter, 2009), 66. Given the wealth of evidence for the use of *hypothesis,* however, this chapter considers only appearances of the term. To Nünlist's point, however, the same conceptual model and line of argumentation appear without the term *hypothesis*, e.g., Sch. *Od.* 4.1k. Text from Filippomaria Pontani, *Scholia graeca in Odysseam vol. 2—Scholia ad libros γ-δ* (Edizioni di storia e letteratura, 2010), 175–176. On the related use of the verb ὑποτίθεσθαι, see D. Holwerda, "Bedeutung des Wortes ΥΠΟΘΕΣΙΣ," 178–181. While the abstract noun *hypothesis* developed into a relatively stable term of art, the uses of the verb are more plastic.

17. Sch. Soph. *Ajax* 1a. Text from Petrus N. Papageorgius, *Scholia in Sophoclis tragoedias vetera* (Leipzig: Teubner, 1888), 1. For a discussion of this definition, see Roos Meijering, *Literary and Rhetorical Theories in Greek Scholia* (E. Forsten, 1987), 116. See also D Holwerda, "Bedeutung des Wortes ΥΠΟΘΕΣΙΣ,'" in *Miscellanea Tragica in Honorem J.C. Kamerbeek* (Hakkert, 1976), 173–198.

scholion helpfully defines the elements of a *hypothesis* as "whom the story is about, and where is the scene, and what [the main character] does"—that is, a story's key characters, settings, and events.[18]

A scholion to Sophocles's *Electra* includes a close parallel: this Sophoclean tragedy begins with a speech from a pedagogue addressed to Orestes, the son of Agamemnon. The speech describes their setting (i.e., Argos), mentions the protagonists (i.e., Orestes and Electra), and foreshadows the play's main event (i.e., avenging a murdered father). Alongside this first line, a scholion reads:

> We often observe that the ancients show us the constituent-parts of their *hypotheses* in the beginnings [of their plays]. Even now it is made clear to whom the speech was addressed and who was a necessary character.[19]

Like the *Ajax* scholion, this commentator uses *hypothesis* language to assert that Sophocles introduces the most important parts of his play in its opening scene. The first lines of both plays, according to these ancient readers, describe the story's main characters, settings, and events. In the mind of these readers, these narrative elements constitute a story's *hypothesis.*

The scholion to *Electra* draws special attention to the way Sophocles introduces the "necessary" (*ἀναγκαῖον*) characters at the beginning of his play. The same story, after all, can be told with a different cast: Chrysothemis, a less famous sister of Orestes, plays a role in Sophocles's *Electra* but does not appear in Euripides's version. According to the commentator preserved in this scholion, however, certain characters who feature in both plays—like Orestes and Electra—are "necessary" to the *hypothesis.*

---

18. On the use of *hypothesis* language in Sophocles's prologues, see Meijering, *Literary and Rhetorical Theories in Greek Scholia*, 116–117.

19. Sch. Soph. *El.* 1a. Text from Georgios Xenis, *Scholia Vetera in Sophoclis "Electram"* (De Gruyter, 2010), 104.

This use of the term explains Dio Chrysostom's assertion that the three Athenian *Philoctetes* share "the same *hypothesis*."[20] Dio noted many differences between the plays. But all three *Philoctetes* shared the characters, settings, and events that Dio deemed necessary. Thus, Dio and these Sophoclean scholia reflect a shared use of the term *hypothesis* to refer to basic elements of a story.[21] As will soon become clear, readers most often found it useful to speak of basic narrative elements when discussing stories that exist in more than one version.

The *Hypothesis* of Pluriform Narratives

The idea of a *hypothesis* appears most often in discussions of pluriform narratives. It is the multiplicity of versions and the inevitable diversity of their contents that motivated readers to identify some elements (and not others) as fundamental to a story—that is, to imagine a narrative *hypothesis*. This idea of a basic story has purely descriptive uses. At the same time, however, the idea of a *hypothesis* served an evaluative purpose, acting as a notional standard to which a specific work could be compared. In both use cases, the term *hypothesis* pointedly distinguishes a story in the abstract from specific instantiations of that story.

The invocation of a *hypothesis* is sometimes merely descriptive. One scholion attached to a plot summary of Euripides's *Orestes*, for instance,

---

20. Dio uses the term *hypothesis* a second time in this same oration on the three *Philoctetes*. In an even closer parallel to the two Sophoclean scholia considered above, Dio states that "Odysseus clearly and precisely presents the dramatic *hypothesis*" in the prologue to Euripides's *Philoctetes* (52.12). This parallel use of the term *hypothesis* corroborates my claim that Dio is using the term in the same technical sense as the scholiasts throughout. The same construction (την δραματικήν ὑπόθεσιν) can be found in the scholia (e.g., Sch. Eur. *Troad* 1129).

21. This is a "lexical (as opposed to a "stipulative") definition" as described by Richard Robinson, *Definition* (Oxford University Press, 1963). This chapter is an attempt to describe in my own language how the term was used in a particular set of historical circumstances. As discussed below, the same term is used differently in other discursive contexts.

states: "Here, Euripides begins in the middle of the *hypothesis*."[22] This scholion goes on to report that other plays by Sophocles and Euripides depict events that occur (in the narrative world) before the beginning of Euripides's *Orestes*. In this scholion, then, a reader has used the term *hypothesis* precisely to distinguish the plot (or *syuzhet*) of Euripides's *Orestes* from the story as it was known from several other works. In this case, the notion of a narrative *hypothesis* allowed a reader to say that Euripides began his play halfway through the story itself (as this reader understood it).

Similar use is made of *hypothesis* in the scholia to other authors. A scholion to Sophocles's *Antigone* notes that Polynices assault on Thebes is describe in brief "because the *hypothesis* is well-known."[23] As with the Euripidean scholion above, this reader uses the term *hypothesis* to compare a specific text to a story as it was known from other sources. Similarly, one of the old scholia to the *Iliad* praises Homer for "omitting nothing from the *hypothesis*," while another praises a character, Odysseus, for "cutting short what is disagreeable of the *hypothesis*."[24] In all these examples, the concept of a *hypothesis* allows readers to

22. Sch. Eur. *Orestes* Arg. 7a. Text from Wilhelm Dindorf, *Scholia Graeca in Euripidis tragoedias*, vol. 2 (Oxonium, Typ. Acad., 1863), 6.

23. Sch. Soph. *Antigone* 110. Text from Petrus N. Papageorgius, *Scholia in Sophoclis Tragoedias Vetera* (Leipzig: Teubner, 1888), 222. See the discussion in Daniel Squire, "An Edition and Translation of the Scholia to Sophocles Antigone 1-581, with Commentary on the Scholia Vetera" (University of California, Berkeley, 2022), 29–30.

24. Sch. *Il.* 9.688b. Text from Hartmut Erbse, *Scholia Graeca in Homeri Iliadem (Scholia vetera)*, vol. 2, *Scholia ad libros E—I continens* (De Gruyter, 1971), 542. Sch. *Il.* 2.494-877. Hartmut Erbse, *Scholia Graeca in Homeri Iliadem (Scholia vetera)*, vol. 1, *Praefationem et scholia ad libros A—D continens* (De Gruyter, 1969), 288. The scholion from Book 9 makes it especially clear that *hypothesis* is meant to distinguish the abstract story from the present work by proceeding to enumerate story elements from the larger epic cycle (e.g., the abduction of Helen, the death of Achilles) that are referenced in the *Iliad* but not narrated. In these examples, the *hypothesis* consistently refers to the *fabula* as distinct from the *syuzhet*.

describe the relation of one version of a story to a wider narrative tradition.[25]

Just as often, however, the term *hypothesis* is used with a normative sense. The idea of an underlying story provides a standard—if only in the mind of the reader—against which a specific work can be judged. For instance, the *arrangement* (οἰκονομία) of a particular work may be said to accord with a *hypothesis* or threaten to destroy it. "The *hypothesis* would have been destroyed," says one scholiast, if Sophocles had portrayed Electra shutting herself away in mourning for the death of her brother.[26] The decision to place Electra lying at the gates, the scholiast notes, was a matter of *arrangement* (using the adverb οἰκονομικῶς). By implication, then, Sophocles could have told the story another way. This commentator asserts, however, that Electra must be present at the gates to meet the disguised Orestes, deliver an elegy, and ally herself with her brother. In this case, a reader praises Sophocles's arrangement for preserving the *hypothesis*.

A similar scholion to Sophocles's *Ajax* praises the playwright for describing Odysseus as uncertain about Ajax's responsibility for a crime. Sophocles "does this well," according to the scholiast, "so that the *hypothesis* still holds together."[27] Other scholia commend authorial choices as "according to the *hypothesis*" (κατὰ τὴν ὑπόθεσιν).[28] In these cases, readers use adherence to an imagined *hypothesis* as grounds for praising an author.

---

25. The same scholia use *hypothesis* language to describe how the author (or a character) chooses to reveal a *hypothesis* (e.g., Sch. Soph. *El.* 94; *Aj.* 34, 38). The term also appears in Homeric and dramatic scholia to simply refer to the content of a story as a whole (e.g., Sch. *Il.* 24.804a).

26. Sch. Soph. *El.* 817. Text from Xenis, *Scholia Vetera in Sophoclis "Electram,"* 211.

27. Sch. Soph. *Ajax* 23a. Text from Papageorgius, *Scholia in Sophoclis tragoedias vetera*, 4.

28. See, for example, Sch. Soph. *Oed. Col.* 1760. On what is probably a distinct use of the same construction (e.g., Eur. *Or.* 141a), see D. Holwerda, "Bedeutung des Wortes ΥΠΟΘΕΣΙΣ," 190-1.

But readers are not always so complimentary.[29] Indeed, the distinction between a work and its *hypothesis* is most clear when commentators are critical. A scholion to Euripides's *Alcestis* provides one such case. At this point in the play, Alcestis is already dying. Her servant describes Alcestis, held in the arms of her husband, scarcely able to breathe (Euripides, *Alcestis*, 205). And yet, a few lines later, the chorus describes Alcestis walking out of her house. One ancient reader disapproved: "Not well (done); For according to the *hypothesis*, it is necessary that these actions be seen as inside."[30] In the opinion of this reader, Euripides's way of telling the story clashed with how the story ought to be told—that is, Euripides's *Alcestis* clashed with its *hypothesis*.

Other unwelcome authorial choices—real or imagined—threaten to "destroy the *hypothesis*".[31] At the climactic reveal of Orestes in Sophocles's *Electra*, one reader remarks "it is necessary that Orestes appear, since if he were silent, the constitutive-parts of the *hypothesis* would be destroyed."[32] The author of this scholion imagines

29. On the scholia as witnesses to scholarly controversies, see Clinton Douglas Kinkade, "Sophocles' Ancient Readers: The Role of Scholarship on the Reception of Greek Tragedy" (PhD dissertation, Duke University Press, 2021).

30. Sch. Eur. *Alc.* 233. Text from Eduard Schwartz, *Scholia in Euripidem*, vol. 2 (Berolini: G. Reimer, 1887), 224. Against reading *hypothesis* as always referring to the *mise en scène*, see Holwerda, "Bedeutung des Wortes ΥΠΟΘΕΣΙΣ," 173-98; on his reading of this scholion, see 176–177.

31. René Nünlist notes that most imagined changes, which, according to a scholiast, would "destroy the hypothesis" concern the *fabula*, not "the present plot in particular" (*The Ancient Critic at Work*, 67). Nünlist, however, suggests that other scholia use the same construction to discuss the arrangement of a particular work (rather than the *fabula*). From this, Nünlist concludes that *hypothesis* is not used consistently to distinguish *fabula* from the plot of a specific work. On one hand, we should not expect perfect consistency in the use of technical terminology by all ancient readers—see Nünlist's own remarks on the lack of such consistency in the scholia (*The Ancient Critic at Work*, 3). And probably, Nünlist has found exceptions—Sch. *Il.* 3.369a, for example, may be a counterexample to my characterization of the term's use. Nevertheless, the majority of the Homeric and dramatic scholia as well as commentators across different genres use the term to refer to the fundamental or underlying story in pointed contrast to a specific work. See also Nünlist's comments on the relationship between *hypothesis* and *economy* (*The Ancient Critic at Work*, 24n5).

32. Sch. Soph. *El.* 1174. Text from Xenis, *Scholia Vetera in Sophoclis "Electram,"* 247.

another version of the play where Orestes maintains his disguise while Electra mourns her brother's death. This change, the scholion asserts, would ruin the story. Similarly, a scholion to Euripides's *Hippolytus* says that the chorus of Trojan women must promise not to give away Phaedra's plan to frame Hippolytus. If everyone knew that Hippolytus was innocent, according to this reader, "the *hypothesis* would be destroyed."[33]

Remarks of the same sort appear in the Homeric scholia.[34] One reader asks why Menelaus did not draw Paris's sword during their duel in book three. The reader offers a few different answers, including that "the poet saved Paris through Aphrodite for the sake of [the story's] arrangement (οἰκονομίαν), since the [substance] of the *hypothesis* would be destroyed by his death."[35] This reader invokes a *hypothesis* to reject an imagined retelling of the *Iliad* where Menelaus kills Paris. Another ancient reader accuses Homer himself of endangering the *hypothesis* by allowing Ajax to nearly kill Hector.[36] Hector, of course, must live to fight Achilles. In all these examples—and many more could be supplied—the idea of a basic story serves as a standard for judging different versions.[37]

---

33. Sch. Eur. *Hipp.* 710. Text from Wilhelm Dindorf, *Scholia Graeca in Euripidis tragoedias* (Oxford: Typ. Acad., 1863), 1:157. Examples could be multiplied (e.g., Sch. Soph. *Aj.* 389c, 462; Eur. *Hipp* 713).

34. On the value of the scholia for Homeric literary criticism in our period, see N. J. Richardson, "Literary Criticism in the Exegetical Scholia to the Iliad: A Sketch," *Class. Q.* 30.2 (1980): 265–87; Dickey, *Ancient Greek Scholarship*, 18–23.

35. Sch. *Il.* 3.369 (D Scholia). Helmut van Thiel, ed., *Scholia D in Iliadem: secundum codices manu scriptos*, Elektronische Schriftenreihe der Universitäts- und Stadtbibliothek 7 (Köln: Universitäts- und Stadtbibliothek Köln, 2006), 177.

36. Sch. *Il.* 7.262. Text from Erbse, *Scholia Graeca in Homeri Iliadem (Scholia vetera)*, vol. 2, *Scholia ad libros E—I continens*, 271. See also Sch. *Il.* 22.437b. Hartmut Erbse, *Scholia Graeca in Homeri Iliadem (Scholia vetera)*, vol. 5, *Scholia ad libros Y—O continens* (De Gruyter, 1977), 347.

37. One scholion declares that an apparently minor change to Andromache's story would destroy the *hypothesis* (Sch. *Il.* 22.437b). Another that "the whole arrangement of the *hypothesis*" would be destroyed if Telemachus learned his father was returning (Sch. *Od.* 1.*Hyp* 328).

The way ancient readers use the concept of a *hypothesis* to evaluate narrative traditions is most clearly articulated in a scholion about a contradiction between Homer's *Odyssey* and Sophocles's *Electra*. Sophocles depicts Electra blaming Clytemnestra for the murder of Agamemnon (*Electra*, 446). Homer, however, clearly attributes Agamemnon's murder to Aegisthus (*Od.* 3.250). Some ancient readers, it seems, faulted Sophocles for diverging from the Homeric version of the story.[38] But one scholiast defended Sophocles.

> It was enough to agree on the whole with what happened (τῷ πράγματι). For each person has the authority to make each part happen as they wish, unless they harm the whole *hypothesis*.[39]

This ancient reader argued that there is nothing scandalous about Homer and Sophocles attributing the murder of Agamemnon to different people. Such differences in detail, according to this scholion, fall within the scope of an author's creative license.[40] Authors are permitted to "make things happen" (πραγματεύσασθαι) as they wish. At the same time, this reader clarifies that such creative differences are acceptable only so long as they do not threaten the fundamental story. Like the scholia reviewed above, this reader imagines a basic story, existing independent of either Homer's epic or Sophocles's drama, that can be used to evaluate whether a change is acceptable.[41]

---

38. On the critical reception of Sophocles and Euripides, see Kinkade, "Sophocles' Ancient Readers." This passage is treated at 131–132.

39. Sch. Soph. *El.* 446. Text from Xenis, *Scholia Vetera in Sophoclis "Electram,"* 175.

40. For parallels to this idea of poetic license, see Meijering, *Literary and Rhetorical Theories in Greek Scholia*, 62–67.

41. Aristotle already articulates a tension between authorial license and a commitment to preserving some core of "traditional stories" (παρειλημμένους μύθους), though without *hypothesis* language (*Poetics* 14). See *Aristotle: Poetics. Longinus: On the Sublime. Demetrius: On Style*, trans. Stephen Halliwell, et al. Loeb Classical Library 199 (Harvard University Press, 1995), 74–76.

What belongs to the *hypothesis* is, of course, a normative judgment. Agamemnon must be murdered. But *how* he dies, according to one reader, falls within the purview of authorial creativity. The very existence of this scholion suggests that other readers did not agree. Like the commentator cited in the scholion of Euripides's *Alcestis,* some ancient reader probably thought that Sophocles's choice destroyed the *hypothesis.* What counts as legitimate variation and what is essential to a story is (and would always have been) a site of contention. Among other things, *hypothesis* language allows disputants to name the contested territory.

Tradition and the Narrative *Hypothesis*

A tradition is an inherited behavior or belief, something regarded as already established or given.[42] There is no necessary relationship between the concept of a narrative *hypothesis* and tradition. In practice, however, most readers regarded narrative *hypotheses* as traditional. That is, readers generally considered the content of a *hypothesis* as given and, therefore, beyond the power of any individual to change. In fact, it was this traditional character of a narrative *hypothesis* that made it possible for readers to charge an author with contradicting or misrepresenting it.

Philodemus of Gadara was a philosopher and poet in Rome during the first century BCE. He wrote extensively on literary criticism and aesthetics. Philodemus's five-volume *On Poetry* bears witness to a series of controversies over the evaluation of poetry: What are the virtues unique to poetry? How does form relate to meaning? For which aspects of a work should a poet be held responsible? These debates involved complex analytic vocabularies for describing different aspects of a composition. As we would expect, *hypothesis* language features in several of these debates.

---

42. My use of the term "tradition" is indebted to the conceptual analysis in Edward Shils, "Tradition," *Comp. Stud. Soc. Hist.* 13.2 (1971): 122–59.

Philodemus is "a critic of critics," a scholar principally concerned with other scholarship.[43] As such, his *On Poetry* is a catalog of, and commentary on, Hellenistic literary criticism as it was known to him.[44] The omnibus character of Philodemus's book makes it an important source for reconstructing Hellenistic approaches to literature across the centuries before the advent of Christianity.[45] The books cited by Philodemus were the kind of books available to readers in the first and second centuries CE.[46] For present purposes, Philodemus and his interlocutors illustrate how readers imagined narrative *hypotheses* as traditional.

In the first two books of *On Poetry*, Philodemus's primary opponents are the "euphonists," literary critics who emphasized form over content.[47] These critics argued that the particular virtue of poetry was

43. Diskin Clay, "Framing the Margins of Philodemus and Poetry," in *Philodemus and Poetry: Poetic Theory and Practice in Lucretius, Philodemus, and Horace* (Oxford University Press, 1995), 7–10.

44. My understanding of *On Poetry* is indebted to Richard Janko's reconstruction and synopsis. Richard Janko, *Philodemus: On Poems, Book 1* (Oxford University Press, 2003), esp. 190–193; Richard Janko, *Philodemus: On Poems, Book 2: With the Fragments of Heracleodorus and Pausimachus*, Philodemus Translation Series (Oxford University Press, 2020).

45. Philodemus's own writings were discovered in the Villa of the Papyri, destroyed in 79 CE. His work was known to the late second/early third-century Diogenes Laertius (*Lives* 10.3) and probably influenced one of Diogenes's contemporaries, Sextus Empiricus. On Philodemus's work as a reflection of more widespread developments in late Hellenistic rhetorical theory, see Robert N. Gaines, "Cicero, Philodemus, and the Development of Late Hellenistic Rhetorical Theory," in *Philodemus and the New Testament World*, ed. John T. Fitzgerald, Dirk Obbink, and Glenn Stanfield Holland (Brill, 2004), 197–220.

46. Philodemus himself relied on digests of older scholarship. Maria Gaki, however, argues that the euphonist critics were known to (and, in some cases, influential on) Dionysius of Halicarnasus (first century BCE), Demetrius (first century CE), Longinus (first century CE), and Quintillian (first century CE). Michael McOsker, *The Good Poem According to Philodemus* (Oxford University Press, 2021), 70; Maria Gaki, "Euphony in Theory and Practice: Sweet Sound in Composition" (PhD dissertation, University of Cincinnati, 2022).

47. On the euphonists, see Gaki, "Euphony in Theory and Practice," esp. 59–160.

the sound produced by the choice (ἐκλογή) and arrangement (σύνθεσις) of words. Accordingly, they denigrated the importance of a poem's content (διάνοια/ (δια)νοήμα).[48]

Philodemus describes the position of Heracleodorus, one such euphonist critic, as follows:

> They claim that 'the poetic [art] sometimes adapts a common *hypothesis* (κοινὴν ὑπόθεσιν) for itself, and arranges it (i.e. a *common hypothesis*) and the traditional [*hypothesis*] (δεδομένην)—and discovers specific parts of content and wording from what is common (κοινοῦ).'[49]

Thus, Heracleodorus claims that a poet derives the content of their work from a "common" or "traditional" *hypothesis.* "One should not praise the poet," the same critic concluded, "if the story (μῦθος) or *hypothesis* is good."[50] The poet, according to Heracleodorus, was not responsible for these traditional aspects of their work. Rather, the poet deserved credit only for the euphonious arrangement of words.

Throughout his *On Poetry*, Philodemus argues for a more holistic account of poetry: both style and substance can agitate the soul (ψυχαγωγία); form and content are not always so easily distinguished. In his response, however, Philodemus grants that the poet inherits a substantial part of their content as a "common" or "traditional" *hypothesis.* Philodemus must qualify, however, that this traditionalism does not detract from the poetic art:

> . . . just as in the manual disciplines, we don't think worse of a craftsperson for how much material they stole from another

48. On distinct uses of these terms, see Gaki, "Euphony in Theory and Practice," 91.

49. Philodemus, *On Poetry*, 2.30. Text from Janko, *Philodemus*: *On Poems, Book 2*, 192.

50. Philodemus, *On Poetry*, 1.42. Text from Janko, *Philodemus: On Poems, Book 1*, 230–231.

> craftsperson and worked it well. Likewise, we don't think this way about poetry, if someone takes an unworked (ἀπόητον) *hypothesis* to add their own interpretation.[51]

Thus, Philodemus compares the poet to a carpenter who steals raw material from another carpenter to make a work of his own. The thieving carpenter's product is no less excellent for having been built with the same materials already used by another. So too a poem that retells an old story is not necessarily inferior. Philodemus proceeds with a few examples:

> We think this way not only about small *hypotheses* but even if the author takes the common *hypotheses* (κοινά) about Troy or Thebes from another author, it is as if they dissolve the story and, somehow assembling it again, add their own preparation.[52]

Philodemus invokes the Trojan War and the Theban cycle as paradigmatic "common *hypotheses.*"[53] These stories were forever being rewritten. Although such a *hypothesis* is shared with other works, each author's elaboration on those basic story elements is a matter of art. Poetry, according to Philodemus, should be judged not only for the sound of its words but also for the author's "preparation" (κατασκευή) of a traditional *hypothesis.*

We do not need to adjudicate between Heracleodorus and Philodemus to see the relevance of this debate for understanding the function of *hypothesis* language. Despite holding different theories of poetics, these two readers agree in using *hypothesis* language to refer to inherited aspects of a story. The narrative *hypothesis* is traditional for both.

---

51. Philodemus, *On Poetry*, 2.44–45. Text from Janko, *Philodemus: On Poems, Book 2*, 215.

52. Text from Janko, *Philodemus: On Poems, Book 2*, 217.

53. Philodemus goes on to cite Sophocles and Euripides, in particular, as authors who improved upon their traditional *hypotheses* (*On Poetry*, 2.45).

In the fifth book of *On Poetry,* Philodemus cites two other literary critics who use *hypothesis* language: Heraclides of Pontus and Neoptolemus of Parium.[54] The "material" (ὕλη) of poetry, says Heraclides, is "a wealth of persons and characters, stories and *hypotheses,* and truth."[55] Philodemus is puzzled by Heraclides's inclusion of "truth," but otherwise seems to agree with this generalization. Philodemus adds that good poetry requires "selection" (ἐκλογή) from among *hypotheses* (*On Poetry*, 5.10). The sole manuscript of *On Poetry* then becomes highly fragmentary but Philodemus appears to have illustrated the importance of exercising care when choosing a *hypothesis* by comparing stories shared by Homer and Sophocles. Again, both Philodemus and his interlocutor are happy to use *hypothesis* language to refer to an imagined repository of traditional narratives.

Finally, Philodemus tells us that Neoptolemus of Parium used *hypothesis* language in drawing a distinction between the "content" (διανοήματα) and "wording" (σύνθεσις τῆς λέξεως) of a poem (*On Poetry*, 5.13–14). The *hypothesis,* according to Neoptolemus, furnishes a poem's content (*On Poetry*, 5.14). On this basis, Neoptolemus seems to have argued that the poet should not be held responsible for matters of content (*On Poetry*, 5.15). Philodemus is critical of this approach as well. Picking up a thread from his response to Heraclides, Philodemus reasserts that a poet should be judged for their choice of *hypotheses.* Poets, according to Philodemus, may choose "inferior *hypotheses*" ([ὑπ]οθέσεις φαῦλαι) by mistake (*On Poetry*, 5.15). Philodemus thus argues that the merits of a poem's *hypothesis* should be considered in evaluating an author's work. Even when asserting the

54. For a useful summary of these critics, see McOsker, *The Good Poem According to Philodemus,* 99–102, 107–110.

55. The conjunction of *hypothesis* with "story" (μῦθος) in Book 1 and 5.8–9 suggests something approaching *but short of* synonymy. Mirroring the relationship of ἦθος to πρόσωπον in the preceding pair, probably *hypothesis* refers to a more specific set of plot points than μῦθος. Philodemus expresses bemusement at the inclusion of "truth" in this list (5.9) but, given Heraclides elevation of the pedagogic potential of poetry over other artistic virtues (5.1), this probably refers to the educational content that Heraclides expected poetry to deliver.

poet's responsibility for a *hypothesis*, Philodemus's reasoning assumes the preexistence of narrative *hypotheses* as a store of traditions from which authors might choose. Both critics regard the content of a *hypothesis* as given.

The anthological character of Philodemus's work allows us to survey the use of *hypothesis* language across several Hellenistic critics. Philodemus and his many interlocutors all treat *hypotheses* as traditional—*given* and, to a certain extent, outside the poet's control. These readers disagreed in their approaches to evaluating poetry but shared an understanding of the term *hypothesis*.[56]

History and the Narrative *Hypothesis*

Homer's epics and Sophocles's tragedies were not histories. Even though many readers regarded the events of the Theban Cycle and Trojan War as broadly historical, the relevant literature was not understood as properly historical in genre.[57] That is to say, first- and second-century readers brought different expectations to an encounter with Homer than to an encounter with Herodotus.[58] The notion of a narrative *hypothesis*, however, cuts across such generic boundaries. Readers of historical literature also used the idea of a *hypothesis* to make sense of pluriform retellings of the past.

Dionysius of Halicarnassus was a Greek historian in the city of Rome at the end of the first century BCE. He wrote a history of the Roman Empire, biographies of Attic orators, and treatises on

56. The scholia to Homer (e.g., *Il.* 8.429) and Pindar (e.g., *Olympian Odes*, 2.39b) likewise discuss the *hypothesis* as traditional materials to be transformed into authorial works.

57. The details were forever in dispute but, apart from a few notable exceptions (e.g., Eratosthenes of Cyrene *apud* Strabo), Hellenistic and Roman readers assumed that the broad contours of these stories really occurred. See, for instance, the discussion of Herodotus, *Histories* 2.116–117 in Bruno Currie, *Herodotus as Homeric Critic* (Histos, 2021). On the different (and sometimes not so different) standards for poetry and history, see Meijering, *Literary and Rhetorical Theories in Greek Scholia*, 57–98.

58. Carolyn R. Miller, "Genre as Social Action," *Quarterly Journal of Speech* 70, no. 2 (1984): 151–167.

rhetoric. Dionysius's critical reflections on Greek historiography provide valuable insights into the language and categories that late Hellenistic readers and writers used to think about historical literature. In particular, Dionysius makes repeated use of *hypothesis* language to describe and evaluate histories—especially those written on the same subject.

In his *Letter to Gnaeus Pompeius*, Dionysius responds to a request for his appraisal of the classical historians, Herodotus and Xenophon (*Pomp.* 3.1). Dionysius answers by citing one of his own, otherwise lost treatises, called *On Imitation.*[59] In this earlier work, Dionysius had judged Herodotus, Thucydides, Xenophon, Philistus, and Theopompus to be the historians most worth imitating. He goes on, then, to describe the methods of writing history in order to judge the relative merits of these great historians:

> The first and, probably, most necessary work of all for the writer of any history is to select a *hypothesis* that is noble (καλὴν) and pleasing to those who will read it. It seems to me that Herodotus did this better than Thucydides.[60]

Thus, Dionysius agrees with Philodemus that an author should be judged for their selection of a *hypothesis* and not only their treatment of it. The philhellenic Dionysius preferred Herodotus's account of the "deeds of the Greeks and Barbarians" to the infighting of Thucydides's *Peloponnesian War.*

Dionysius, then, makes a clarification important for understanding the scope and contours of a narrative *hypothesis.* Thucydides, according to Dionysius, wrote on a single *hypothesis*, while Herodotus selected

---

59. On the relationship of this quotation to the surviving epitome, see Malcolm Heath, "Dionysius of Halicarnassus *On Imitation,*" *Hermes* 117 (1989): 370–373.

60. Dionysius, *Pomp.*, 3.2. Text from Stephen Usher, *Dionysius of Halicarnassus: Critical Essays*, vol. 2, *On Literary Composition. Dinarchus. Letters to Ammaeus and Pompeius.* Loeb Classical Library 466 (Harvard University Press, 1985), 372. Thank you to Jimmy Meyers for drawing my attention to this passage.

"many, dissimilar *hypotheses*" to combine into one work (*Pomp.* 3.14).[61] If the term *hypothesis* referred to just any subject material of any given work then Dionysius's clarification would be senseless. But, as the dramatic scholia made clear, a narrative *hypothesis* had a particular shape and content in the minds of readers. It was, according to a few scholia, the essential characters, settings, and events of a particular narrative. It makes sense for Dionysius, then, to speak of primary characters, settings, and events in Thucydides's *Peloponnesian War*, but not in Herodotus's *Histories*. Dionysius describes Herodotus's work, rather, as a collection of many *hypotheses* since the sprawling and eclectic treatment of ancient Mediterranean civilization and history was too wide-ranging to be characterized as a composition on any single *hypothesis*. Just as in discussions of poetry and drama, readers of historical literature imagined narrative *hypotheses* with specific content and shape.

In the same passage, Dionysius describes the process of writing a history. This useful account of the authorial process further clarifies the scope of historical *hypotheses*. First, Dionysius's ideal historian selects a *hypothesis* (*Pomp.* 3.2). Second, the historian decides where to begin and end their narrative (3.8). Third, they decide which events to include and what to omit (*Pomp.* 3.11). Fourth, they arrange events in their presentation (3.13). Finally, Dionysius's historian must determine their "disposition" (διάθεσις) toward the events (3.15). It follows from this description of history writing that the selection of a *hypothesis* underdetermines where a particular work begins and ends, what is included, how a work is arranged, and the author's judgment on the matter. Two works may be said to share a *hypothesis* despite beginning in difference places, including different events, treating those events in different orders, and reaching different conclusions about the subject.

61. Text from Usher, *Dionysius of Halicarnassus*, 380. Elsewhere, Dionysius's *On Thucydides* draws attention to Thucydides's selection of a single *hypothesis* for his history in contrast to earlier historians (7). A lacunose scholion to Thucydides's *History* uses *hypothesis* language to make (what appears to be) a similar point (2.1). In a suggestive parallel, Aristotle argues in *Poetics* that the unity and coherence of a narrative distinguishes poetry from history (8–9).

For Dionysius, the narrative *hypothesis* picked out only the most basic elements of a historical narrative.

Lastly, Dionysius illustrates the usefulness of *hypothesis* language for discussing pluriform narratives. Herodotus, according to Dionysius, wrote on "the same *hypothesis*" (τὴν αὐτὴν ὑπόθεσιν) as two previous historians, Hellanicus and Charon (3.7).[62] Thucydides, in contrast, chose a different *hypothesis* from Herodotus because "he did not want to write [about] the same things as others" (3.6).[63] Dionysius uses the term *hypothesis* to refer to the fundamental narrative shared by overlapping histories.

Dionysius's account of writing makes him a useful source for understanding the categories that readers brought to historical literature. But he is not unique in any of these respects. Didorus Siculus, a contemporary of Dionysius, speaks of both "fictional" (1.2.2) and "historical" (1.3.5) *hypotheses*.[64] Strabo, a first-century historian and geographer, describes Homer as "poetically preparing" an historical *hypothesis* (*Geography* 1.2.11).[65] Elsewhere, he invokes this *hypothesis* in evaluating competing interpretations.[66] Josephus, a Jewish historian of the late first century, uses *hypothesis* language to describe the historical subject matter underlying both Jewish scripture and his *Antiquities* (Preface 1/4).[67]

---

62. Text from Usher, 374.

63. Text from Usher, 374.

64. Text from C. H. Oldfather, trans., *Diodorus Siculus, Library of History*, vol. 1. Loeb Classical Library 279 (Harvard University Press, 1933), 8.

65. Stefan Radt, *Strabons Geographika Band 1* (Vandenhoeck & Ruprecht, 2002), 50.

66. Strabo defends the plausibility of Callimachus's identification of Gaudos and Corcyra as the historical sites of Odysseus's journeys against the accusation of earlier scholars that this identification was "against the Homeric hypothesis" (*Geography* 1.2.37). Text from Radt, *Strabons Geographika Band 1*, 110.

67. Probably, Dionysius would have described the Jewish Scriptures as containing multiple *hypotheses*—and, indeed, Josephus elsewhere speaks of a *hypothesis* related to the life of a specific character (*Antiquities* 6.350). We should, of course, expect variety

Late Hellenistic and Roman readers used the idea of a *hypothesis* to think about retellings of the past. As with the literary critics, the term serves to distinguish the narrative from any particular account of that narrative. Ancient readers recognized that historians could write very different versions of the same persons, places, and events. They used *hypothesis* language to pick out the basic elements that readers imagined underlying these overlapping histories.

The Prevalence of the Narrative *Hypothesis*

The idea of a narrative *hypothesis* seems to have emerged from the criticism of Athenian drama in the early Hellenistic period.[68] By the turn of the millennium, however, it was widespread. Readers applied *hypothesis* language to a variety of narrative traditions in the first few centuries of the common era. The notion of a *hypothesis* underlying different versions of the same story was not simply a piece of technical vocabulary in dramatic criticism but also a feature of the standard model used to imagine pluriform literature.

Plutarch of Chaeronea was a rough contemporary of the canonical evangelists. In his *Life of Alexander*, Plutarch says that a section of Alexander's journey "has become for many the written *hypothesis* of histories" (*Alex.* 17.6). Like Dionysius, Plutarch identifies historical events as the shared *hypothesis* of multiple books. In another work, Plutarch juxtaposes "stories that take wicked *hypotheses*" with "the poets and musicians" who "take their *hypotheses* from [the lives of people] who are prudent and sensible" (*How to Study Poetry* 20.A). In this passage

---

in the imagined scope of such an abstraction. For Josephus's rhetorical purposes in *Antiquities*, it is useful to describe the history of his people as a single *hypothesis*.

68. Wesley Trimpi identifies the origin of the idea in Aristotle's use of the verb τίθεσθαι (and derived forms) in *Poetics* and on analogy with the nominal *hypothesis* in logical and rhetorical discourse. Wesley Trimpi, "The Ancient Hypothesis of Fiction: An Essay on the Origins of Literary Theory," *Traditio* 27 (1971): 1–78. Particularly instructive is Aristotle's use of related terminology to describe the basic outline of a story in contrast to the kind of detail supplied when composing "episodes" (*Poetics* 17). See the discussion at Trimpi, "The Ancient Hypothesis of Fiction," 43–46.

too, it is the lives of historical people that provide a narrative *hypothesis.* Elsewhere, Plutarch calls the story of a sunken city known to Solon and Plato "the Atlantic *hypothesis*" (*Solon* 32.1) and reports that plot-driven comedies were called "*hypotheses*" to distinguish them from simplistic farces (*Table Talk* 7.8).[69] Thus, Plutarch used *hypothesis* language to describe the basic narrative elements of histories and lives as well as fictions.[70]

Herodian of Antioch wrote his *Roman History* in the first half of the third century. After introducing Severus Alexander, Herodian declines to enumerate all the emperor's deeds, sayings, and stratagems. "Many authors and poets have written sufficient histories," says Herodian, "making the life of Severus into the *hypothesis* of their entire work" (*Roman History* 2.15.6). Several other authors, according to Herodian, have already written lives of Severus. Herodian intends, rather, to treat the most important deeds of multiple emperors, over a broader span of time. Again, this historian refers to the shared subject matter of a pluriform literary tradition as a *hypothesis.* And, strikingly for the study of gospel literature, it is a biographical *hypothesis.*[71]

Diogenes Laërtius was the third-century author of the *Lives and Opinions of Eminent Philosophers*, a collection of philosophical biographies. In his biography of Plato, Diogenes gives a lengthy disquisition on the different methods of arranging the Socratic dialogues. In the first century of the common era, a grammarian named Thrasyllus of

---

69. This use of *hypothesis* as a genre title is clear case of synecdoche. It is the significance of the *hypothesis* to certain comedies that earns them this label. This is a clear parallel to the use of *hypothesis/argumentum* as the name for a genre of plot summaries (see the discussion of Dicaearchus's summaries below).

70. I discuss nonnarrative uses of *hypothesis* language in the next section. These are also common in Plutarch (e.g., the rhetorical use at *Timoleon* 10.14).

71. As widely noted, the genre of biography was not well defined in antiquity and was often regarded as a subcategory of history. Joseph Geiger, *Cornelius Nepos and Ancient Political Biography* (Steiner, 1985), 12–15. Moreover, it is not clear that ancient interpreters understood the gospels as βίοι in a generic sense (see the discussion of Justin Martyr in chapter 4). Nevertheless, the subject matter of the gospels is the life of a historical person.

Mendes, says Diogenes, published the dialogues in sets of four, called "tetralogies." His first tetralogy consisted of the *Euthyphro*, *Apology*, *Crito*, and *Phaedo*. These four dialogues are often grouped today under titles like "The last days of Socrates" because of the attention they give to Socrates's biography. According to Diogenes, this first tetralogy "has a common *hypothesis*, for [Thrasyllus] wishes to describe what the life of the philosopher should be" (*Lives* 3.57). Thrasyllus, according to Diogenes, fashioned these Platonic dialogues into a kind of biography of Socrates. Diogenes, therefore, refers to the historical events that underly these dialogues (i.e., the basic events of Socrates's life) as a *hypothesis*.[72]

Plutarch, Herodian, and Diogenes Laërtius illustrate how the narrative use of *hypothesis* language persisted from the Hellenistic period through the first, second, and third centuries CE. Examples could be multiplied. As these ancient readers illustrate, however, the idea of a narrative *hypothesis* was not restricted to specialized commentaries or treatises on specific genres. It was, rather, part of the mental furniture for educated readers in the late Hellenistic period and the Roman principate.

The Literary *Hypothesis* in Nonnarrative Genres

This way of thinking about books was native to narrative literature. Nevertheless, the concept of a *hypothesis* so pervaded Hellenistic literary culture that readers of philosophical, medical, and rhetorical literature adapted the term to their own purposes. The use of *hypothesis* language across these nonnarrative genres further illustrates the availability of this idea to all kinds of first- and second-century readers.

Whereas certain characters, settings, and events constitute the *hypothesis* of a narrative tradition, the *hypothesis* of nonnarrative literature is usually a specific set of topics, methods, or lines of argument. Dio Chrysostom says that Zeno, his student Persaeus, and some other authors all wrote treatises on Homer "according to the same *hypothesis*"

72. See Jaap Mansfield, *Prolegomena: Questions to Be Settled Before the Study of an Author, or a Text*, Philosophia Antiqua 61 (Brill, 1994), 67–70. As discussed in the following chapter, Athenaeus compares Platonic dialogues with Xenophon's works "on the same *hypothesis*" (*Deipnosophists* 11.112).

(*Oration* 53.4).[73] This common *hypothesis* consisted of specifying which aspects of the Homeric epics were true (κατὰ ἀλήθειαν) and which were imagined (κατὰ δόξαν). Just as Dio used *hypothesis* to refer to the common plot elements in the three *Philoctetes*, so Dio uses *hypothesis* to pick out a stratum of subject matter shared by these nonnarrative treatises. Similarly, the first-century Pseudo-Longinus introduces his work on aesthetics by contrasting it with Caecilius of Calacte's work, written "on the same *hypothesis*" (1.1). Both books were titled *On the Sublime* and, judging from Pseudo-Longinus's criticisms of Caecilius's lost work, they touched on many of the same topics.

Galen, a physician and philosopher from the second century CE, employs *hypothesis* in the same sense to describe literary traditions in medical literature.[74]

> [Hippocrates] entitled a medical book, "Concerning Surgery." It would have been better, however, to entitle it "About the Things Concerning Surgery," as some entitle the books of Diocles, Philotimus, and Mantius. For although these men wrote on the same *hypothesis* in each book, the title in many copies is lacking the preposition and article—they are entitled simply "Concerning Surgery." But in a few... (*Hipp, Off. Med.* 1.1)[75]

Three earlier authors, Galen reports, wrote books entitled "(*About the Things*) *Concerning Surgery*." All three, according to Galen, were written on the same *hypothesis*. Like Dio and Longinus, Galen uses *hypothesis* to refer to a substrate of shared content across several nonnarrative works, written by different authors, with the same (or nearly the same) title.

In another work, *On Hippocrates' "Regimen in Acute Diseases,"* Galen describes the composition of a new book on an established *hypothesis*.

73. Text from Crosby, *Dio Chrysostom: Discourses 37–60*, 360.

74. For an excellent introduction on Galen as both doctor and philosopher, see Vivian Nutton, *Galen: A Thinking Doctor in Imperial Rome* (Routledge, 2020).

75. Text from Kühn 18b 629–630.

> A second book written in the place of an older book is said to be "re-prepared" (ἐπιδιεσκευάσθαι) when they have the same *hypothesis* and most of the words—some of these [words] removed from the former composition, some added, and some subtly changed. But, for the sake of clarity, if you want an example of this, you have the second *Autolycus* of Eupolis composed (διεσκευασμένον) from the first. And so also the doctors from Cnidos published (ἐξέδοσαν) the second *Cnidian Opinions* in the place of the former—some things being entirely the same, some things added, some things removed, even as also things were changed. This, therefore, is the second book, which Hippocrates, having compared, says is more medical than the former" (*HVA* 1.4).[76]

Although this passage uses *hypothesis* language, it is important to acknowledge that Galen is describing something more than composition on a common *hypothesis*. The practice that Galen describes as "re-preparation" (ἐπιδιεσκευάσθαι) includes substantial verbal borrowing in addition to an inherited *hypothesis*. This compositional procedure is a distinctive feature of technical literature, often criticized by outside readers as a kind of plagiarism. Whether this practice has any relevance for the study of gospel literature lies beyond the scope of the present project.[77] These details aside, Galen uses the term *hypothesis* to describe the content shared between these books with the same title. Moreover, he explicitly connects the phenomenon back to dramatic criticism by

76. Text from Antoine Pietrobelli, ed., *Galien, Oeuvres: Tome IX, 1re Partie: Commentaire Au Regime Des Maladies Aigues d'Hippocrate: Livre I* (Les Belles Lettres, 2019), 8; Kühn 15.424.

77. Loveday Alexander's study of the Lukan prologue suggests that the conventions of technical literature may have influenced the composition of the synoptic gospels. Loveday Alexander, *The Preface to Luke's Gospel: Literary Convention and Social Context in Luke 1:1–4 and Acts 1:1*, Society for New Testament Studies 78 (Cambridge University Press, 1993). See also Sharon Lea Mattila, "A Question Too Often Neglected," *New Testament Studies* 41, no. 2 (1995): 199. I make this case at length in Ian Nelson Mills, "Rewriting the Gospel: The Synoptics Among Pluriform Literary Traditions" (Doctor of Philosophy, Duke University, 2021).

his use of the playwright Autolycus's *Eupolis* as an analogy.[78] Galen is evidently aware that this use of *hypothesis* language has been appropriated from narrative genres.

The term *hypothesis* had a specialized use in discussions of rhetoric.[79] This rhetorical use of the term is distinguished by a dialectical relationship with another technical term: *thesis*. An explanation of this pair can be found in the earliest Greek and Latin rhetorical manuals. Aelius Theon's *Progymnasmata* and Quintilian's *Institutes of Oratory*, both treatises on rhetoric from the first century CE, divide speeches into two types: those answering indefinite questions (e.g., Should a man marry?) and those answering definite questions (e.g., Should Cato marry?). The former class of speeches are said to concern a specific *thesis*, while the latter concern a *hypothesis*.[80] Notably, Quintilian transliterates these Greek terms, rather than attempting a translation into Latin.[81] The use of *thesis* in rhetorical literature is not dissimilar to the English derivative "thesis," referring to the subject of a speech. A *hypothesis*, by way of contrast, is more specific. Theon and Quintilian explain that

78. It seems Eupolis, an Athenian playwright, staged two different versions of his *Autolycus*. See Julius Pollux *Onomasticon* 7.202 and the scholia to Aristophanes's *Thesmophoriazusas* (941, 942b). These should not be confused with the two plays titled *Autolycus* by Euripides.

79. Sextus Empiricus (discussed in the next section of this chapter) pointedly distinguished this use of *hypothesis* from the narrative use associated with dramatic criticism. It seems clear to me, however, that a common set of semantic conventions governs both uses of the term. What I am calling the rhetorical use of *hypothesis* is further discussed in Meijering, *Literary and Rhetorical Theories in Greek Scholia*, 114–116. There is yet another use of *hypothesis* in rhetorical discourse, roughly equivalent to *propositium*. See Meijering, *Literary and Rhetorical Theories in Greek Scholia*, 107–111; Trimpi, "The Ancient Hypothesis of Fiction," 22–27.

80. Theon, *Progymnasmata* 1; Quintilian, *Institutes* 3.5.5–7. Although this distinction is common in rhetorical literature, it is not maintained with perfect consistency (e.g., Theon, *Progymnasmata* 2 at Leonhard von Spengel, *Rhetores graeci* (Lipsiae: sumptibus et typis B.G. Teubneri, 1854), 2:70.

81. Notably, Quintillian does not translate *hypothesis* with *argumentum* but with *causa*. On the subsequent conflation of *hypotheses* with *argumenta*, see the discussion of Dicaearchus's summaries in the next section of this chapter.

a *hypothesis* entails particular "facts, persons, time, etc . . ." (*Institutes* 3.5.7; *Progymnasmata* 1).[82] This list of elements is strikingly similar to the definition of *hypothesis* found in the Sophoclean scholia discussed above. Despite the disciplinary specificity of the rhetorical use of *hypothesis*, it clearly drew upon many of the same semantic conventions.[83]

Likewise, the audience of rhetorical performances used *hypothesis* language to describe the features held in common across multiple, distinct works. Lucian of Samosata (125–180 CE), for example, accuses an orator of pretending to speak extemporaneously on the well-known *hypothesis* of Pythagoras's exclusion from the Eleusinian mysteries (*Mistaken Critic* 5). Similarly, Plutarch (46–119 CE) complains about orators giving innumerable speeches on the same *hypothesis* (*Timoleon* 10.4). Isocrates, says Philostratus in his *Lives of the Sophists* (170–250 CE), was accused of plagiarism (literally, "a crime") for composing an oration "from the works of Gorgias on the same *hypothesis*" (*Vit. soph.* 1.17).[84] As in drama, poetry, and history, the term *hypothesis* functions as an organizing category in rhetorical criticism for describing the relationship between multiple works in a pluriform tradition.

The notion of a constitutive *hypothesis* underlying a literary tradition proved useful to late Hellenistic readers of all kinds of books. Although the term had a technical use in narratological discourse, it was applied *mutatis mutandis* to literary traditions in philosophy, medicine, and rhetoric. Readers and writers from various intellectual subcultures drew on a common store of semantic conventions in using *hypothesis* language to describe a stratum of content that constituted a

82. Text from Donald A. Russell, *Quintilian. The Orator's Education, Volume I: Books 1-2*, Loeb Classical Library 124, ed. Jeffrey Henderson (Harvard University Press, 2002), 40–41.

83. Notably, the idea of further specificity is not suggested by the prefix 'υπο-.' This rhetorical use of the term probably developed, therefore, under the influence of the narratological use, discussed above.

84. Text from Wilmer Cave France Wright, *Philostratus and Eunapius: The Lives of the Sophists* (Putnam, 1922), 52–55. Rhetorical critics would undoubtably charge the synoptic evangelists with plagiarism as well. See, however, scholarship on technical literature in note 77.

literary tradition. In sum, this way of thinking about pluriform books was pervasive in antiquity.

Other Uses of the Term *Hypothesis*

The term *hypothesis* had a variety of uses, and the narrative sense outlined above is far from the most common. More often, the word refers to a belief or supposition—from which the English term *hypothesis* is derived. And several other uses are identifiable. Readers in antiquity, however, recognized relevant distinctions between different uses of this term.

Sextus Empiricus, a second-century philosopher, offers an illuminating discussion of the semantic range of the word *hypothesis*. This bit of lexicography appears, surprisingly, not in a treatise on Greek literature but, rather, in an argument against the epistemic pretensions of ancient mathematicians. Sextus was a Pyrrhonian skeptic and, in the third book of his *Against the Scholars*, he sets out an argument against deriving the principles of geometry from a set of undemonstrated axioms.[85] These geometric axioms are called *hypotheses*—a fact that prompts immediate clarification.

> And for the sake of good order, it should be noted preliminarily that *hypothesis* means many and various things. Now, it is enough to name three . . .[86]

Sextus prefaces his argument against the mathematicians by acknowledging the polysemy of *hypothesis*. As noted above, the term's etymology suggests one thing positioned under something else. This deverbative noun, connoting a spatial relationship, evidently afforded diverse metaphorical applications, each suited to different disciplinary discourses. Sextus offers three examples.

85. See R. J. Hankinson, *The Sceptics* (Psychology Press, 1998), 70–71.

86. Text from R. G. Bury, *Sextus Empiricus: Against the Professors*, Loeb 382 (Harvard University Press, 1949), 244.

> According to one convention, it is the dramatic plot (ἡ δραματικὴ περιπέτεια). Accordingly, we say that there is a tragic or comic *hypothesis*, and *hypotheses* of the myths of Euripides and Sophocles by a certain Dicaearchus, not referring to anything other by *hypothesis* than the plot of the drama. And according to another custom of meaning, *hypothesis* in rhetoric refers to engagement in a controversy over particular details. In this way, the sophists are accustomed often to say "a *hypothesis* is required." And as yet a third use, we call the starting point of an argument the *hypothesis*."[87]

Sextus, arguing against the geometers, is concerned with the third use of the term. In logical contexts, *hypothesis* means something like "assumption" or "premise." It is this logical use that appears in the common idiom "καθ' ὑπόθεσιν," roughly meaning "let us suppose . . ." or "if, for the sake of argument, we assume . . ."[88]

The second sense of *hypothesis* mentioned by Sextus is that associated with rhetoric, discussed above in connection with Theon, Quintillian, and others. Sextus notes that the term *hypothesis* refers to the subject matter of speeches with greater specificity of detail. Sextus makes a point to distinguish this rhetorical sense of *hypothesis* from the narrative sense but, like the many uses surveyed above, it refers to traditional subject material with specified content. The rhetorical and narrative senses of the term are clearly related.

The narrative *hypothesis* is the first sense listed. Importantly, Sextus raises this use of the term only to distinguish it from the logical use that concerns him. As such, Sextus's definition is somewhat less clear than the authors considered above. Sextus simply identifies *hypotheses* with the "plots" (περιπέτεια) of drama and myth.[89] This broad definition

87. Text from Bury, *Sextus Empiricus*, 244.

88. See, for instance, the cognate accusative in Plutarch, *On the Delays of Divine Justice*, 17.

89. In his *Poetics*, Aristotle uses this term to refer to a sudden change of fortunes. This is evidently not how Sextus uses the term. See Gertjan Verhasselt, "The Hypotheses of Euripides and Sophocles by Dicaearchus," *Greek, Roman, and*

covers the use outlined above, but it allows for the misconception that *hypothesis* refers to the "arrangement" (οἰκονομία) or "constitution" (σύστασις) of a particular work.[90] Rather, readers consistently use *hypothesis* language to talk about the story as distinct from its presentation in any particular work.

Sextus illustrates this use of *hypothesis* in dramatic criticism by pointing to a famous collection of plot summaries published by Aristotle's student, Dicaearchus.[91] The original summaries composed by Dicaearchus are mostly lost to us, but they inspired a genre of prolegomena, called *hypotheses* in Greek or, more appropriately, *argumenta* in Latin.[92] Confusingly, Dicaearchus's use of *hypothesis* as a title for his summaries is related to the narratological sense of the term and, yet, distinct: Plot summaries lay out the content of a specific work, often attending to that work's distinctive features. A narrative *hypothesis*, by way of contrast, refers to the shared elements of a narrative tradition. Despite the historical connection noted by Sextus, the plot summaries, called *hypotheses/argumenta*, are not identifiable with a narrative *hypothesis* as the term is used by readers in the late Hellenistic period and Roman principate.

Byzantine Studies 55 (2015): 615. See also the discussion in R. Kassel, "Hypothesis," in *ΣΧΟΛΙΑ: Studia Ad Criticam Interpretationemque Textuum Graecorum et Ad Historiam Iuris Graeco-Romani Pertinentia Viro Doctissimo D. Holwerda Oblata*, ed. W. J. Aerts et al (E. Forsten, 1985), 53–59.

90. On οἰκονομία, see Nünlist, *The Ancient Critic at Work*, 23–28.

91. On the work of Dicaearchus, see D. C. Mirhady, "Dicaearchus of Messana: The Sources, Text and Translation," in *Dicaearchus of Messana: Text, Translation, and Discussion*, ed. W. W. Fortenbaugh and E. Schütrumpf, Rutgers University Studies in Classical Humanities 10 (Routledge, 2018), 6–123; Verhasselt, "The Hypotheses of Euripides and Sophocles by Dicaearchus." On this genre of prolegomena, see Rudolf Pfeiffer, *History of Classical Scholarship from the Beginnings to the End of the Hellenistic Age* (Clarendon Press, 1968), 193–96; Bruce Metzger, *A Textual Commentary on the Greek New Testament*, 3rd ed. (United Bible Societies, 1971), 25–26; Dickey, *Ancient Greek Scholarship*, 26, 42.

92. The relationship of the Latin *argumentum* to the Greek *hypothesis* is discussed at length in an excursus at the end of chapter 2.

Sextus's lexographic excursus highlights a few key points. First, Sextus draws attention to the polysemy of "*hypothesis*." Different disciplines used the word in different ways during the first, second, and third centuries. It is particularly important to exclude the logical sense of the term when considering the word's attested uses. Second, Sextus provides further evidence that the narrative use of *hypothesis* was widely recognized as a piece of technical vocabulary in ancient literary criticism. His definition is vague, but it corresponds with the use of the term found in other late Hellenistic authors. Finally, Sextus raises the confusing comparison with the genre of Dicaearchean summaries, also called *hypotheses/argumenta*. These uses of the term are historically related but importantly distinct.

Conclusion

Hellenistic and Roman readers at the turn of the millennium had their own vocabulary to describe the complicated interrelations of multiple (distinct) books that together constituted a literary tradition. The term *hypothesis* picked out a notional stratum of basic content held in common across multiple works. Authors used the idea of a *hypothesis* to describe the relationship of their own work to its predecessors. Readers, likewise, used the idea to describe and evaluate pluriform traditions. The content of a *hypothesis* was typically imagined as traditional. At the same time, the identification of certain parts of a story as "basic" is necessarily a normative judgement. The idea that certain elements of a story were *given* (and others were not) allowed readers to legitimize variation between stories as well as critique versions they disapproved of.

This way of thinking about pluriform literature was native to discourse around narrative traditions, specifically dramatic criticism. It proved useful, however, to readers and writers of various narrative and non-narrative genres. The idea that literary traditions were composed of distinct books that shared a substratum of nonnegotiable content became something like a "standard model" in the bookish imagination of the first and second centuries. As we will see, it is sometimes possible to recognize this model shaping the thought of readers even where explicit *hypothesis* language is absent.

It was in this Greek-speaking milieu that the gospels were read, transmitted, and composed. Christians were shaped by, and in turn, shaped the cultural matrices of the Roman Empire, including contemporary literary cultures. Early Christian readers and writers brought the same interpretive categories to the gospels that Dio Chrysostom, Dionysius of Halicarnassus, and Plutarch brought to other Greek books. There is every reason to expect, therefore, that Christians imagined narrative *hypotheses* abstracted out of their own books. Thankfully, there is no need to speculate about whether the idea of a narrative *hypothesis* conditioned the reception of the gospels since early Christian commentators use the term explicitly to theorize the plurality of gospels, the unity of Christian teaching, and the boundaries between accepted and rejected versions of the story of Jesus.

CHAPTER TWO

The Gospel *Hypothesis* in Irenaeus of Lyon

"Being more or less intelligent does not permit someone to change the *hypothesis* itself."

—Irenaeus of Lyon, *Against Heresies*

Introduction

IRENAEUS OF LYON is the first surviving author to reflect at length on the multiplicity of gospels. Many Christians in the second century knew and used more than one gospel, but Irenaeus was the first to articulate a rationale for a collection of four (and only four). Confronted by Christians who regarded only one gospel as authoritative, Irenaeus sought to legitimize the pluriformity of gospel literature. Confronted by Christians who regarded other gospels as authoritative, Irenaeus sought to limit that pluriformity. Like the Hellenistic and Roman readers surveyed in the previous chapter, the idea of a literary *hypothesis* allowed Irenaeus to articulate the extent and limits of legitimate variation in the narrative tradition about Jesus's life.

Irenaeus's appeal to a *hypothesis* is not his most famous argument related to the collection of gospel literature. Best known is, perhaps, his appeal to the symbolic significance of the number four.[1] Just as there

1. See, for instance, T. C. Skeat, "Irenaeus and the Four-Gospel Canon," *Novum Testamentum* 34, no. 2 (1992): 194–199. More recently Francis Watson, *Gospel Writing: A Canonical Perspective* (Eerdmans, 2013), 453–472, 553–603. On the usefulness of a quadriform cosmos for the Christian bibliographic imagination, see Jeremiah Coogan, "Reading (in) a Quadriform Cosmos: Gospel Books in the Early

are four winds and four corners of the earth, says Irenaeus, so too there are exactly four gospels. The protocanonical logic reflected in this line of argument sits uneasily alongside Irenaeus's invocation of the gospel *hypothesis.*[2] Also well-known is Irenaeus's frequent appeal to the "rule of faith."[3] The term translated as "rule" (κανών) refers to a standard of measure—historically, a tool used by tradespeople. This "rule of faith," Irenaeus claims, is a kind of baptismal confession, handed down by Jesus's disciples as a standard for evaluating Christian theology.[4]

Irenaeus's argument that only Matthew, Mark, Luke, and John preserve the same *hypothesis* is, by comparison, less well known.[5] Despite their differences in detail and scope, Irenaeus claims that these four gospels individually and equally transmit the same *hypothesis.* Other so-called gospels, by way of contrast, destroy the *hypothesis.*

Christian Bibliographic Imagination," *Journal of Early Christian Studies* 31, no. 1 (2023): 85–103.

2. Though I differ on particular points of interpretation, Kenneth Laing presents compelling evidence that Irenaeus was not entirely consistent about the authority and status of the gospels as scripture. Kenneth Laing, *Irenaeus, the Scriptures, and the Apostolic Writings: Re-Evaluating the Status of the New Testament Writings at the End of the Second Century*, The Library of New Testament Studies 659 (T&T Clark, 2022). Similarly, I conclude that Irenaeus sometimes discusses the pluriformity of the gospels in ways that are inconsistent with his own notion of a fourfold gospel.

3. Key passages for Irenaeus's understanding of the "rule of faith" are *Against Heresies* 1.22.1 and 3.11.1 as well as *Demonstration of the Apostolic Preaching* 6. A passage sometimes identified with the rule of faith at 1.10.1 is discussed at length below. For a parallel use, see Tertullian, *Prescription Against Heretics* 12–13.

4. On the use of this "rule of faith" as a baptismal confession, see Irenaeus, *Against Heresies* 1.9.4. Everett Ferguson, "Functions of the Rule of Faith," in *The Rule of Faith: A Guide* (Cascade Books, 2015).

5. The importance of *hypothesis* language in *Against Heresies* has not, of course, been overlooked by specialists. I cite many of these studies below but, in particular, I extend many of the conclusions already reached in Anthony Briggman, "Literary and Rhetorical Theory in Irenaeus, Part 1," *Vigiliae Christianae* 69, no. 5 (2015): 500–527; Anthony Briggman, "Literary and Rhetorical Theory in Irenaeus, Part 2," *Vigiliae Christianae* 70, no. 1 (2016): 31–50. My differences with Briggman are discussed in note 41.

Additionally, Irenaeus uses the idea of a narrative *hypothesis* to discuss methods of interpretation and the origin of heretical myths. In each of these contexts, it is clear that Irenaeus simply takes the concept of a narrative *hypothesis* for granted. The idea of a basic story that constitutes a narrative tradition is clearly just part of how Irenaeus thinks about books.

Concepts shape our thinking even when they are not made explicit. The history of scholarship on Irenaeus's use of *hypothesis* language has quite understandably focused on actual appearances of the term. But this overlooks the widespread practice of using the title of one work as a shorthand for a relevant *hypothesis*. Irenaeus sometimes uses the term *gospel* not only to refer to the Christian message of salvation or as the title of specific books but also to invoke the *hypothesis* of the gospels. Recognizing this use of the term in *Against Heresies* reveals the extent to which the idea of a *hypothesis* pervades Irenaeus's thinking about the gospel tradition.

Irenaeus's Education

Irenaeus was a late second-century bishop of Lugdunum (modern-day Lyon) in the Roman province of Gaul. His most important work, *On the Detection and Overthrow of So-Called Gnosis* (conventionally, *Against Heresies*), was a critique of rival Christianities and an articulation of his own orthodoxy. Many of Irenaeus's opponents boasted a particular "knowledge" (γνῶσις) underlying their distinctive interpretations of Christian scripture.[6] As such, education, expertise, and methods of reading were sites of contention between Irenaeus and his cultured rivals. It is a surprise, then, that in the preface to his work, Irenaeus apparently denies his own sophistication.

> You will not expect rhetorical art (which we have not learned) from us who reside among the Celts and mostly engage in

6. On "gnosticism," see Michael Allen Williams, *Rethinking "Gnosticism": An Argument for Dismantling a Dubious Category* (Princeton University Press, 1999).

> barbaric dialects—nor power of composition (which we have not practiced), nor excellence of composition nor persuasiveness (which we do not know).[7]

We should not take Irenaeus at his word. Downplaying one's own training and skill is itself a rhetorical *topos* that dates back at least to Socrates's disavowal of his own abilities in Plato's *Apology*.[8] Scholarship on the level of education displayed in *Against Heresies* has mostly contradicted Irenaeus's modest self-presentation.[9]

In ways large and small, Irenaeus's work betrays an author steeped in Greek literary culture. He has apparent first-hand knowledge of Homer (*AH* 1.12.2), Hesiod (*AH* 2.21.2), Plato (*AH* 2.23.2), Pindar (*AH* 2.21.2), and a lost work of the Hellenistic playwright Antiphanes (2.14.1–2). It is true that Irenaeus's knowledge of philosophy was largely (though perhaps not exclusively) indebted to the doxographical tradition—handbooks containing summaries of different schools of thought.[10] But this too reflects a practice typical of the educated class during the second sophistic.

---

7. Text from Adelin Rousseau and Louis Doutreleau, eds., *Irénée de Lyon: Contre les hérésies, Livre 1*, vol. 2., Sources chrétiennes 264 (Éditions du Cerf, 1979), 25.

8. Robert M. Grant, "Irenaeus and Hellenistic Culture," *Harvard Theological Review* 42, no. 1 (1949): 47. The archetypical disavowal of rhetorical sophistication is Socrates's self-presentation in Plato's *Apology* (17b–d). It is a common feature of Attic oratory (e.g., Lysias, *On the Property of Aristophanes* (19)1; Isocrates, *Antidosis* 15.15, 26, 36; Isaeus, *Aristarchus* (10)1), adopted by Roman authors (Dio Chrysostom, *1st Oration* 9, *42nd Oration* 2–3; Hermogenes, *On Style* 2.6).

9. A modest estimate of Irenaeus's education comes from William R. Schoedel, "Philosophy and Rhetoric in the Adversus Haereses of Irenaeus," *Vigilae Christianae* 13, no. 1 (1959): 22–32. Scholarly reevaluations are cited in the following notes.

10. Grant contrasts Irenaeus's rhetorical acumen with "the slightness of his acquaintance with philosophy." Grant, "Irenaeus and Hellenistic Culture," 42. But see Anthony Briggman, "Revisiting Irenaeus' Philosophical Acumen," *Vigiliae Christianae* 65, no. 2 (January 1, 2011): 115–124.

Whether taught or self-studied, Irenaeus displays undeniable familiarity with Hellenistic and Roman rhetorical conventions.[11] The structure of Irenaeus's argumentation corresponds, more or less, to Ciceronian ideals.[12] Likewise, he makes frequent use of classical *topoi*, known to Roman authors by way of *progymnasmata*—handbooks of rhetorical theory and exercises.[13] In a point of special importance for our investigation, scholars have long recognized that Irenaeus uses the technical vocabulary of Hellenistic literary criticism. For instance, Irenaeus uses the term *economy* (οἰκονομία) to describe the organization of a text or narrative more than a hundred times in *Against Heresies*.[14] The term originally referred to the management of a household and then, by extension, the management of the state. But, as illustrated in the previous chapter, literary critics used this term to describe the organization of literary works.[15]

---

11. Among the first to argue for Irenaeus's rhetorical sophistication was D. B. Reynders, "La polémique de saint Irénée Méthode et principes," *Recherches de théologie ancienne et médiévale* 7 (1935): 5–27. For an updated treatment, see Briggman, "Literary and Rhetorical Theory in Irenaeus, Part 1"; Briggman, "Literary and Rhetorical Theory in Irenaeus, Part 2."

12. On the structure Irenaeus's argumentation, see Schoedel, "Philosophy and Rhetoric in the Adversus Haereses of Irenaeus," 27. Brendan Harris attributes further agreements between Irenaeus and the rhetorical techniques endorsed Cicero to the former's use of rhetorical handbooks. Brendan Harris, "Irenaeus's Engagement with Rhetorical Theory in His Exegesis of the Johannine Prologue in Adversus Haereses 1.8.5–1.9.3," *Vigiliae Christianae* 72, no. 4 (2018): 405–420.

13. Schoedel, "Philosophy and Rhetoric in the Adversus Haereses of Irenaeus," 30–31. See also the *topoi* discussed in D. Jeffrey Bingham, "Paideia and Polemic in Second-Century Lyons: Irenaeus on Education," in *Pedagogy in Ancient Judaism and Early Christianity*, ed. Karina Martin Hogan, Matthew Goff, and Emma Wasserman (SBL Press, 2017), 338–343.

14. Adhémar d'Alès, "Le mot OIKONOMIA dans la langue théologique de Saint Irénée," *Revue des Études Grecques* 32 (1919): 1–9; Robert M. Grant, *Irenaeus of Lyons* (Routledge, 1997), 36–37; Anthony Briggman, "Literary and Rhetorical Theory in Irenaeus, Part 1," 517–523.

15. In the previous chapter, I consistently translated the term οἰκονομία as "arrangement." See, in particular, the discussion of Sch. Soph. *El.* 817. On the use of this term

Irenaeus was not extraordinary. He was not a Clement of Alexandria, engaging contemporary philosophical movements on their own terms. Neither is Irenaeus the equal of Origen, at the bleeding edge of philological scholarship.[16] Rather, Irenaeus's *Against Heresies* reflects a more-or-less normal education for a member of the Roman literati.[17] But therein lies Irenaeus's value for understanding early readers of the gospels. Irenaeus is not performing some remarkable feat of intellectual gymnastics in applying the idea of a *hypothesis* to gospel literature. He is, rather, describing the gospels according to a standard model of pluriform literary traditions in his culture of reading.

The Valentinian *Hypothesis*

Rewriting Pagan Myths

Irenaeus makes frequent use of *hypothesis* language in the first two books of *Against Heresies*. Like the Hellenistic literary critics surveyed in the previous chapter, Irenaeus uses the term *hypothesis* to refer to (what he understands as) fundamental elements held in common across multiple instantiations of the same story. While the term appears in a wide variety of rhetorical contexts in *Against Heresies*, Irenaeus's debt to contemporary literary criticism is nowhere more explicit than in his critique of Valentinian Christians.

The label "Valentinian" is an exonym for a group of Christians whose intellectual genealogy can be traced back to a mid-second-century Roman teacher named Valentinus.[18] Many of the so-called Valentinians

---

in rhetorical theory, see René Nünlist, *The Ancient Critic at Work: Terms and Concepts of Literary Criticism in Greek Scholia* (Cambridge University Press, 2009), 23–28.

16. Bernhardt Neuschäfer, *Origenes als Philologe*, 2 vols. (Friedrich Reinhardt, 1987).

17. On Greek education in the Roman Empire, see Raffaella Cribiore, *Gymnastics of the Mind: Greek Education in Hellenistic and Roman Egypt* (Princeton University Press, 2005).

18. Christoph Markschies, *Valentinus Gnosticus? Untersuchungen zur valentinianischen Gnosis; mit einem Kommentar zu den Fragmenten Valentins*. Wissenschaftliche

actually known to Irenaeus were followers of a more recent teacher, named Ptolemy.[19] While there were theological differences between the followers of Valentinus, the movement was marked by a cosmogony that explained the physical universe as the creation of an inferior power (identified with the God of Jewish scripture) and an emphasis on knowledge.

In the second book of *Against Heresies*, Irenaeus uses the term *hypothesis* to describe the (purported) origin of the Valentinian creation myth. Valentinian Christians, Irenaeus asserts, rewrote pagan myths the same way that playwrights rewrote their mythological sources. After summarizing the procession of divine powers from The One, which some Valentinians named "Depth" (βυθός), Irenaeus claims that a better version of the story told by the Valentinians could be found in another source—Antiphanes's *Theogony*.

> Antiphanes, one of the old comic-poets, spoke much more realistically and agreeably in the *Theogony*. Indeed, he speaks about Chaos sent out by Night and Silence . . . they have transferred these things (which everywhere are made into comedies in theatres by actors with the clearest voices) into their own *hypothesis*—truly, indeed, teaching the very same *hypotheses*, only changing the names. (2.14.1–2)[20]

Antiphanes was a fourth-century BCE playwright of the Middle Comedy. Like the Athenian playwrights, Antiphanes sometimes took traditional myths as his subject material. For instance, Antiphanes

---

Untersuchungen zum Neuen Testament 65 (Mohr, 1992); Einar Thomassen, *The Spiritual Seed: The Church of the "Valentinians"* (Brill, 2006).

19. See Irenaeus, *Against Heresies* 1.Preface.2. Ptolemy's isagogic *Letter to Flora* is preserved in Epiphanius, *Panarion* 33.3.1–7.10.

20. Text from Adelin Rousseau and Louis Doutreleau, eds., *Irénée de Lyon: Contre les hérésies, Livre 2*, vol. 2., Sources chrétiennes 294 (Éditions du Cerf, 1982), 130–32. The Latin term used in both instances is *argumentum*; see the excursus on the translation of *hypothesis* in *Against Heresies* at the end of this chapter.

seems to have written his own version of *Philoctetes*, already written and rewritten by the three Athenians.[21] *Theogony*, as Irenaeus's summary suggests, was Antiphanes's account of the origin of the gods. The best-known work in this narrative tradition was, of course, Hesiod's *Theogony*, but the myth was frequently retold.[22] Like the Valentinian cosmogony, this narrative tradition featured the origin and subsequent generation of supernatural entities from mysterious primal powers. Irenaeus argues, therefore, that a comic poet had already written a more compelling version of the Valentinian story. Irenaeus claims to have found the origin of his opponents' cosmogony in pagan mythology.[23]

After summarizing Antiphanes's play, Irenaeus restates his claim with *hypothesis* language. He asserts, first, that the Valentinians transferred certain narrative elements from the theogony tradition into "their own *hypothesis*" (*suum argumentum*). This initial claim does not suggest that Antiphanes and the Valentinians are telling the same story, but that both stories share some fundamental features. But then, Irenaeus corrects himself (*immo vero*) in order to make a stronger claim. Valentinian Christians, says Irenaeus, propound "the very same *hypotheses*" (*eisdem argumentis*) as the pagans, only changing the names of

21. S. Douglas Olson, *Fragementa Comica. Antiphanes Frr. 101-192*, Fragmenta Comica 19.2 (Verlag Antike, 2022), 113–115.

22. Marco Antonio Santamaría, "Our Co(s)Mic Origins: Theogonies in Greek Comedy," *Arch. für Relig.* 21–22.1 (2020): 369–86; Stephen Scully, *Hesiod's Theogony: From Near Eastern Creation Myths to Paradise Lost* (Oxford University Press, 2015).

23. The theogony tradition is just one of many sources that Irenaeus proposes for the Valentinian myth. Throughout the first book of *Against Heresies*, Irenaeus claims that the Valentinians derived their system from earlier gnostic groups, including the Basilideans. And in the section that follows, Irenaeus argues that the Valentinians derived their system from the speculations of pagan philosophers. Irenaeus may shift between proposals as a matter of rhetorical convenience but, at the same time, they are not mutually exclusive.

dramatis personae.[24] So, Irenaeus concludes, these heretical Christians do not merely borrow from pagan playwrights but, in fact, retell the same myths using different names.

There can be no question that Irenaeus here uses the term *hypothesis* in the narrative sense often associated with literary criticism.[25] Irenaeus begins the discussion by comparing Valentinians to Hellenistic playwrights who rewrite traditional narratives. Then, after offering a narrative summary, Irenaeus uses the term *hypothesis* to refer to basic, narrative elements shared across multiple versions of the same story. At first, Irenaeus's accusation assumes that the pagan theogony tradition and the Valentinian cosmogony have distinct *hypotheses* with elements of the former borrowed by the latter. Then, Irenaeus revises his accusation to suggest that Valentinian authors, in fact, share common *hypotheses* with pagan mythographers. The key elements (i.e., the *hypothesis*) of the Valentinian story of salvation, according to Irenaeus, is simply a rewritten pagan myth.

Irenaeus's arguments exhibit many of the key characteristics of the use of *hypothesis* language in late Hellenistic literary criticism. It is clear from Philodemus, for instance, that a narrative *hypothesis* was imagined as traditional. Irenaeus accuses his opponents of reusing traditional myths. At the same time, Dio and the scholia invoke the notional *hypothesis* while acknowledging differences between versions of a story. Irenaeus, likewise, acknowledges that Antiphanes and the Valentinians used different names for their cosmic powers. And Irenaeus certainly would have expected his readers to recognize that the stories differed in other respects. Irenaeus used the idea of a narrative *hypothesis* to

24. The use of the plural *hypotheses* suggests that Irenaeus has multiple myths in mind. And, indeed, only a few paragraphs later Irenaeus also accuses the Valentinians of stealing the plot of the Pandora myth from Herodotus (2.14.5).

25. Epiphanius's paraphrase of Irenaeus's argument corroborates this interpretation (*Panarion* 2.30.4.5–10). Epiphanius lists poets who rewrote the same "tragic *hypothesis*" (τὴν τραγικὴν ὑπόθεσιν) in succession. Karl Holl, *Epiphanius I Ancoratus und Panarion haer. 1-33* (De Gruyter, 2013), 389.

articulate his claim that, despite obvious differences, the Valentinians reused a pagan creation myth.

The Valentinian *Hypothesis*
Interpreting the Gospels

In the preface to his *Against Heresies*, Irenaeus says that his entire heresiological undertaking was inspired by reading Valentinian "commentaries" (1.Preface.2).[26] Judging from what little survives of these commentaries, Valentinian interpreters used then-popular methods for the allegorical interpretation of traditional myths.[27] Stoic, Platonic, and other philosophical schools had long looked to the Homeric epics and other myths for theological, cosmological, and moral instruction hidden sometimes within narrative minutia.[28] Heraclitus the Grammarian (first century CE), for instance, interpreted Zeus's threatening speech about dangling his wife, Hera, from Mount Olympus with an anvil on each foot as an allegory for the creation of the universe (*Homeric Problems*

26. The closest thing to a surviving example of such commentaries are Origen's quotations of Heracleon's *Commentary on John*. The surviving fragments of this work corroborate Irenaeus's characterization of these commentaries. See Ansgar Wucherpfennig, *Heracleon Philologus : Gnostische Johannesexegese im zweiten Jahrhundert* (Mohr Siebeck, 2002); A. E. Brooke, *The Fragments of Heracleon* (Gorgias, 2004). For a collection of Valentinian fragments, see Geoffrey Smith, *Valentinian Christianity: Texts and Translations,* (University of California Press, 2020).

27. For an excellent recent treatment, see Lewis Ayres, "Irenaeus vs. the Valentinians: Toward a Rethinking of Patristic Exegetical Origins," *Journal of Early Christian Studies* 23, no. 2 (2015): 153–187.

28. For an introduction and history of allegorical interpretation in Greek and Roman literature, see Peter Struck, *Birth of the Symbol: Ancient Readers at the Limits of Their Texts* (Princeton University Press, 2014). On allegorical interpretation among the Stoics, in particular, see Mikolaj Domaradzki, "Stoic Allegoresis: The Problem of Definition and Influence," *Classical Philology* 117, no. 1 (2022): 139–162. For a treatment of how this approach to texts shaped the reception of Jewish and Christian scripture, see David Dawson, *Allegorical Readers and Cultural Revision in Ancient Alexandria* (University of California Press, 1991). The tension between allegorical reading and viewing works as expressions of a common *hypothesis* is discussed at length in chapter 3.

40). These anvils, says Heraclitus, refer to the two elementary principals: water and earth. Similarly, a Valentinian commentator interpreted the number of hours mentioned in Jesus's Parable of the Vineyard (Matt 20) as an intimation of the number of Aeons (i.e., spiritual powers emanated from the primal monad) belonging to the divine Pleroma (*AH* 1.1.3). Though strange to modern eyes, Valentinian methods of reading scripture could boast a long and distinguished pedigree in philosophical and other elite literary circles.[29]

Irenaeus's response to this way of reading the gospels, likewise, drew on conventional lines of argumentation against allegorical interpretation. Aristarchus of Samothrace, the Alexandrian librarian, was famous for his opposition to *allegoresis* as an interpretive strategy.[30] Aristarchus, one commentator reports, "did not want to allegorize anything in Homer . . . but understood everything according to what part of the story had been shown and said beforehand."[31] Narrative context, according to Aristarchus, weighs against the allegorical interpretation of particular details.[32] Irenaeus adopts a similar line of argument, contending that the allegorical explanations advanced by Valentinian interpreters "go beyond the order (τάξις) and sequence (εἱρμός) of the

29. On the philosophical use of allegorical reading, see also Luc Brisson, *How Philosophers Saved Myths: Allegorical Interpretation and Classical Mythology* (University of Chicago Press, 2008). The same interpretation of the Homeric anvils is found in the first century in Lucius Annaeus Cornutus's *Compendium of Greek Theology* 26.

30. On Aristarchus and allegorical interpretation, see Francesca Schironi, *The Best of the Grammarians: Aristarchus of Samothrace on the Iliad* (University of Michigan Press, 2018), 138–142. Ayres draws attention to the rhetoric of obviousness in antiallegorical argumentation and notes additional parallels with antiallegorical interpreters in the Roman period. Ayres, "Irenaeus vs. the Valentinians," 169–180.

31. Eustathius, *Commentary on the Iliad* 40.25-34. Text from Schironi, *The Best of the Grammarians*, 141.

32. One scholion describes Aristarchus as skeptical of interpretation that concern "matters beyond what is said" (εξω των φραζομενων), a line of argument that also resembles Irenaeus's critique of the Valentinians (Sch. D. *Il.* 5.385). Helmut van Thiel, ed., *Scholia D in Iliadem*, 242.

scriptures" (*Against Heresies* 1.8.1) and "tear-out words, phrases, and parables from here and from there, in order to adapt the *logia* of God for their myths" (1.8.1).[33] Instead, Irenaeus argues, incidental details in the gospels should be read as part of the surrounding story.

In the course of this argument, Irenaeus found the idea of a narrative *hypothesis* useful for drawing a contrast between Valentinian exegetical methods and his own way of reading scripture.

> You see, beloved, the method by which they deceive themselves: they abuse the scriptures in their attempts to put together a fiction (πλάσμα) from them. . . . And each of the things they have said have been taken from the truth and, by exploiting the names, brought over into their own *hypothesis* (ἰδία ὑπόθεσις), so that according to them in all these [aforementioned verses] John does not mention our Lord Jesus Christ. (*Against Heresies* 1.9.1–2)[34]

The passage of scripture under debate is the Johannine prologue. Valentinian interpreters, according to Irenaeus, understood words like "life," "light," and "human" as found in John 1:4 to reveal the existence of the primordial Aeons. But it is absurd, Irenaeus argues, to read this introduction to Jesus's life as wholly concerned with entities other than Jesus. The Valentinians, he says, have plucked these words and phrases out of their narrative context in order to assemble, what Irenaeus calls, "a fiction" (πλάσμα) and "their own *hypothesis* (ἰδία ὑπόθεσις)."[35]

Irenaeus, then, illustrates this claim by comparing Valentinian exegesis to a genre of creatively rewritten poetry—the Homeric cento.

---

33. Text from Rousseau and Doutreleau, *Irénée de Lyon: Livre 1*, vol 2., 112–113, 116.

34. Text from Rousseau and Doutreleau, *Irénée de Lyon*, 2:137.

35. The pointed juxtaposition of the Valentinian *hypothesis* with the life of Jesus suggests that Irenaeus has in mind the *hypothesis* of the gospels in particular. See the discussion in note 41 below.

> So, gathering together words and names that are scattered about, they change them (as we have already shown) from a natural to an unnatural meaning, like those who put forward any-random-thing (τυχούσας) as *hypotheses* and then try to make them [appear] well-thought-up from Homer so that foolish people think that the newly concocted *hypothesis* is what Homer really composed. And many are persuaded by the arranged sequence of the passages so that they suppose Homer might have composed these things in this way.[36]

The cento to which Irenaeus alludes is a genre of poetry consisting entirely of lines copied verbatim from another poetic *oeuvre*. A cento could be written on any subject but surviving examples suggest they were playful exercises, intended to demonstrate the poet's facility with some traditional corpora.[37] Like the comparison to a comic playwright, then, Irenaeus's comparison of Valentinian exegesis to a genre of playfully rewritten poetry is probably intended to belittle his opponents.

Irenaeus proceeds to quote a Homeric cento.[38] This short poem is composed entirely of lines copied out of Homer's *Iliad* and *Odyssey* but, in its novel arrangement, briefly describes one of Hercules's famous labors. "What simpleton," asks Irenaeus, "could be persuaded by such things and so believe that Homer composed these [verses] on this *hypothesis?*"[39] And yet, says Irenaeus, Valentinian interpreters treat the

36. Text from Rousseau and Doutreleau, *Irénée de Lyon*, 2:147.

37. This understanding of the cento is indebted to Ausonius's explanation in the preface to his *Carmen Nuptialis*. Anna Lefteratou, however, emphasizes the variety of motivations for composing a cento—especially Christian examples. Anna Lefteratou, *The Homeric Centos: Homer and the Bible Interwoven*, Oxford Studies in Late Antiquity (Oxford University Press, 2023), 7–52, esp. 16.

38. On the composition of this cento by someone other than Irenaeus, see R. L. Wilken, "The Homeric Cento in Irenaeus, 'Adversus Haereses' I, 9,4," *Vigiliae Christianae* 21 (1967): 25–33, esp. 29.

39. Text from Rousseau and Doutreleau, *Irénée de Lyon: Livre 1*, vol. 2, 149–150.

gospels the same way that the author of a cento treats the Homeric epic. An appropriately trained reader of a Valentinian commentary, according to Irenaeus, "will recognize the names, phrases, and parables but will not recognize their blasphemous *hypothesis*."[40]

The curious case of a cento inverts the typical relationship between *hypothesis* and text. Instead of describing multiple versions of a shared basic story, Irenaeus describes a shared text (i.e., Homeric lines) with different *hypotheses* (i.e., the Trojan War and Herculean labors). Still, Irenaeus uses the term *hypothesis* to distinguish a notional story from any particular textualization thereof.

But the concept of a narrative *hypothesis* is not useful only to explain the cento. Irenaeus raises the analogy in order to map these categories onto the interpretation of the gospels. According to Irenaeus, the labors of Hercules is to the text of the *Iliad* as the Valentinian myth is to the text of the gospels. Just as any educated reader will recognize that the cento preserves Homer's language with a foreign *hypothesis*, so too should Irenaeus's reader recognize that Valentinian interpreters have misappropriated the language of the gospels. It follows, then, that the story of the Trojan War is to the *Iliad* as the story of Jesus's life (i.e., the *hypothesis* of the gospels) is to the gospels.

Throughout these anti-Valentinian polemics, Irenaeus uses the term *hypothesis* in a thoroughly narrative sense. Irenaeus uses "fiction" (πλάσμα)" and "myth" (μύθος) as almost synonyms for the Valentinian *hypothesis*, characterizes it as a rewriting of the pagan theogony, and compares it to a cento about the labors of Hercules. The term does not refer to a theological system, supposition, or creedal statement. It is, rather, a story.

Just as Hellenistic literary critics most often use the term *hypothesis* to organize and evaluate stories that exist in more than one version, so too Irenaeus's use of *hypothesis* language is occasioned by pluriform narrative traditions. The Valentinian creation myth is not identifiable with any single work but, rather, a story found in many different texts. Likewise, Irenaeus's chosen analogies—the origin of the gods, the labors

40. Text from Rousseau and Doutreleau, *Irénée de Lyon*, 2:150–151.

of Hercules, and the Trojan War—are famously pluriform narratives. It is the existence of multiple versions that makes it useful to have language that distinguishes the story itself from any instantiation thereof.

In the examples considered so far, Irenaeus is concerned with the mistreatment of scripture by his theological opponents. These polemical uses of the term demonstrate how the idea of a narrative *hypothesis* structures Irenaeus's thinking about narrative traditions. But even in these polemics, Irenaeus is thinking about the gospels as books with a shared *hypothesis* of their own. Indeed, he has already revealed the content of that gospel *hypothesis* in his objection that Valentinian interpretation of John turns the gospel into a story about something other than "our Lord Jesus Christ" (*Against Heresies* 1.9.2). Indeed, the whole logic of Irenaeus's argument against the Valentinians takes for granted that the gospels have a *hypothesis* of their own.

The Hypothesis of the Gospels

Irenaeus does not use *hypothesis* language only when describing the stories, books, and interpretive practices of others. So far, Irenaeus has left the true *hypothesis* of the gospels mostly implicit in his critique of the Valentinians. But Irenaeus goes on to be perfectly explicit. Immediately following his discussion of the Homeric cento, Irenaeus instructs the reader how to interpret the gospels according to their true *hypothesis*.[41]

41. Paul Blowers, Frances Young, and Anthony Briggman, (among others) have highlighted the idea of a *hypothesis* in Irenaeus's constructive thought. Paul M. Blowers, "The Regula Fidei and the Narrative Character of Early Christian Faith," *Ecclesiology: The Journal for Catholic and Evangelical Theology* 6, no. 2 (1997): 199–228; Frances M. Young, *Biblical Exegesis and the Formation of Christian Culture* (Baker Academic, 2002), 17–21; Briggman, "Literary and Rhetorical Theory in Irenaeus, Part 1"; Richard A Norris, "Theology and Language in Irenaeus of Lyon," *Anglican Theological Review* 76, no. 3 (1994): 285–295. These interpreters have generally understood Irenaeus's *hypothesis* as the narrative structure of all scripture/history. This interpretation is correct in so far as Irenaeus sees Christ as the goal of all history and scripture. Moreover, Irenaeus understands the canonical gospels as speaking to the whole history of salvation (e.g., the debate over John 1:1–18 outlined above). But (apart from the polemical uses described above) Irenaeus uses *hypothesis* language only to describe the basic story of the gospels (not all of scripture). This is made clear by Irenaeus's pointed

Irenaeus begins by articulating the faith "received from the apostles and from their disciples" (*Against Heresies* 1.10.1).[42] The content of that faith, says Irenaeus, are the persons of the trinity, the life of Jesus, and its implications for the final judgement. Here, Irenaeus draws special attention to the narrative of Jesus's life—outlining the virgin birth, passion, resurrection, and ascension as key events.[43]

Having established that the story of Jesus's life is traditional (i.e., passed down from the disciples), Irenaeus appeals to the *hypothesis* to explain the proper interpretation of the gospels.[44]

> Being more or less intelligent does not permit someone to change the *hypothesis* itself and invent another God besides the maker and creator and sustainer of all this (as if God were not sufficient to accomplish all this)—or another Christ or

---

contrast of the Valentinian *hypothesis* with the life of Jesus Christ (*Against Heresies* 1.9.2). Likewise, Irenaeus juxtaposes the "blasphemous *hypotheses*" of the Valentinians with "the gospel" (3.16.5, see discussion below). Finally, the passage identified by Briggman himself as the summary of Irenaeus's *hypothesis* (1.10.1) includes the persons of the trinity (i.e., the *dramatis personae*) and an enumeration of the events of Jesus's life (not all of biblical history).

42. Text from Rousseau and Doutreleau, *Irénée de Lyon,: Livre 1*, vol. 2, 155. Briggman argues plausibly that the account given at 1.10.1 is Irenaeus's notion of the *hypothesis*, not the rule of faith. Briggman, "Literary and Rhetorical Theory in Irenaeus, Part 1," 506–509. Frances Young identifies 1.10.1 as the "rule of faith" but notes its narrative character and focuses on the life of Jesus rather than all of scripture (see my disagreement with Briggman et al. in note 41). Frances Young, *Art of Performance: Towards a Theology of Holy Scripture* (Darton, Longman & Todd, 1990), 49–51. See also Paul M. Blowers, "The Regula Fidei and the Narrative Character of Early Christian Faith," *Pro Ecclesia: A Journal of Catholic and Evangelical Theology* 6, no. 2 (May 1997): 199–228.

43. The outline is reminiscent of the scholia that identify the *hypothesis* with primary characters, settings, and events (e.g., Sch. Soph. *Ajax* 1a 13,3–7). I argue below that Irenaeus refers back to this passage as the *hypothesis* that unites the gospels. Probably, Irenaeus imagined Jesus's promised second coming as part of the life of Jesus.

44. The discussion of Philodemus in the previous chapter showed that narrative *hypotheses* were, likewise, regarded as traditional. The Homeric scholia reflect similar assumptions about the *hypothesis* (e.g., Sch. *Il.* 8.429).

> another only-begotten. Rather, one ought to work out [the meaning of] what is found in the parables, and to make them agree with the *hypothesis* of the faith; and, by this interpretation, narrate the activity (πραγματείαν) and economy (οἰκονομίαν) of God—namely what was accomplished for humankind.[45]

The shift from a summary of what the disciples passed down about Jesus to Irenaeus's instructions for the proper interpretation of parables is not, as it might appear, a change of subject. Rather, the *hypothesis* that Irenaeus describes as "change[d]" by the Valentinians and used in the interpretation of parables is nothing other than the narrative of Jesus's life as outlined in the preceding passage. The parables, Irenaeus will proceed to argue, should be interpreted as about the life of Jesus (i.e., the *hypothesis* of the gospels).

The Homeric scholia preserve a striking parallel to Irenaeus's appeal to the *hypothesis* as a guide for interpreting parables. An extended simile in the *Iliad* compares two Greek warriors to lions who snatch away a goat from some dogs (*Il.* 13.198). Zenodotus, the Alexandrian scholar, proposed substituting "two goats" (αἶγε) for the lions, since lions are not known to cooperate.[46] A scholion, however, proposes an alternative to emending the text.

---

45. Text from Rousseau and Doutreleau, *Irénée de Lyon, Livre 1*, vol. 2, 160–163. Irenaeus goes on to enumerate additional subject matter which he understands as related in the parables, including the fall of angels and humanity, the structure of the cosmos, the different covenants, the incarnation of Jesus, and the coming judgement.

46. Sch. *Il.* 13.198a[1]. Text from Hartmut Erbse, *Scholia Graeca in Homeri Iliadem (Scholia vetera). Volumen III: Scholia ad libros K—Z continens* (De Gruyter, 1974), 3:438. Or, perhaps, this was the received reading in Zenodotus's edition. See Klaus Nickau, *Untersuchungen zur textkritischen Methode des Zenodotos von Ephesos* (De Gruyter, 1977), 6–19; Franco Montanari, "Zenodotus, Aristarchus, and the Ekdosis of Homer," in *Editing Texts = Texte Edieren*, ed. Glenn W. Most, Aporemata ; Bd. 2 (Vandenhoeck & Ruprecht, 1998), 1–21; Martin L. West, "Zenodotus' Text," in *Studies in the Text and Transmission of the Iliad*, by Martin L. West (K.G. Saur, 2001), 33–45.

> Or that what [is found] in the parable ought to be interpreted according to the *hypothesis*, not as entirely true.[47]

Another version of the same comment reads:

> What [is found] in the parable should be interpreted according to the *hypothesis*. For lions do not cooperate with one another. Rather, when one lion has snatched [the goat], the other, upon meeting it, snatches it—each dragging the catch toward itself.[48]

These parallel scholia reflect somewhat different approaches to the Homeric simile. The first scholion directs the reader to interpret the passage according to the logic of the story in contrast to the behavior of actual lions. In the story, the Greek warriors are cooperating, so whatever the behavior of actual lions, the lions of the parable should be understood as cooperating. The second scholion also insists on reading the parable "according to the *hypothesis*" but uses the behavior of actual lions to interpret the manner in which the Homeric warriors were cooperating. These parallel scholia, despite the differences between their approaches, both use *hypothesis* language to insist that the Homeric parable be understood as part of the story in which it was embedded.

Irenaeus likewise insists that Jesus's parables should be interpreted as providing information about the narrative of Jesus's life in which they were embedded. The Valentinians, according to Irenaeus, interpreted the parables as relating information about cosmic powers and the origin of the universe. He characterizes this allegorical approach as "changing the *hypothesis*" because the Valentinians understood the parables to be telling a story about something other than Jesus's life. Instead, Irenaeus instructs his reader to interpret the parables as "agree[ing] with" the

47. Text from Erbse, *Scholia Graeca in Homeri Iliadem (Scholia vetera). Volumen III: Scholia ad libros K—Z continens*, 3:438.

48. Sch. *Il.* 13.198a². Text from Erbse, *Scholia Graeca in Homeri Iliadem (Scholia vetera). Volumen III: Scholia ad libros K—Z continens*, 3:438.

story of the gospels—that is, God's salvation of humankind through the life of Jesus.

Irenaeus and the Valentinians are reading the same text but reaching different conclusions about its meaning. Irenaeus appeals, therefore, to something (imagined as) distinct from the text itself. The idea of a basic story (i.e., a *hypothesis*) as found in various written and oral media provides that external point of reference for Irenaeus's argument.[49] Irenaeus will go on to argue that the same basic story is passed down through the preaching of the church universal and in each of the four gospels.

Irenaeus makes a similar argument in the second volume of his *Against Heresies*. Valentinian commentators, says Irenaeus, found some deeper significance in the repeated use of the number thirty in the gospels. Jesus was thirty years old when he began his public ministry (Luke 3:23), and the landowner hired thirty workers in the parable of the vineyard (Matt 20:1–16). These passages, according to the Valentinians, were a figurative indication of the number of primordial divine powers.[50] Likewise, Valentinians had identified the number thirty in nature, which they took as corroboration of their theology (*Against Heresies* 2.24.5). In his response to both lines of reasoning, Irenaeus invokes the *hypothesis* of the gospels (*Against Heresies* 2.25.1).

> All things have been done by God with great wisdom and diligence, suited and arranged for clarity; his Word accomplished whatever happened in antiquity and in recent times. They ought to connect these things not to the number thirty but to the underlying *hypothesis* or to reason.[51]

---

49. Elsewhere, Irenaeus imagines a scenario in which the apostles did not leave any writings and argues that the life of Jesus would nevertheless be known through the preaching of the church (3.4.1–2). See further discussion of Irenaeus's appeal to multiple media below.

50. This point of Valentinian exegesis is raised repeatedly in *Against Heresies* (1.1.3, 3.1; 2.10.2, 12.1, 7).

51. Text from Rousseau and Doutreleau, *Irénée de Lyon, Livre 2*, vol. 2, 250.

God, according to Irenaeus, did not conceal the truth either in nature (i.e., what the Word accomplished in antiquity) or in the gospel (i.e., what the Word accomplished in recent times).[52] Instead of a misguided preoccupation with the number thirty, says Irenaeus, Christians should relate the aspects of nature to "reason" (*rationi*) and details in the gospels to the "underlying *hypothesis*" (*subiacenti . . . argumenta*).[53]

Irenaeus continues the argument by calling Valentinian methods arbitrary and suggesting they could easily be manipulated.

> And they ought not to accept the investigation of God from numbers and syllables, since this is uncertain because of their multiplicity and variety. And because any *hypothesis*, contrary to the truth, could be prepared by anyone, right now, drawn from these very pieces of evidence, since they can be turned in many directions. But they ought to adapt those numbers and the things which are created to the underlying *hypothesis* of the truth.[54]

The Valentinian method of interpretation, he says, would allow anyone to invent a new *hypothesis* at any time and support that concocted story with random details from the gospels. Irenaeus juxtaposes this kind of fraudulent *hypothesis* with the "*hypothesis* of the truth." The true *hypothesis*, the juxtaposition implies, is not a recent or ad hoc fabrication. And it is not derived from arbitrarily selected narrative details. It is, rather, an inherited (i.e., traditional) and widely known story. This basic narrative

52. The relevant section begins by enumerating the objects of interpretation: "the placement of names, call of the apostles, work of the lord, and composition of what has been made" (2.25.1). The first three items are elements of the gospel tradition. The fourth refers to creation. Text from Rousseau and Doutreleau, *Irénée de Lyon*, 2:250.

53. The Latin adjective *subiacenti* probably does not represent a distinct Greek term but an attempt to capture the full sense of *hypothesis*. See the appendix on Latin translation of *hypothesis* at the end of this chapter.

54. Text from Rousseau and Doutreleau, *Irénée de Lyon, Livre 2*, vol. 2, 250–252.

of Jesus's life, says Irenaeus, ought to frame the reader's interpretation of any particular passage from the gospels.

The *Hypothetic* Use of "Gospel"

The term *hypothesis* appears repeatedly in Irenaeus's description of both literary traditions and interpretive practices. It is one of several pieces of rhetorical vocabulary evidently integrated into Irenaeus's way of seeing the world. But concepts can shape someone's thinking even when not explicitly named. The idea of a *hypothesis* informs Irenaeus's imagination of gospel literature even where the word does not actually appear.

Readers and writers in the late Hellenistic and Roman principate—Irenaeus's contemporaries—often referred to the *hypothesis* of a narrative tradition by the title (or something approximating the title) of an important work in that tradition. This word or phrase functioned as a shorthand for the *hypothesis.* This shorthand was used to characterize subsequent works in the same narrative tradition whether or not those works actually used it as their title.

Athenaeus's *Deipnosophists* (meaning, "The Dinner Experts") is a fictional dialogue filled with anecdotes, literary allusions, and quotations about food and drink. The conversation of one dinner party turns to the appropriateness of large drinking vessels (11.504d-e). One guest appeals to Socrates's drinking habits, as portrayed by Xenophon.

> If one considers these words of the noble Xenophon, they will be able to recognize the jealousy which the most brilliant Plato had toward him. Or, possibly, these men were contentious from the beginning since they perceived each other's unique virtue and, probably, they competed to be first in rank as we can perceive not only from what they said about Cyrus but also from [what they said] on the same *hypothesis*. For, indeed, both men wrote *Symposia*. And in them, [Plato] expels the flute girls, while [Xenophon] brings them in. And [Xenophon's

> Socrates], as mentioned above, refuses to drink with big cups, while [Plato] depicts Socrates drinking with the wine-cooler until dawn.[55]

This dinner guest alleges a rivalry between Plato and Xenophon not only from their different opinions about Cyrus the Great but from the works they wrote "on the same *hypothesis*."[56] The examples he provides are the Socratic *Symposia*. Plato and Xenophon had each written a philosophical dialogue featuring Socrates at a drinking party, titled *The Symposium*. At least for the sake of this rhetorical point, Athenaeus considered these works sufficiently similar to be described as sharing a single *hypothesis*. For our purposes, it is Athenaeus's reference to *Symposia*—in the plural—that suggests that ancient readers had another way of talking about a shared *hypothesis*, without the rhetorical jargon. Immediately after using the term *hypothesis* explicitly, Athenaeus uses the shared title of two different works to refer to their narrative tradition.

The point is clearer in Diogenes Laertius's parallel discussion of Socratic literature. In his biography on Plato, Diogenes gives the following description of the same literary rivalry (*Lives of the Eminent Philosophers* 3.34).

> And it seems Xenophon was not well-disposed toward [Plato]. In any case, they have written similar books in rivalry: a *Symposium*, a Socratic *Apology*, and ethical *Memorabilia* — as well the *Republic* and the *Education of Cyrus*.[57]

55. Text from S. Douglas Olson, *Athenaeus. The Learned Banqueters*, vol. 5, *Books 10.420e-11*, Loeb Classical Library 274 (Harvard University Press, 2009), 466–469.

56. The inferred rivalry between works on the same *hypothesis* is discussed at length in chapter 5.

57. Text from Tiziano Dorandi, ed., *Diogenes Laertius: Lives of Eminent Philosophers*, Cambridge Classical Texts and Commentaries (Cambridge University Press, 2013), 262.

Whereas Athenaeus speaks of *Symposia* (in the plural) written on the same *hypothesis*, Diogenes speaks of two authors, each writing a *Symposium* and an *Apology*.[58] The singular noun in *Diogenes* does the same work as Athenaeus's explicit use of *hypothesis* language. That is, Diogenes uses the shared title of two distinct works to refer to a basic story constituted by certain shared narrative elements. The terms *Symposium* or *Apology* might refer to the title of a work or, as in this case, the *hypothesis* of several works.

The narrative traditions surrounding the Trojan War provide additional illustrations of a title being used as a shorthand for a *hypothesis*. Several ancient commentators were interested in Homer's literary predecessors. Aelian, a rough contemporary of Irenaeus, attributes the origin of the *Iliad*'s narrative tradition to someone named Oeagrus (*Varia* 14.21).[59]

> There was a certain poet, Oeagrus, [who lived] after Orpheus and Musaeus, who is said to have been first [to write] the Trojan War, daring to take up this greatest *hypothesis*.[60]

In this passage, Aelian makes explicit use of *hypothesis* language to describe the narrative tradition about the Trojan War.[61] But then, in

58. Diogenes's reference to the ethical *Memorabilia* of Plato is probably illuminated by Thrasyllus's claim—preserved by Diogenes himself—that the first four Platonic dialogues share a "common *hypothesis*" (κοινὴν υποθέσιν) concerning the life and death of Socrates (*Lives of the Philosophers* 3.57). See Mansfield, *Prolegomena*, 67–70. As in Athenaeus's account, the *Republic* and *Education of Cyrus* are two works that disagree without being written on the same *hypothesis*.

59. A certain "Oeagrus" was king of Thrace and father of Orpheus (Apollodorus, *Bibliotheca* 1.3.2). Since Aelian says the named Oeagrus came after Orpheus, this cannot be the same figure. A certain 'Syagrus' (Σύαγρος) is named as a contemporary critic of Homer by Diogenes of Laertius (*Lives of the Philosophers* 2.46).

60. Text from Nigel G. Wilson, *Aelian. Historical Miscellany*, Loeb Classical Libary 486 (Harvard University Press, 1997), 468.

61. The Suda makes comparable use of *hypothesis* language to describe the relationship of Dictys of Crete's prose history of the Trojan war to Homer's *Iliad* (Δ 1117).

the same work, Aelian uses "Iliad" as a shorthand for that same narrative tradition, when discussing another of Homer's predecessors (11.2).

> And they say that Dares the Phrygian, whose Phrygian Iliad I know is still preserved, was before Homer.[62]

Aelian refers to the work of Dares as a "Phrygian Iliad," with *Iliad* referring to a basic story shared with Homer's poem.

Likewise, the second-century grammarian Ptolemy Chennus says Dares "wrote the Iliad before Homer."[63] Probably, "Iliad" was not the title of Dares's work. It seems to have circulated, rather, as *The History of the Destruction of Troy*.[64] Both Aelian and Ptolemy, then, use the word *Iliad* to refer to a narrative tradition in which Dares and Homer both participated. That is, these second-century authors used *Iliad* for the same purpose that, in his earlier discussion of Oeagrus, Aelian had used the word *hypothesis*.[65] Just like *Symposium* and *Apology* could refer to the basic story of a narrative tradition in which Plato and Xenophon both participated, so too *Iliad* could refer to the *hypothesis* of multiple books. In all these cases, the title of a particularly important work in a narrative tradition serves as a shorthand for its *hypothesis*.

Irenaeus uses the term *gospel* in multiple senses.[66] In pre-Christian literature the term referred to the announcement of good news. Often

62. Text from Wilson, *Aelian. Historical Miscellany*, 332.

63. Ptolemy's *New History* survives only as abbreviated in Photius, *Library* 190. Text from René Henry, *Photius Bibliothèque Tome III (Codices 186-222)* (Société Les Belles Lettres, 1962), 53.

64. Only a Latin translation survives of the original Greek. See Andreas Beschorner, *Untersuchungen zu Dares Phrygius*, Classica Monacensia 4 (Gunter Narr, 1992). Since titles in antiquity are especially fluid, we cannot be sure how these books were known to Aelian and Ptolemy.

65. The same use of "Iliad" as a shorthand for the *hypothesis* is probably also at work in Athenaeus's reference to an "Egyptian Iliad" written by a certain Hippocrates (3.101).

66. My analysis is deeply indebted to Annette Y. Reed, "EUAGGELION: Orality, Textuality, and the Christian Truth in Irenaeus' Adversus Haereses," *Vigiliae*

cited as background for Christian uses of the term are its appearance in imperial propaganda and, as a verb, in the eschatological promises of Greek *Isaiah*. Throughout his letters, Paul uses *gospel* to refer to the message about Jesus Christ. The term appears with the same sense in the gospels to describe Jesus's own preaching. This use of the term *gospel* may be called "*kerygmatic*" from the Greek work *kerygma*, meaning "preaching." And, indeed, Irenaeus sometimes uses the term *gospel* in a strictly *kerygmatic* sense (e.g., *Against Heresies* 3.9.3, 14.1).

The Gospel according to Mark, however, planted the seeds for a new use of the term. The opening line of Mark is "The beginning of the gospel of Jesus Christ." Since books in antiquity—including Jewish and Christian texts—were sometimes titled after their opening lines, "The Gospel of Jesus Christ" may have been the work's original title.[67] Whatever the author intended, this is how many early readers understood the passage.[68] The term *gospel*, then, was quickly reappropriated as the title of a book. This use of the term may be called *titular* or *bibliographic*. To wit, Irenaeus frequently refers to specific books as "gospels" (e.g., *Against Heresies* 3.11.7).

Christianae 56, no. 1 (2002): 11–46. Though I do not share Reed's reticence to identify bibliographic uses of *gospel* in Irenaeus (especially for ἐν + dative clauses), my proposal is an attempt to explain the transformed use of *gospel* in Irenaeus which Reed acutely identified as referring to "a group of written sources." Reed, "EUAGGELION," 38–42, esp. 40.

67. See, for instance, the discussion in Johannes Munck, "Evangelium Veritatis and Greek Usages as to Book Titles," *Studia Theologica* 17, no. 2 (1963): 133–138. This is not, however, a universal practice in Roman times. Aulus Gellius, as noted by Geoffrey Smith, considers titles to be authorial paratexts (*Attic Knights* Pref. 3–10). Geoffrey S. Smith, *Guilt by Association* (Oxford University Press, 2015), 57n17. See also Tim Whitmarsh, "The Greek Novel: Titles and Genre," *American Journal of Philology* 126, no. 4 (2005): 587–611. The opening verse of Mark is discussed at greater length in chapter 5.

68. Chris Keith, *The Gospel as Manuscript: An Early History of the Jesus Tradition as Material Artifact* (Oxford University Press, 2020), 111–121; Graham Stanton, *Jesus and Gospel* (Cambridge University Press, 2004), 56–58; Jack Dean Kingsbury, *Matthew: Structure, Christology, Kingdom* (Fortress Press, 1991), 130. I discuss the evidence for the pre-Irenaean usage of *gospel* as a title in chapters 4 and 5.

Irenaeus also uses the term *gospel* in a third, distinct sense.[69] Like his contemporaries Diogenes Laertius, Claudius Aelianus, and Ptolemy Chennus, Irenaeus uses the title of an important work—namely "the gospel"—as a shorthand for the *hypothesis* of its narrative tradition. This third category might be called a *hypothetic* sense of the term *gospel*.

In the third book of *Against Heresies*, Irenaeus articulates his positive account of the pluriform gospel tradition. As such, the *hypothetic* use of the term *gospel* appears throughout. This third sense of the term is perhaps most clear when Irenaeus explicitly contrasts "the gospel" with the "blasphemous *hypotheses*" of his opponents (e.g., *Against Heresies* 3.16.5).[70] But the term does not appear only in heresiological polemic. Irenaeus also uses the term in a *hypothetic* sense in order to articulate his own understanding of gospel literature.

In the preface to the third volume of *Against Heresies*, Irenaeus promises to prove the falsity of the heretics from the scriptures themselves. In the very first line of this argument, then, Irenaeus makes an appeal to the pluriformity of the gospel tradition (3.1.1).

> Indeed, we did not learn about the plot of our salvation through anyone other than those persons through whom the gospel came to us—[the gospel] which they preached for a certain time and then later, by the will of God, passed on to us in the scriptures to be the foundation and column of our faith.[71]

69. As noted above, the importance of this transformed use of *gospel* in Irenaeus's thought was highlighted in Reed, "EUAGGELION," 38–42.

70. Irenaeus argues that "the gospel" features the birth and death of Jesus while the "blasphemous *hypotheses*" of his opponents divide Jesus into multiple characters. Adelin Rousseau and Louis Doutreleau, eds., *Irénée de Lyon: Contre les hérésies, Livre 3*, vol. 2. Sources chrétiennes 211 (Éditions du Cerf, 1974), 308. The term *gospel* in this passage transparently refers to the *hypothesis* of the now-canonical gospels.

71. Text from Rousseau and Doutreleau, *Irénée de Lyon*, 2:20. I take *dispositionem* to be the Latin translation of οἰκονομία —a standard term in Greek literary theory for a work's plot.

From the very start, Irenaeus emphasizes the transmission of a singular "gospel" through multiple media and in more than one version. Repeating an argument from the second volume of *Against Heresies*, Irenaeus claims that the written gospels preserve the same story that the apostles preached.[72] Then, in the following lines, Irenaeus names each of the four canonical gospels and briefly describes the situation of their authorship. All four written gospels, Irenaeus insists, "indeed all equally and each one of them have the Gospel of God" (*Against Heresies* 3.1.1).

The singular "gospel" in this passage cannot be identified with either the preaching of the apostles (i.e., the *kerygmatic* sense) or any particular book (i.e., the *bibliographic* sense). In fact, Irenaeus pointedly distinguishes this singular "gospel" from the several written gospels. The singular "gospel," says Irenaeus, is independently transmitted through these different media.[73] Each of the four gospels contains "the gospel."

This description of gospel literature makes perfect sense if Irenaeus's reference to a singular "gospel" is understood as a shorthand for the *hypothesis* of the gospels. The same basic story, says Irenaeus, is preserved "equally" (*pariter*) and "individually" (*singuli eorum*) in all four gospels. Irenaeus's claim to have learned "the plot of our salvation" from this singular gospel makes it clear that Irenaeus is thinking in narrative terms. That "plot" (*dispositio*) is the incarnation, life, death, and resurrection of Jesus—i.e., the basic story of the gospels. Although the term does not actually appear in this passage, the concept of a narrative *hypothesis* clearly structures Irenaeus's way of thinking about the pluriformity of the gospel tradition.

In a subsequent passage, Irenaeus uses the notion of a gospel *hypothesis* to legitimize the use of more than one gospel. He begins the section by raising the specter of a Christian who would reject the Gospel

72. On the place of apostolic tradition in Irenaeus's thought, see Andre Benoit, "Ecriture et Tradition chez saint Irenee," *Revue d'Histoire et de Philosophie Religieuses* 40, no. 1 (1960): 32–43.

73. The emphasis on the *individual* preservation of the gospel *hypothesis* in all four gospels suggests that the singular "gospel," for Irenaeus, is not a composite of the four (as canonical interpretation would sometimes have it).

according to Luke. To reject Luke, says Irenaeus, is to "throw away the gospel" (3.14.3).

> For we learned through [Luke] many important elements of the gospel, such as the birth of John, the history about Zacharias, the appearance of the angel to Mary, the exclamation of Elizabeth, the descent of the angels to the shepherds and what was said by them, the testimony of Anna and Simeon concerning the messiah, that at twelve years old he was left in Jerusalem, the baptism of John and how old the Lord was when baptized, and that it was in the fifteenth year of Tiberius Caesar.[74]

Luke's gospel, observes Irenaeus, preserves "many and important parts of the gospel." This description is premised on some meaningful distinction between gospel books and the singular "gospel." Irenaeus, then, enumerates "the parts of the gospel" specially preserved by Luke. These features of the gospel are not points of theology or doctrine, but details of Jesus's life. Here too it seems inescapable that Irenaeus used *gospel* in a *hypothetic* sense. The same kind of argument proved useful to Irenaeus in his argument against Marcion in the second book of *Against Heresies.* Irenaeus accuses the heresiarch of "mutilating" (*circumcidens*) Luke's Gospel by excising passages that associate Jesus with the God of Israel (1.27.2).

> [Marcion] persuaded his disciples that he himself was more truthful than those apostles who transmitted the gospel — delivering [to his disciples] not a gospel but a fragment of the gospel.[75]

Marcion's biography of Jesus was titled simply "the Gospel."[76] But Irenaeus wants to insist that Marcion's version was not a legitimate

74. Text from Rousseau and Doutreleau, *Irénée de Lyon, Livre 3*, vol. 2, 266–269.

75. Text from Rousseau and Doutreleau, *Irénée de Lyon, Livre 1*, vol. 2, 350.

76. See, for instance, Tertullian, *Prescription* 4.2 and *Adamantius Dialogue* 4–8.

version of that pluriform narrative tradition. He appeals, therefore, to the *hypothetic* "gospel" as communicated through oral and written media by the apostles. Marcion's gospel, claims Irenaeus, does not preserve this basic narrative. Rather, in the language of the scholiasts, Marcion has destroyed the *hypothesis*. In both passages, Irenaeus uses "gospel" in a *hypothetic* sense to defend the multiplicity of the gospels.

Just as scholiasts spoke of playwrights beginning their drama halfway through the relevant *hypothesis*, so too Irenaeus imagines different gospels addressing different parts of a shared *hypothesis*. And just as scholiasts defended differences between versions of a story as upholding the *hypothesis*, so too Irenaeus asserts that each of the four gospels transmits the same *hypothetic* gospel. Throughout *Against Heresies*, then, Irenaeus uses the idea of a gospel *hypothesis* to defend the multiplicity of the gospels as well as limit its variety.[77]

The Four Aspects of the Gospel

Irenaeus's thinking about gospel literature was certainly not just a regurgitation of already existing notions about narrative *hypotheses*. On the contrary, Irenaeus makes claims about the gospels that are simply unparalleled in Hellenistic and Roman discussions of pluriform literature. In particular, Irenaeus makes the surprising assertion that the gospel *hypothesis* has a strictly limited number of instantiations (*Against Heresies* 3.11.8).

> It is not possible for there to be any more or fewer gospels. Since there are four parts of the world in which we live and four general winds . . ., it is appropriate that [the church] should

77. Additional examples of the *hypothetic* use of *gospel* in the third book of *Against Heresies* include 5.1, 11.7, 14.4, 15.1, and 16.5. To this could be added, Irenaeus's explicit use of *hypothesis* language in his critique of the Marcosians (1.20.3). The purpose of this chapter is not, however, to give a comprehensive account of Irenaeus's hermeneutics but to illustrate how the concept of a *hypothesis* structured Irenaeus's understanding of gospel literature.

> have four pillars blowing immortality in every direction and revivifying people. . . . the one who appeared to all people gave to us the four-form gospel.[78]

Irenaeus says that it is only possible for there to be exactly four gospels. This is not part of the standard model for thinking about pluriform narrative traditions. No Hellenistic reader ever claims that there is a precise number of plays that must be written about the murder of Agamemnon. Irenaeus's argument is, rather, a *post hoc* rationalization for the number of gospels used by the churches with which he is affiliated.

This line of argument differs in emphasis from Irenaeus's appeal to a shared *hypothesis*. Irenaeus had argued that each of the gospels "equally" and "individually" maintained the *hypothesis* (see especially 3.1.1). Mark by itself, according to Irenaeus, transmits the gospel no less than Matthew or Luke. But, building on his novel idea of a four-form gospel, Irenaeus now argues that Christians should have all four gospels.

> Vain, ignorant, and audacious are those who disregard the form of the gospel—those who purport that there are either more or fewer faces of the gospel than what I have already said.[79]

According to Irenaeus, there can be no more or fewer than four gospels. There is some tension between this novel claim and the model of gospel literature he draws on elsewhere: If each of the gospels preserves the *hypothesis* individually, why should all four gospels be necessary? The answer, according to Irenaeus, lies beyond the standard way of thinking about a pluriform tradition and its *hypothesis* in Hellenistic literature. There must be four gospels, says Irenaeus, because we inhabit a fourfold cosmos, and so on. Still, this protocanonical account of gospel literature

78. Text from Rousseau and Doutreleau, *Irénée de Lyon, Livre* 3, no. 2, 160–162.

79. Text from Rousseau and Doutreleau, *Irénée de Lyon*, 2.2:170–171.

denies what he had previously affirmed—that each gospel individually preserves the *hypothesis*.

The idea of a *hypothesis* does not explain all of Irenaeus's thinking about gospel literature. Irenaeus used other conceptual categories, which have hardly been addressed. But Irenaeus's famous—though surprisingly brief—argument that four and only four gospels can exist is not indebted to widespread ways of thinking about the *hypothesis* of narrative traditions. It is, by all appearances, an innovation, and Irenaeus elsewhere still reflects ordinary ways of thinking about the *hypothesis* of pluriform literature.

Conclusion

The idea of a narrative *hypothesis* featured prominently in the earliest surviving reflection on the pluriformity of the gospels. Though it may have originated as a piece of technical vocabulary, the notion of a shared *hypothesis* was part of the standard model for thinking about such literary traditions at the turn of the millennium. Irenaeus's use of *hypothesis* language, therefore, does not reflect any particular erudition. In fact, Irenaeus never explains the term to his readers. The idea of a basic story—with all its prescriptive and descriptive connotations—was simply the normal way to think about such books.

Irenaeus illustrates how the idea of a *hypothesis* can inform a reader's imagination of a literary tradition even where the term itself is absent. Like several contemporary authors, Irenaeus sometimes uses the title of one work as a shorthand for the relevant *hypothesis*. Alongside its *kerygmatic* and *titular/bibliographic* senses, then, Irenaeus sometimes uses the term *gospel* in a *hypothetic* sense.

Like the scholiasts and other late Hellenistic readers, Irenaeus uses the idea of a *hypothesis* to both legitimize and limit variation in a narrative tradition. Each gospel, according to Irenaeus, "equally and individually" passes along the *hypothesis*. The differences between the gospels—for instance, the episodes unique to Luke—maintain the same basic story. By way of contrast, Marcion's gospel transgresses acceptable limits on the pluriformity of the narrative tradition. Marcion, according to Irenaeus, destroys the *hypothesis.*

None of these ideas is unique to Irenaeus.[80] The conceptual categories were inherited from Hellenistic literary criticism. And readers after Irenaeus would apply the same standard model for narrative traditions to the gospels. Nevertheless, Irenaeus occupies a special place in the reception history of the gospels. The prevalence of *hypothesis* language in Irenaeus's account of gospel literature is strong evidence that early readers used this idea to make sense of the multiplicity of gospels.

Excursus

Translating the Narrative Hypothesis *into Latin*

Irenaeus wrote his *Against Heresies* in Greek. Only one volume out of five, however, survives in the original language.[81] Thankfully, the entire work is preserved in a good Latin translation as well as sections in Syriac and Armenian. The incomplete preservation of Irenaeus's Greek, however, presents a problem for studying Irenaeus's use of the term *hypothesis.* The concept of a narrative *hypothesis* developed out of Greek dramatic criticism, and there is no precise equivalent in the Latin language. For this reason, many previous studies of the word *hypothesis* in *Against Heresies* have restricted themselves to appearances of the term in the surviving Greek. Unfortunately, some of the most revealing instances of the term appear in Irenaeus's later volumes—where the Greek is seldom extant. It is necessary, therefore, to carefully consider how the term *hypothesis* can be recognized in translation.

In the first book of *Against Heresies*, the Latin translator used three different terms to render *hypothesis* in its narrative sense. These are *argumentum/argumentatio*, *materia*, and *regula*. The use of three different words to render *hypothesis* is itself instructive. None of these

80. The notion of a tetraform gospel, by way of contrast, might be Irenaeus's invention.

81. Additional Greek fragments and quotations preserve other portions of the work (e.g., P.Oxy. 405 corresponding to *AH* 3.9.3).

is conceptually equivalent to *hypothesis* but each has some overlap in sense or function.

Where the Greek is extant, *argumentum* is the most common translation of *hypothesis*. It is a noun derived from the verb *arguo*, meaning "to show or demonstrate," and the instrumental suffix *-mentum*. Etymologically speaking, then, *argumentum* suggests the means by which something is shown. It is, of course, treacherous to infer usage from etymology but, as the examples below illustrate, the conventional uses of *argumentum* in narrative and literary discourses reflect the term's etymology.

A whole section of Quintilian's *Institutes* is dedicated to *argumenta* (5.10). But Quintilian is concerned with a very different sense of the term, more or less corresponding to the English "argument" or "demonstration."[82] In the course of that discussion, however, Quintilian mentions other uses of the word (5.10.9-10).

> But *argumentum* means more things as well. Stories (*fabulae*) composed to be acted on the stage are called *argumenta*. Also, Pedianus says, "the *argumentum* is as follows. . .," explaining the theme of Cicero's speeches. Also, Cicero himself writes to Brutus, "Being afraid, lest perhaps we transfer something from there to our Cato, though the *argumentum* was not similar. From this it is apparent that everything destined to be written is so called."[83]

Quintilian is emphasizing the many and varied uses of the term. As such, he cites instances of *argumentum* applied to drama, speeches, and biographies.[84] From these, he concludes that the subject of any writing can be called an *argumentum*.

---

82. The text is lacunose precisely where Quintilian defines his use of the term, but editors plausibly reconstruct "that which pertains to proof." Text from Donald A. Russell, *Quintilian: The Orator's Education*, vol. 2, *Books 3-5*, Loeb Classical Library 125 (Harvard University Press, 2002), 370.

83. Text from Russell, *Quintilian*, 370.

84. On the genre of Cicero's *Cato,* see note 85. The passage continues with an application to epic poetry.

There are similarities between Quintilian's examples and the literary use of *hypothesis* language, but his quotation from Cicero illustrates the key difference between the two ideas. Cato the Younger's suicide provoked a flurry of quasi-biographical literature, praising or denigrating the senator. When Cicero wrote his own biography of Cato, then, he had to be careful not to plagiarize these earlier works.[85] He qualifies this statement, however, by asserting that his work's *argumentum* does not resemble other lives of Cato. But were Cicero writing in Greek, he could not say the same thing about the *hypothesis* of his work. As the use of the term by Herodian of Antioch, Diogenes Laertius, and others illustrates, biographies of the same person—however different—are said to share a *hypothesis*. Cicero, by way of contrast, uses *argumentum* to refer to the particularities of his version of Cato's life. As the root *arguō* suggests, the *argumentum* is the presentation of the story. The *hypothesis* (as also suggested by its etymology) is an underlying story in contrast to any particular presentation.

The first definition offered by Quintilian, then, is frustratingly vague. The term *argumentum*, says Quintilian, refers to stories (*fabulae*) written for the stage. Probably the same sense of *argumentum* appears in one early rhetorical handbook (*Rhetorica ad Herennium* 1.8/13) and Cicero's *On Invention* (1.19). Terrence and Plautus, likewise, often speak of *argumenta* for specific plays in their prefaces.[86] But the best-known use of *argumentum* in this narrative sense is the plot summaries found in the manuscript tradition. These summaries, the descendants of Dicaearchus's *hypotheses*, were discussed briefly in chapter 1, in connection with Sextus Empiricus. These *argumenta* describe the plot of a specific work, often drawing attention to its distinctive features. The narrative *hypothesis* in Hellenistic literary criticism does the opposite, referring to the basic elements of a story shared across different versions.

85. Aulus Gellius and a scholion call Cicero's work a *vita* of Cato (*Attic Nights* 13.20.14; Sch. Juvenal 6.338). C. P. Jones, "Cicero's 'Cato,'" *Rheinisches Museum für Philologie* 113, no. 2/3 (1970): 188–196.

86. For example, Terentius, *Andria* prol. 6 and Plautus, *Amphitruo* Prol. 96.

It is undoubtably the use of *argumentum* in Latin literary criticism to refer to the content of a story that suggested the term to Irenaeus's Latin translator.[87] It captures the narrative dimension of *hypothesis* and appears frequently in contexts where Irenaeus is referring to the Valentinian creation myth. It fails, however, to capture the distinction between the abstract story and the present work.[88]

The Latin *materia* is used once to translate *hypothesis* in the first book of *Against Heresies* (1.23.2). This Latin term, meaning "material," captures another dimension of the narrative *hypothesis*. Irenaeus uses it to refer to a cosmogenic story about Simon of Samaria as the raw material out of which the sect of Simonians was formed. While *materia* does not have the narrative connotations of *hypothesis*, it does connote something foundational, constitutive, or underlying. This aspect of *hypothesis* was made explicit in Philodemus's discussion of the poetic art.

> . . . just as in the manual disciplines, we don't think worse of a craftsperson for how much material they stole from another craftsperson and worked it well. Likewise, we don't think this way about poetry, if someone takes an unworked (ἀπόητον) *hypothesis* to add their own interpretation.[89]

Philodemus uses *hypothesis* language to characterize the underlying stories that poets and playwrights are constantly reworking into their own versions. Likewise, one of his Hellenistic interlocutors, Heraclides of Pontus, refers to *hypotheses* as the "material" (ὕλη) of poetry (*On*

87. The second most common Latin translation of *hypothesis* in Irenaeus's *Against Heresies* is, in fact, *argumentatio*. This closely related term does not have a conventional use in narrative discourse. It is, however, part of the standard vocabulary in rhetorical theory, referring to the section of a speech where claims are demonstrated with arguments and evidence. And like *argumentum*, it is derived from the verb *arguo*, "to show." Probably, its use is explained by the resemblance to *argumentum*.

88. In a revealing passage, the Latin translator rectifies this failing of *argumentum* as a translation of *hypothesis* by modifying it with the participle *subiacens* (*Against Heresies* 2.25.1).

89. Text from Janko, *Philodemus: On Poems, Book 2*, 215.

Poetry 5.10). The Latin translation *materia*, then, captures how readers thought about *hypotheses* as constitutive of *but distinct from* particular works.

Late Hellenistic and Roman readers—including Irenaeus—used the notion of a *hypothesis* to evaluate different versions of a story. But neither *argumentum* nor *materia* have the normative implications associated with a narrative *hypothesis*. As such, the Latin translator of Irenaeus occasionally used the Latin *regula* (literally, "rule") to translate *hypothesis* (1.20.3; 31.1). This is, of course, the translator's typical rendering of "rule" (κανών), as in the proto-creedal "rule of faith" (1.22.1, 3.11.1). The decision to translate *hypothesis* with the Latin term for a measuring instrument reflects the translator's knowledge that the notional *hypothesis* played an evaluative role in the criticism of narrative traditions.

Irenaeus's Latin translator was attuned to the nuances of *hypothesis* language. The Latin language had no precise equivalent for the way the term was used in Hellenistic literary criticism. The translator, therefore, used several different words that each captured a different aspect of how *hypothesis* language was used. The Latin *argumentum* reflects the association of *hypothesis* with narratives, *materia* the distinction between a present work and its constitutive elements, and *regula* its normative or evaluative functions.

CHAPTER THREE

The Gospel *Hypothesis* in Early Christian Literature

> "But also give an answer about the *hypothesis* of Christ, oh mythmaker of this fiction. If Simon the Cyrene was crucified, our salvation is not through Jesus but through Simon."
>
> —Epiphanius of Salamis, *Panarion* 2.24.8.6

Introduction

THAT SOME BASIC story underlies every retelling was the standard model for thinking about narrative traditions in the late Hellenistic period and Roman Principate. Readers of poetry, drama, and history used the idea of a narrative *hypothesis* to describe and evaluate different versions of the same story. Irenaeus, the first author to reflect at any length on the multiplicity of gospels, likewise used the idea of a *hypothesis* to describe, legitimize, and limit the gospel tradition. But Irenaeus was not the only early reader to think about the gospels in this way.

Across the centuries, other gospel readers used the concept of a narrative *hypothesis* for their own apologetic, polemical, and theological purposes. Greek-speaking Christians after Irenaeus invoked a notional *hypothesis* to organize the same pluriform tradition. This use of *hypothesis* language was not the jargon of high-minded scholarship or theological hairsplitting. It was, rather, a commonplace—the result of viewing gospels through the lens of Hellenistic book culture.

As ideas about Christian scripture changed over time, so too did the language and concepts used to think about the gospels. The notion of a literary *hypothesis* became less common as interpreters stopped thinking about the gospels like other kinds of books. The idea of a New Testament canon and the associated assumptions on which allegorical interpretation is premised left readers with little use for normative appeals to the gospel *hypothesis*.[1] Still, the use of *hypothesis* language to describe and evaluate gospels from the second through the sixth century demonstrates the applicability of this conceptual category to the gospel tradition for readers educated in Hellenistic literary culture.

Clement of Alexandria

Clement of Alexandria was a junior contemporary of Irenaeus, writing from the opposite end of the Roman Empire.[2] As a teacher in the intellectual capital of the Hellenistic world, Clement was steeped in the literary and philosophical culture of his age. His works are packed with allusions to Greek literature and current philosophical ideas. It is no surprise, then, to find that the concept of a *hypothesis* informs Clement's thinking about the gospels (and other narrative traditions).

Clement wrote a series of major works—the *Protrepticus*, *Paedagogus*, and *Hypotyposeis*—which together constitute a philosophical curriculum.[3] Unfortunately, it was the now-lost *Hypotyposeis* that

1. The use of *hypothesis* language more or less maps onto a conventional dichotomy between rhetorical criticism and allegorical interpretation. I follow Peter Struck in understanding this division as a useful heuristic, even as both approaches to interpretation are many times used by the same interpreters. Struck's observation that the two approaches are premised on different assumptions about the text is foundational to the argument of this chapter. Struck, *Birth of the Symbol*, 1–13. A strict dichotomy is rightly problematized by H. Clifton Ward, and the treatment of Clement in this chapter only supports that analysis. H. Clifton Ward, *Clement and Scriptural Exegesis: The Making of a Commentarial Theologian* (Oxford University Press, 2022), 1–29.

2. For an accessible introduction, see Eric Osborn, *Clement of Alexandria* (Cambridge University Press, 2008).

3. Bogdan G. Bucur, "The Place of the Hypotyposeis in the Clementine Corpus: An Apology for 'The Other Clement of Alexandria,'" *Journal of Early Christian Studies* 17, no. 3 (2009): 313–335. Jane M. F. Heath would interject the *Stromata* as third in a sequence of four. J. M. F. Heath, *Clement of Alexandria and the Shaping*

treated scripture and its interpretation.[4] The extant works are filled with Clement's reading of scripture but he only rarely addresses the kind of elementary exegetical issues that Irenaeus confronted in his dispute with the Marcionites and Valentinians.[5] If Clement wrote any sustained reflection on the nature of gospel literature, it has not survived.[6]

Clement's most explicit use of *hypothesis* language appears in his only surviving homily, "Who is the Rich Man That Will Be Saved?"[7] This treatment of wealth begins with the episode of the Rich Young Ruler, found in all three synoptic gospels. A young man, the story begins, asks Jesus how to inherit eternal life (6.2).

> [Jesus] was asked about those things for the sake of which he descended—the things he was instructing, the things he

---

of Christian Literary Practice: Miscellany and the Transformation of Greco-Roman Writing (Cambridge University Press, 2020), 382–393.

4. On the surviving evidence, see Jana Plátová, "How Many Fragments of the Hypotyposes by Clement of Alexandria Do We Have?," *Studia Theologica* 18 (2016): 1–17.

5. On Clement as "transitional" in the history of gospel collections, see Francis Watson, *Gospel Writing*, 418-436. Clifton Ward argues that Clement's theology throughout emerges from his exegesis of scripture. Ward, *Clement and Scriptural Exegesis*. Ward notes the importance of a notional *hypothesis* for the grammarian's inquiry into a work's "textual context" (28–29) but does not discuss the passage treated below.

6. Stevens argues persuasively that even those preserved fragments from the *hypotyposeis* on the origin of the gospels are only partially attributable to Clement. Luke J. Stevens, "The Evangelists in Clement's Hypotyposes," *Journal of Early Christian Studies* 26, no. 3 (2018): 353–379. If Clement employed *allegoresis* like Origen (discussed in the next section of this chapter), we might, in fact, find that Clement had little use for the idea of a *hypothesis* in his lost exegetical treatise.

7. The identification of *Quis Dives Salvetur* as a homily is found already in the manuscripts. Eusebius of Caesarea calls it merely a λόγος (*Ecclesiastical History* 6.13.3). Plátová argues that the work is a combination of two separate homilies with an editorial introduction. Jana Plátová, "Clement of Alexandria's Homily 'Quis Dives Salvetur?' And Its Pastoral Challenges for Alexandrian Christians," *Vox Patrum* 85 (2023): 7–22.

> was teaching, the things he was causing to happen—in order to display the *hypothesis* of the gospel, because it is the gift of eternal life.[8]

Clement interprets the question as a general inquiry into the story of salvation. In short, why did Jesus come? The answer, according to Clement, is "the *hypothesis* of the gospel." He glosses this *hypothesis* as the instructions, teachings, and actions of Jesus. The gospel *hypothesis* (i.e., the life of Jesus) is the gift of eternal life.

Beyond just the appearance of the term, however, it is clear from the context that the idea of a *hypothesis* is here shaping Clement's account of gospel literature. Clement introduces the episode with an extremely brief discussion of his sources (5.1).[9]

> These things are written in the Gospel according to Mark and in all the others which agree. Although, perhaps, each differs a little with respect to expressions, all [the gospels] show the same harmony of meaning (τὴν αὐτὴν τῆς γνώμης συμφωνίαν).[10]

For his primary source, Clement selects the Gospel according to Mark. There are differences, he acknowledges, between the gospels, but their meaning is the same. Recognizing the discrepancies between the gospels while, at the same time, insisting on a fundamental unity neatly parallels the scholiast's assertion that every author "has the authority to make each

8. Text from O. Stählin et al., *Clément d'Alexandrie Quel riche sera sauvé?*, Sources Chrétiennes 537 (Les Éditions du Cerf, 2011), 116–118.

9. On the gospel text presented by Clement, see Matteo Monfrinotti, "Quis dives salvetur? Ricezione ed esegesi Di Mc. 10,17-31," *Augustinianum* 53, no. 2 (2013): 305–335; Jana Plátová, "The Text of Mark 10:29–30 in Quis Dives Salvetur? By Clement of Alexandria," in *The Process of Authority: The Dynamics in Transmission and Reception of Canonical Texts*, ed. Jan Dušek, Deuterocanonical and Cognate Literature Studies 27 (De Gruyter, 2016), 253–270.

10. Text from Stählin et al., *Clément d'Alexandrie Quel riche sera sauvé?*, 119.

part happen as they wish, unless they harm the whole *hypothesis*."[11] Clement first asserts that the gospels tell the same basic story, and then identifies the salvific life of Jesus as that *hypothesis*. The differences in expression between the gospels, according to Clement, do no harm to the *hypothesis*.

Just as the concept of a *hypothesis* structured Irenaeus's account of the gospels in the absence of the term, so too Clement relied on this paradigm for understanding pluriform traditions in his occasional discussions of gospel literature elsewhere. This influence is most clearly discernable when Clement, like Irenaeus, uses the title "gospel" as a shorthand for the *hypothesis*.

Near the beginning of his *Pedagogus*, Clement appeals to scripture to explain his use of the term *pedagogue* (literally, "child-trainer") for Jesus. The scriptures, says Clement, refer to those who worship the one, true God as children. In support of this claim, Clement cites passages scattered throughout the Jewish and Christian scriptures—including several quotations from the gospels (1.5.12).

> Scripture praises us in many different ways, giving diversity to the simplicity of faith with various figures and names. In the gospel, for instance, it says, "the Lord, standing on the shore, called out to the disciples—who were, by chance, fishing—'Children, do you have some food?'" (John 21:4–5), speaking of the disciples who were already mature as children. And it is said "They brought children to him" to put hands on them to bless them. And when the disciples prevented them, Jesus said "Permit the children and do not prevent them from coming to me. For the kingdom of heaven belongs to such as these" (Matthew 19:14). What the saying meant, the Lord will explain, saying "Unless you repent and become as little children, you will not enter into the kingdom of heaven" (Matthew 18:3).[12]

11. Text from Xenis, *Scholia Vetera in Sophoclis "Electram,"* 175.

12. Text from M. Marcovich, ed., *Clementis Alexandrini Paedagogus* (Brill, 2002), 9–10.

Clement attributes three sayings of Jesus—two from Matthew and one from John—to "the gospel." His use of the singular "gospel" is a choice. Afterall, Clement uses the plural elsewhere (e.g., *Stromata* 3.13). And given the introduction of these gospel quotations as "scripture," Clement must have books (not the *kerygmatic* "gospel") in mind. Furthermore, given his knowledge of Matthew and John as distinct gospels under their traditional titles, Clement cannot be using *gospel* as the title of one particular book.[13]

This reference to the singular *gospel*, then, is best understood as referring to the *hypothesis* (or, by metonymy, the tradition constituted by that *hypothesis*) of the gospels. Jesus's treatment of his followers as children in need of instruction is, according to Clement, part of the basic story of Jesus's life. Indeed, the idea of Jesus as a teacher is central to Clement's theological project. If the singular *gospel* is understood as a shorthand for the *hypothesis* in this passage, then Clement is making the entirely comprehensible claim that the teacher-student relationship between Jesus and his followers is fundamental to the story that unites the gospels.

The context of this passage, furthermore, suggests that the idea of a narrative *hypothesis* is shaping Clement's thinking. In the sentence immediately preceding his use of the singular *gospel* (quoted above), Clement emphasizes the multiplicity of expressions for the singular message about Jesus. Using the singular *gospel* in a *hypothetic* sense allows Clement to acknowledge this variety while insisting upon an underlying unity.[14] Thus, it is not merely the use of the singular *gospel* in reference

13. Clement attributes the Matthean genealogy to "the Gospel according to Matthew" (*Stromata* 1.21) and part of the Johannine prologue to "John the Apostle" (*Stromata* 5.12). Clement believes the mainstream church uses four gospels (*Stromata* 3.13). From the *hypotyposeis*, at least the reference to Mark as an evangelist appears to be authentically Clementine. Stevens, "The Evangelists in Clement's Hypotyposes."

14. Clement accomplishes a similar effect with respect to proof texts from the Old Testament by attributing them all to the same "prophetic spirit" or the singular "prophecy." Where Clement uses *hypothesis* language for the gospels (which he believes to have four distinct authors), he instead appeals to common (divine) authorship for the works of Jewish Scripture.

to passages from various gospels that suggests Clement is referring to the gospel *hypothesis*, but the sweep of his argument.

Additional examples could be furnished for Clement. In his *Stromata* (or *Miscellanies*), Clement uses explicit *hypothesis* language to characterize other narrative traditions.[15] Likewise, he repeatedly draws on the shorthand *gospel* when emphasizing the harmonious testimony of scripture.[16] For instance, Clement asserts "we have the Lord as the source of our teaching through the prophets, through the gospel, and through the blessed apostles" (*Strom*. 7.16.95).[17] The use of the singular *gospel* between the plural *prophets* and *apostles* weighs against either a *kerygmatic* or *bibliographic* interpretation of the term. Instead, Clement's insistence on the common testimony of multiple sources of authority suggest *hypothetic* thinking. Probably, Clement is claiming that the basic story of the gospels—whatever the variation between gospels—agrees with the law, prophets, and apostles.

We do not know if Clement used *hypothesis* language in his lost treatise on the interpretation of scripture. But, as his only surviving homily makes clear, he did use the concept of a narrative *hypothesis* to characterize the basic story of the gospels and assert their unity in spite of apparent diversity. Likewise, Clement's use of the singular *gospel* as a shorthand for the *hypothesis* is the best explanation for his thinking in several additional passages. Nowhere does Clement stop to explain the concept; instead, Clement expects his reader and audience to understand this use of *hypothesis* language. By all appearances, then, the idea

15. Clement says the Cainites and the Ophites were named after "*hypotheses* and [those persons] whom they honored" (*Stromata* 7.17). Both were named after mythological figures from the first chapters of Genesis and sectarian retellings of that story. Probably, Clement uses *hypotheses* here to refer to pluriform narrative traditions. He preserves also a fragment of Isidore, the son of the heresiarch Basilides, which alleges that the pagan mythographer Pherecydes of Syros used a Biblical *hypothesis* for one of his stories (*Stromata* 6.6).

16. *Stromata* 4.13, 5.5, 6.11, 7.16; cf. 3.10, 11.

17. Alain le Boulluec, *Clement of Alexandria: Les Stromates, Stromate VII* (Les Éditions du Cerf, 1997), 288

of a *hypothesis* was simply part of how Clement thought about pluriform narrative traditions, including (but not limited to) the gospels.

Origen of Alexandria

Origen of Alexandria was the most important Christian thinker of the third century. He was a philosopher and philologist of the highest caliber, educated alongside other elite Romans in Alexandria. Origen wrote a systematic theology, edited the scriptures, and composed biblical commentaries. In his writings on gospel literature, the Alexandrian drew from different traditions of textual scholarship—including, on at least one occasion, the idea of a narrative *hypothesis*.

Sometime in the late second century, a pagan philosopher named Celsus wrote a critique of Christianity. Celsus read the gospels and, in his treatise, mocked them as contradictory, absurd, and ignoble. Ironically, we know of Celsus's work only because Origen wrote a massive eight-volume response, *Against Celsus*. Halfway through the first volume, Origen tells us that Celsus drew a series of arguments against the gospels from a Jewish critic of Christianity.[18] In one such argument, Celsus's Jewish critic suggests that Jesus could have more clearly demonstrated his divinity by appearing to his enemies after the crucifixion (2.63–67) or miraculously disappearing from the cross (2.68).

Origen responds by insisting that the events of Jesus's death, burial, and resurrection needed to play out exactly as they did (2.69). He apologizes, however, that he cannot offer a better interpretation of these passages in his present work.

> On a better occasion and in a work that prioritized the subject, one might explain better and in a more divine manner those

18. Lincoln Blumell, "A Jew in Celsus' True Doctrine? An Examination of Jewish Anti-Christian Polemic in the Second Century C.E," *Studies in Religion/Sciences Religieuses* 36, no. 2 (2007): 297–315; Maren R. Niehoff, "A Jewish Critique of Christianity from Second-Century Alexandria: Revisiting the Jew Mentioned in Contra Celsum," *Journal of Early Christian Studies* 21, no. 2 (2013): 151–175.

> points of interpretation and, so, rise up to the matters which are symbolic from what was recorded to have happened.[19]

Origen is famous for his allegorical readings of scripture. The Holy Spirit, according to Origen, inspired narratives that are not simply records of what happened, but figures of more profound spiritual truths. In fact, Origen believed that the scriptures were filled with contradictions and historical impossibilities—Origen calls them "stumbling blocks"—to prompt the reader to look for deeper meanings.[20] As further discussed at the end of this chapter, this allegorical mode of reading has less use for the concept of a *hypothesis*, and the term is correspondingly rare in Origen's commentaries.[21]

After directing the reader to find an allegorical interpretation elsewhere, Origen answers Celsus's critique on interpretive grounds that his opponent might accept.

> One could, however, explain the literal [sense] in this way: it was right that he remain, hanging upon the cross. This was to preserve the elements in the *hypothesis* in order—that he should be condemned as a human, die as a human, and be buried as a human.[22]

Origen asserts that all the gospels present the basic details of Jesus's passion as they did in order to protect the *hypothesis*. The fundamental story of the gospel, according to Origen, requires that Jesus be condemned, die, and be buried. This argument resembles the scholiast's

19. Text from Miroslav Marcovich, ed., *Origenes Contra Celsum: Libri VIII*, Supplements to *Vigiliae Christianae* 54 (Brill, 2001), 140.

20. *On First Principles* 4.2.9

21. Origen almost exclusively uses the term *hypothesis* in the suppositional sense that is typical of philosophical literature. I argue below that the rhetorical context explains this other literary use of the term. On Origen's interpretation of the gospels, see Samuel B. Johnson, *The Life of Jesus in the Writings of Origen of Alexandria* (Oxford University Press, 2025).

22. Text from Marcovich, *Contra Celsum*, 140.

claim that to tell a story otherwise would "destroy" the relevant *hypothesis*. Origen, as the surrounding discussion makes clear, is keenly aware of the differences between the gospels, but he uses the idea of a narrative *hypothesis* to appeal to their fundamental story.

Eusebius of Caesarea

Eusebius had the great fortune to be born, educated, and ordained as bishop in Caesarea Maritima.[23] Decades earlier, Origen had been exiled from Alexandria and spent the last twenty years of his life as a teacher in Caesarea. The Christian community in that city inherited Origen's vast library and enjoyed the stewardship of his students. Eusebius was not only shaped by this scholarly patrimony but also made his own significant contributions. He composed a new chronology of human history, invented an apparatus for navigating gospel parallels, and wrote a history of early Christianity.[24]

Eusebius is the first author in our study to be educated in a thoroughly Christian context. For Eusebius, gospel literature was always already what Irenaeus claimed it to be.[25] As such, Eusebius sometimes uses distinctively Christian language where we might expect Hellenistic technical vocabulary. For instance, Eusebius refers to the common subject matter of the gospels as "the evangelical message" (*Demonstration* 1.1).[26] Still Eusebius drank deeply from Hellenistic

23. For an introduction to Eusebius, see Aaron P. Johnson, *Eusebius* (I. B. Tauris, 2014).

24. On Eusebius's chronology, see Anthony Grafton, *Christianity and the Transformation of the Book: Origen, Eusebius, and the Library of Caesarea*, Illustrated edition. (Belknap Press of Harvard University Press, 2008), 133–177. On the Eusebian apparatus, see Matthew R. Crawford, *The Eusebian Canon Tables: Ordering Textual Knowledge in Late Antiquity* (Oxford University Press, 2019); Jeremiah Coogan, *Eusebius the Evangelist: Rewriting the Fourfold Gospel in Late Antiquity*, Cultures of Reading in the Ancient Mediterranean (Oxford University Press, 2022).

25. See Eusebius's citations of Irenaeus at *Ecclesiastical History* 5.8.

26. Ivar A Heikel, *Die Demonstratio Evangelica*, vol. 6, Die griechischen christlichen Schriftsteller der ersten Jahrhunderte 23 (De Gruyter, 1913), 3.

literature, and the idea of a narrative *hypothesis* shapes his imagination of pluriform literary traditions, including the gospels.

Eusebius wrote his *Demonstration of the Gospel* to prove that the elements of Jesus's life fulfilled the prophecies he found in Jewish scripture. The first three volumes of his *Demonstration* establish the respectability of Jewish scripture, defend its appropriation by Christians, and argue for the reliability of the gospels and the quality of Jesus's character.[27] It is not until the middle of the fourth volume, after laying out his account of human salvation, that Eusebius reaches his promised subject. This transition is marked by a restatement of the work's thesis (*Demonstration* 4.15.1–2).

> Therefore, to speak briefly, the *hypothesis* concerning the savior, our Lord Jesus Christ, having an exceptional arrangement, will be supported from the prophetic oracles of the Hebrews, as just a little later their testimony will show: the old proving the new scriptures, and the things of the gospels sealing the testimony of the prophets.[28]

Eusebius refers to the events of Jesus's life as "the *hypothesis* concerning the savior." He immediately glosses *hypothesis* with "new scriptures" and "the things of the gospels." Reading on, Eusebius claims that the elements of the gospel *hypothesis* predicted in the Jewish scriptures include Jesus's name, provenance, incarnation, ethical teaching, conflict with Jewish leaders, apocalyptic prophecies, passion, resurrection, and ascension. Eusebius uses *hypothesis* to refer to the basic story of Jesus's life, abstracted away from any particular gospel book.

On several other occasions, Eusebius uses the similar construction, "the evangelical *hypothesis*" (ἡ εὐαγγελικὴ ὑπόθεσις) with a similar sense. In his treatise, *The Preparation for the Gospel*, for instance, Eusebius

27. Eusebius, in fact, begins to review relevant prophecies at the beginning of book three but quickly becomes preoccupied with these more basic questions.

28. Text from Heikel, *Die Demonstratio Evangelica*, 173.

claims that the falsity of traditional Roman religion is an important aspect of gospel literature (4.4.1).

> I suppose it is clear to everyone that the consideration of the present matters is no little thing but rather contains the greatest and most essential part of the evangelical *hypothesis*. For if it is demonstrated that, before the coming of our savior Jesus Christ, everyone everywhere—Greeks and Barbarians—had not known the true God . . . how could the great mystery of the evangelical arrangement (τῆς εὐαγγελικῆς οἰκονομίας) not be seen as even greater.[29]

By "the gospel *hypothesis*," here, Eusebius refers to "the coming of our savior Jesus Christ." It is glossed, then, as the "evangelical arrangement." Modern readers do not think of a polemic against paganism as an important theme of the gospels. But for Eusebius and many other late antique readers, still surrounded by the institutions, monuments, and adherents of traditional religion, the revelation of Jesus as the incarnation of the one, true God was imagined as a refutation of polytheism.[30] Here too, the idea of a *hypothesis* allows Eusebius to refer the narrative of the gospels in the abstract.

Epiphanius of Salamis

Though less well known today than Origen or Eusebius, Epiphanius of Salamis was famous in the fourth century.[31] He was a monk

29. Text from Edwin Hamilton Gifford, *Eusebius, Evangelicae Praeparationis Libri XV Ad Codices Manuscriptos* (Academic Press, 1903), 1:139–140.

30. As early as Ignatius of Antioch, the Matthean story of the Magi was interpreted as the end of astrological arts (*Ephesians* 19.2–3). More explicitly, Proba's *Cento* depicts Jesus condemning traditional Greek and Roman religion (488–494).

31. In his excellent study of Epiphanius, Andrew Jacobs argues that Epiphanius should be understood as something like a celebrity. Andrew Jacobs, *Epiphanius of Cyprus: A Cultural Biography of Late Antiquity*, Christianity in Late Antiquity 2 (University of California Press, 2016).

in Egypt, an abbot in Palestine, and, finally, appointed bishop of Cyprus. From his island seat, Epiphanius traveled to adjudicate ecclesiastic disputes and wrote popular treatises on theology and biblical interpretation.[32] His appearance in churches abroad attracted crowds, and his books achieved wide circulation already in Epiphanius's lifetime.[33]

In terms of scholarship, however, Epiphanius was no Origen. In fact, he was an avowed critic of the Alexandrian. Among their many differences were diverging approaches to the interpretation of scripture. Epiphanius repeatedly attacks Origen's allegorical reading of biblical narrative.[34] Where Origen found symbolic significances in sometimes-incredible details, Epiphanius insisted on straightforwardly historical readings. Instead of Origen's highbrow philosophical theology, Epiphanius supplied his readers with a veritable miscellany of relevant secular and Christian authorities, etymological and linguistic analyses, and geographic, ethnographic, and historical trivia.[35] This too reflects a kind of learning but, in contrast to Origen, Epiphanius's eclecticism suggests an attempt at popular appeal.

It was precisely when Origen set aside his preferred allegorical method and condescended to answer his pagan critics in terms of "literal" meaning that the notion of a *hypothesis* became useful to him. It is striking, then, that Epiphanius (who insists on reading scripture this way) appeals to a narrative *hypothesis* more than any foregoing author (excluding Irenaeus).[36] Indeed, Epiphanius explicitly contrasts

32. See the brief biography in Jacobs, *Epiphanius of Cyprus*, 8–13.

33. Jerome, *Against John of Jerusalem* 11; *Epistle* 57.2; *Letter of Acacius and Paul* 1.2;

34. Epiphanius, *Ancoratus* 58.3; *Panarion* 64.4.11.

35. Andrew S. Jacobs, "Epiphanius of Salamis and the Antiquarian's Bible," *Journal of Early Christian Studies* 21, no. 3 (2013): 437–464.

36. Epiphanius makes frequent use of *hypothesis* language in other senses—especially the suppositional sense discussed above. Most confusingly, he sometimes employs the term to refer to general subject matter without any of the conventions of meaning outlined in chapter 1. Nevertheless, I argue below that Epiphanius's thinking about the gospels continues to be shaped by the Hellenistic model outlined in chapter 1.

allegorical interpretation with the kind of reading that attends to the *hypotheses* of scripture (*Panarion* 61.6.4).

> But all divine words do not need to be interpreted allegorically to have power. Instead, there is need for contemplation and perception in order to understand the power of each *hypothesis*.[37]

Like the scholion critiquing Zenodotus's emendation of text or Irenaeus in his argument against the Valentinians, Epiphanius uses the term *hypothesis*, here, to point readers to the narrative in which a disputed passage is embedded.

This narrative *hypothesis*, however, is not simply identifiable with any specific work. Epiphanius makes this clear when he appeals to the gospel *hypothesis* to explain his use of parallel passages from different gospels. For instance, Epiphanius appeals to the idea of a *hypothesis* in his defense of the gospels against Manichean claims of contradiction (*Panarion* 66.40.1–4). Why does Matthew describe two demoniacs at Gadara (Matt 8:28–34) while Luke only mentions one (Luke 8:26–39)? Epiphanius proposes various explanations for Luke's omission of the second figure, including speculation that the omitted demoniac did not continue in the faith (*Panarion* 66.40.5–6) or that the third evangelist used a collective singular (*Panarion* 66.41.3). Whatever the reason for the difference, however, Epiphanius ultimately appeals to something beyond the individual gospels (*Panarion* 66.41.4).

> So, the *hypothesis* of the gospel contains multiple [demoniacs]. The one [of two gospels] narrated that one [demoniac] was the blasphemer and one [demoniac] confessed and attained salvation. And you see that all the elements of the truth are clearly there and nothing contradictory is in scripture.[38]

---

37. Text from Karl Holl and Jurgen Dummer, *Epiphanius II Panarion haer. 34–64*, vol. 2. Die griechischen christlichen Schriftsteller der ersten drei Jahrhunderte 2 (Akademie-Verlag, 1980), 386.

38. Karl Holl, *Epiphanius III Panarion Haer. 65-80 De Fide* (Akademie-Verlag, 1985), 78.

Though there are two demoniacs in the basic story, according to Epiphanius, the third evangelist had good reason to omit one from his retelling. This line of reasoning recalls Dio Chrysostom's arguments that different playwrights were justified in adding or omitting certain characters—like Diomedes who accompanies Odysseus only in Euripides's version—from their retelling of the *Philoctetes*.[39] Both readers use *hypothesis* language to distinguish the story itself from a particular articulation of that story.[40]

The concept of a narrative *hypothesis* most clearly shapes Epiphanius's thinking about the gospels in his treatment of the so-called *Alogi* (*Panarion* 51). These Christians, according to Epiphanius, rejected the Gospel of John because it contradicted the synoptics. Epiphanius takes the occasion, however, to treat inconsistencies in scripture in general, providing his own list of omissions, additions, and contradictions among the synoptics (*Panarion* 51.5.9–10; 6.3–5). Despite these differences, Epiphanius insists that the gospels are harmonious. Apparent inconsistencies, says Epiphanius, are authorial choices with stylistic or theological justifications (*Panarion* 51.4.11; 6.2).

After explaining why each evangelist decided to begin their gospel in a different fashion, Epiphanius states: "For the entire *hypothesis* of the gospels is like this."[41] He goes on, then, to illustrate how the wording of Matthew's gospel led some Christians to believe Jesus was the natural son of Joseph, despite contradicting statements in the Gospel of

39. The arguments differ subtly: Dio and the scholiasts tend to think about the elements where legitimate difference is found as not belonging to the narrative *hypothesis*, whereas Epiphanius here seems to think of the *hypothesis* as a master story legitimately described with different language by both. Epiphanius is writing hundreds of years after Dio (and the evangelists). We should not expect perfect synchronic consistency or diachronic stability with such abstract concepts.

40. In parallel passages, Epiphanius appeals to the *hypothesis* (sometimes pointedly contrasted with the wording of the narrative in question) to identify unnamed disciples in a particular story (*Panarion* 51.15.3, 12).

41. Text from Holl and Dummer, *Epiphanius II Panarion haer*, 255. B. A. Williams gives the paraphrase "the whole treatment of the Gospel." But this translation conceals the term *hypothesis* and the plural εὐαγγελίων. B. A. Williams, *The Panarion of Epiphanius of Salamis: De Fide. Books II and III* (Brill, 2013), 31.

John.[42] These critics of the gospels err, according to Epiphanius, for failing to interpret this passage from one gospel in light of the narrative known from other gospels. There follows, then, a series of explanations for additional differences in terms of the compositional context of each evangelist.

Epiphanius's explicit use of the term *hypothesis* in this passage is metonymic, referring to the tradition constituted by a basic story. Still Epiphanius summarizes a discussion of differences between the gospels by pointing to a singular, underlying *hypothesis*. In its rhetorical context, this statement draws attention to the unity that underlies the variety of the gospels. Against these critics of the fourth gospel, Epiphanius uses the idea of a gospel *hypothesis* to defend the pluriformity of the gospel tradition.

Epiphanius elsewhere demands that Basilideans who believe that Simon the Cyrene was crucified in place of Jesus "answer about the *hypothesis* of Christ" (*Panarion* 24.8.6).[43] Epiphanius understandably suggests that substituting Simon for Jesus on the cross threatens the basic story (i.e., *hypothesis*) of the gospels. In another passage, he says copyists "made something defective of the *hypothesis*" by altering Matthew's genealogy (4.8.4).[44] In a third place, Epiphanius refers to Marcion's rewritten version of the third gospel as "the *hypothesis* according to him [composed] from the remains which were saved by him from the gospel" (42.12.1).[45] In all three of these passages, Epiphanius uses the idea of a *hypothesis* to assert limits to acceptable variation among the gospels. These heretics and foolish scribes, according to Epiphanius, have retold the life of Jesus in a way that undermines the fundamental story.

---

42. Epiphanius does not state what passage from the fourth gospel supports the virgin birth. A likely candidate is John 1:13, frequently cited (out of context) in support of Jesus's supernatural conception.

43. Text from Holl, *Epiphanius I Ancoratus und Panarion haer. 1-33*, 265.

44. Text from Holl, *Epiphanius I Ancoratus und Panarion haer. 1-33*, 195.

45. Text from Holl, *Epiphanius II Panarion Haer*, 155. Williams reasonably takes *hypothesis* to refer to the subject of Epiphanius's treatise and not as a reference to Marcion's Gospel. But William's interpretation is not possible in light of the almost exact parallel at *Panarion* 3.42.12.3. Frank Williams, *The Panarion of Epiphanius of Salamis: Book I* (SBL Press, 2016), 339.

Lastly, it's important to note that Epiphanius uses the idea of a *hypothesis* to organize other narrative traditions. He employs the term to introduce a summary of the basic story of the mythical phoenix, which Epiphanius flags as both traditional and pluriform (*Ancoratus* 38). Likewise, Epiphanius uses the term to refer to the myths of various heretics (e.g., *Panarion* 23.4.3; 25.3.6), the general contours of Jewish scripture (4.3.6; 4.7.4) or particular narratives therein (e.g., 42.11 Sch. 25), and a correct account of historical events (e.g., 25.4.10; 66.2.1).

Particularly notable is Epiphanius's use of *hypothesis* language to describe the Manichean account of human origins. Mani narrates the history of human souls in one way and then, according to Epiphanius, "narrates the *hypothesis* concerning the same thing in a different way" (*Panarion* 66.44.2).[46] Epiphanius wants to claim that Mani's two stories contradict. But for this to be true, the stories must be about the same people, places, and events—they must share the same *hypothesis.* Mirroring the scholiasts' typical usage, then, Epiphanius employs the idea of a *hypothesis* to refer to the underlying unity of two contradictory stories.

These final examples illustrate that Epiphanius is not claiming something special about the gospels by the mere use of *hypothesis* language. Of course, Epiphanius does believe the gospels are special, and he sometimes uses *hypothesis* language to say so. Still, Epiphanius imagines all kinds of narrative traditions as expressions of a shared *hypothesis.* When Epiphanius applies the concept of a narrative *hypothesis* to the gospels, he is drawing on the standard language for pluriform literary traditions in antiquity.

Cosmas Indicopleustes

A century after Epiphanius and nearly a half millennium after the gospels were written, Greek-speaking readers can still be found who use the idea of a narrative *hypothesis* to think about gospel literature and the

46. Text from Holl, *Epiphanius III Panarion Haer,* 81.

life of Jesus. One such author is Cosmas Indicopleustes, a sixth-century merchant from Alexandria. His *Christian Topography*, ostensibly a geographic treatise, is filled with reflections on Christian scripture.

In the fifth book of this work, Cosmas makes an extended argument for the harmony of the prophets, gospels, and apostolic writings. Halfway through this discussion, he provides a synopsis of each of the four gospels, including the occasion of their composition, opening lines, and an outline of their narratives (*Top.* 190–205). This is the kind of material that would be used in the Dicaearchean plot summaries, often called *hypotheses* (or, more appropriately, *argumenta*) in the manuscript tradition of the gospels.[47] But these are outlines of individual gospels—not the basic story underlying multiple gospels. Notably, Cosmas does not call these summaries *hypotheses.*

In the very next section of his treatise, however, Cosmas uses the idea of a narrative *hypothesis* to refer to the basic narrative shared across the gospels. Cosmas compares Peter's preaching in the book of Acts to the work of gospel authors. The apostle Peter, says Cosmas, shared "the same goal" (τὸν αὐτὸν . . . σκοπὸν) as the evangelists (5.206). Then, after quoting several descriptions of Jesus's life from the speeches in Acts (2:22–24, 32–36, 3:19–21, 10:38–43), Cosmas uses *hypothesis* language to describe these speeches.

> Consider here how the whole *hypothesis* of the gospels is circumscribed into a few lines, saying concerning [Jesus] that he was raised in Nazareth, and that he was a man from God (like a second Adam) and that through him God worked wonders and that, by divine allowance, he was killed by the lawless, and that God raised him up immortal and unchangeable (for it says: "destroying the pains of death") and that, by divine

47. On Dicaearchus's *hypotheses,* see the final section of chapter 1. On *argumentum,* see the excursus at the end of chapter 2. These very summaries were later repurposed as *hypotheses/argumenta* in New Testament manuscripts. See the recent discussion in Mina Monier, "Mark's Endings in Context: Paratexts and Codicological Remarks" *Religions* 13, no. 6 (2022), 3–6.

> power, being exalted he went up into heaven and sent down from there the Holy Spirit (5.207).[48]

In this passage, Cosmas speaks of a single *hypothesis* held in common by multiple gospels and pithily articulated in Peter's speeches. The content of that *hypothesis* is specified: Jesus's provenance, character, miracles, death, and resurrection. Like Irenaeus, Clement, and so many others, Cosmas uses the term *hypothesis* to refer to the fundamental story of Jesus's life, variously instantiated in (but not identical to) several written gospels and the preaching of the early church.

Not Like Other Books

Allegorical interpretation, as practiced by pagans, Jews, and Christians alike, was premised on certain assumptions about the text to be interpreted.[49] No reader in antiquity assumed that every piece of writing was permeated with philosophical, theological, and scientific knowledge. Appropriate objects of allegorical interpretation were thought to be, in some sense, *divine*.[50]

To consider only a few examples, Heraclitus, a first-century grammarian, begins his defense of allegorical interpretation by asserting that Homer himself was "divine" (3.1) and concludes with an insistence on the inspiration of Homer's poetry (79.13).[51] Philo of Alexandria, a Jewish advocate of allegorical reading, says the law of Moses was "truly

---

48. Text from Wanda Wolska-Conus, *Cosma Indicopleusta Topographie Chretienne.*, vol. 2. Sources Chrétiennes 159 (Les Éditions du Cerf, 1970), 309.

49. On different working assumptions of rhetorical and allegorical reading, see Struck, *Birth of the Symbol*, 1–13.

50. For evidence of one debate over the appropriateness of interpreting Christian scripture allegorically, see Melissa Sellew, "Achilles or Christ? Porphyry and Didymus in Debate over Allegorical Interpretation," *Harvard Theological Review* 82, no. 1 (1989): 79–100.

51. D. A. Russell and David Konstan, *Heraclitus: Homeric Problems*, Writings from the Greco-Roman World 14 (Society of Biblical Literature, 2005), 130.

divine" (*Life of Moses* 2.12) and "prophesied by inspiration" (2.34, see also 68).[52] Lastly, Origen defends the allegorical interpretation of the Pentateuch by asserting that Moses "ascended over all creation and united himself to the creation of all things" and possessed "a divine spirit" (*Against Celsus* 1.19).[53]

To read the gospels allegorically, then, was to read them as something more than ordinary books. The evangelists, insists Origen, were divinely inspired in the same manner as the authors of Jewish scripture (*On First Principles* 4.16).

> The Holy Spirit orchestrated these things, not only for those scriptures which were written up until the advent of Christ but . . . did the very same also in the gospels and the apostles. For, indeed, those narratives which He inspired through them were not put together without his wisdom, which we have already explained. So, indeed, he intermingled not a few things which interrupting or breaking the historical arrangement of the narrative call the attention of the reader (by the impossibility of it) to consider its inner meaning.[54]

Differences between the gospels, according to Origen, were not merely instances of permissible variation or authorial license. Rather, Origen understood every difference as an opportunity to seek a deeper level of meaning. Each variation in the parallel narratives was an inspired symbol of some profound truth.

A reader with these assumptions about the text has relatively little use for the idea of a narrative *hypothesis.* Hellenistic literary critics used *hypothesis* language, in part, to excuse acceptable variation and indict what was unacceptable in the retelling of a story. Irenaeus and other

---

52. Text from Leopold Cohn and Paul Wendland, *Philonis Alexandrini Opera quae supersunt. Ediderunt Leopoldus Cohn et Paulus Wendland* (Georg Reimer, 1902), 4:203, 207.

53. Text from Marcovich, *Contra Celsum*, 21.

54. John Behr, *Origen: On First Principles* (Oxford University Press, 2017), 516.

early readers adopted this notion to make sense of their own pluriform narratives. There are innumerable, acknowledged differences between Matthew, Mark, Luke, and John but, according to Irenaeus, they each preserve the same *hypothesis*. Basilides's version of the gospel story, by way of contrast, destroys the *hypothesis* (according to Epiphanius) despite its close resemblance to the canonical gospels. But a reader like Origen does not wish interpreters to look past differences to focus on a shared basic story. The differences, according to Origen, are due to divine inspiration. Likewise, a reader who takes for granted the canon of scripture need not appeal to a *hypothesis* to exclude alternative versions of a story. For Origen, it is simply the case that the church has four gospels.[55] These different assumptions explain the distribution of *hypothesis* language in the history of Christian interpretation.

Conclusion

Early readers of gospels used *hypothesis* language to organize the gospels because that was the way Hellenistic and Roman readers thought about narrative traditions. Readers like Irenaeus and Epiphanius describe the gospels with the same conceptual categories as other retold stories. But Christians gradually stopped reading the gospels like normal books. Origen uses the idea of the *hypothesis* when he condescends to meet Celsus on his own interpretive grounds. Eusebius and Cosmas primarily use *hypothesis* language descriptively. Once the singular *gospel* was reconceptualized as one work in four volumes with one divine author, there was little need to appeal to a basic story abstracted away from the text.

Nevertheless, the application of *hypothesis* language to the gospels by these early readers supports the relevance of that concept to gospel literature in literary imaginations shaped by Hellenistic reading culture. Irenaeus's appeal to the gospel *hypothesis* is not an idiosyncratic invocation of an obscure piece of technical vocabulary. Rather, it made sense to different readers across several centuries to describe and evaluate gospels in these same terms.

55. See, for instance, Origen's matter of fact dismissal of alternative gospels in his commentary on the Lukan prologue.

CHAPTER FOUR

Reading the Gospels Before Irenaeus

"Since I was provided with this gospel by them, I was able to go through it and discover that most of it belonged to the true account of the savior."

—Serapion of Antioch

Introduction

DID IRENAEUS RADICALLY reimagine the gospels? His notion of a fourfold gospel is certainly innovative. No other reader in the Hellenistic world stipulates that a narrative tradition has only a specific number of instantiations. And gospel readers before Irenaeus did not share this idea. But the argument for a fourfold gospel makes up only a small part of Irenaeus's account of gospel literature.[1] Throughout the rest of *Against Heresies*, Irenaeus describes the gospels with the same language that other Hellenistic readers used to describe other narrative traditions. Like Dio Chrysostom's description of the three versions of *Philoctetes*, Irenaeus refers to the gospels as distinct books on a common *hypothesis*, identifies their authors, and describes how, when, and where they became public (3.1.1). That is, Irenaeus describes gospels as conventional, Hellenistic literature.[2] Was this way of thinking about gospels another innovation from the age of Irenaeus?

---

1. In chapter 2, I argued that Irenaeus's claims in *Against Heresies* 3.11.8–9 stands in tension with Irenaeus's claim throughout *Against Heresies* that each gospel independently and equally preserves the *hypothesis* of the gospel (e.g., 3.1.1).

2. A flurry of recent scholarship has argued that gospels were regarded by early readers as something less than authored, discrete books in the decades before Irenaeus. D.

There is no explicit or sustained reflection on the multiplicity of gospels from any writer before Irenaeus. It is unsurprising, then, that the term *hypothesis* does not appear in Christian literature from the first half of the second century. Several earlier authors do, however, reveal their conception of gospel literature *en passant*. These incidental remarks suggest that Irenaeus's basic view of the gospels—though not his proto-canonical conception of a fourfold collection—was widespread in the second century. That is, several authors before Irenaeus imagined gospels as discrete books, composed and published by their authors according to the conventions of Hellenistic literary culture. And although they do not use the term *hypothesis*, some of these authors discuss gospels in a way that suggests their imaginations of narrative traditions were shaped by this standard model (i.e., distinct, authorial works on a shared basic story).

Papias of Hierapolis

Papias, a bishop of Asia Minor in the early second century, is the first author to reflect explicitly on the existence of more than one gospel.[3] Unfortunately, Papias's discussion of the gospels is preserved only as fragments in Eusebius's *Church History*. The handful of surviving lines related to Mark and Matthew, nevertheless, contain tantalizing hints at Papias's conception of the pluriform gospel tradition.[4]

C. Parker, *The Living Text of the Gospels* (Cambridge University Press, 1997), esp. 45–47, 117–119, 205; Francis Watson, "How Did Mark Survive?," in *Matthew and Mark Across Perspectives*, by K. A. Bendoraitis and N. K. Gupta (Bloomsbury T&T Clark, 2016), 1–18; Matthew Larsen, *Gospels Before the Book* (Oxford University Press, 2018); Elder, *Gospel Media*, 236–272.

3. Eusebius's *Chronicle* places Papias early in the second century. Stephen C. Carlson, ed., *Papias of Hierapolis Exposition of Dominical Oracles: The Fragments, Testimonia, and Reception of a Second-Century Commentator*, Oxford Early Christian Texts (Oxford University Press, 2021), 136–137. The description of multiple gospels from the Lukan prologue is discussed in chapter 5.

4. Further material from Papias on John's gospel may be preserved in several late antiquity authors without attribution. See the discussion in Charles E. Hill, "What

The first relevant fragment from Papias concerns the origin of the gospel ascribed to Mark.[5]

> Mark, who was Peter's interpreter, wrote whatever he remembered of the things said and done by the Lord accurately but not in order. For he neither heard the Lord nor followed him, but later (as I said) [followed] Peter, who would produce teachings as needed. But [Peter] did not produce a composition of the Lord's *logia*, so that Mark did not err in writing some as he recalled them. For he did one thing with foresight: neither omitting nor falsifying anything among them.[6]

Papias Said About John (and Luke): A 'New' Papian Fragment," *Journal of Theological Studies* 49, no. 2 (1998): 582–629; T. Scott Manor, "Papias, Origen, and Eusebius: The Criticisms and Defense of the Gospel of John," *Vigiliae Christianae* 67, no. 1 (2013): 1–21; Dean Furlong, "Theodore of Mopsuestia: New Evidence for the Proposed Papian Fragment in Hist. Eccl. 3.24.5-13," *Journal for the Study of the New Testament* 39, no. 2 (2016): 209–229.

5. For present purposes, I am unconcerned with the historicity of Papias's traditions. The convoluted etiology of this gospel does, however, seem like an attempt to legitimize a preexisting attribution to someone named Mark. See the argument in Joel Marcus, *Mark 1-8: A New Translation with Introduction and Commentary*, vol. 27 of *The Anchor Bible* (Doubleday, 1999), 17–24.

6. Text from Carlson, *Papias of Hierapolis Exposition of Dominical Oracles*, 116. Carlson reads τῶν κυριακῶν [. . .] λογίων as referring to Old Testament prophecies about Jesus. Carlson, *Papias of Hierapolis Exposition of Dominical Oracles*, 39. The previous clause, however, makes it clear that Papias is explaining why Mark records the words and deeds of Jesus in a different order from Matthew. It makes little sense for Papias to then contrast their treatment of Old Testament prophecies. Moreover, *logia* is the natural antecedent of "any among them" (τι ἐν αὐτοῖς). Thus, Papias is defending Mark against the charge of falsifying these same *logia*. What could it mean for Papias to defend Mark (vis-à-vis Matthew) against the charge of falsifying passages of the Old Testament? By way of contrast, Papias's exact contemporaries protest against the falsification of Jesus's written teachings (e.g., *Epistula Apostolorum* 29.1; Dionysius of Corinth *apud* Eusebius, *Church History* 23.12). Finally, the use of "Dominical *Logia*" to refer to the teachings of Jesus is attested elsewhere (ps-Athanasius, *Discourse Against the Arians* PG 28 445; see also Origen, *Comm. on Matthew* 15.8). That this is the most plausible way to hold together the fragments of Papias, see E. Norelli, *Papia Di Hierapolis: Esposizione Degli Oracoli Del Signore: I Frammenti* (Paoline, 2005), 59–80.

Papias describes Peter as a teacher who produced no "composition" (σύνταξις) of his own. It was left, therefore, to one of his students to publish Peter's teachings "as he recalled them."[7]

This scenario would be familiar to readers in the second century. Famously, Socrates wrote nothing himself. It was, rather, Socrates's followers who published accounts of his life. The teachings of other famous philosophers—including Diogenes of Sinope and Pyrrho—were recorded only by their disciples. Traditions developed that other famous philosophers—including Thales and Pythagoras—wrote nothing themselves, in spite of the fact that many works were then circulating under their names.[8] And this scenario was not just literary convention: Papias's contemporary, Arrian, preserves the only accounts of Epictetus's doctrine, and only Lucian passed on the life of his teacher, Demonax.[9] Papias's readers would recognize the description of Mark recording the doctrines of his unpublished teacher as perfectly conventional.

Papias's account of composition subtly complicates the authorial attribution of this gospel. The gospel is, according to Papias, Peter's

---

7. Candida Moss reads Papias as a description of Peter composing the gospel by dictation to Mark. On Moss's reading, Mark plays a servile role as interpreter, scribe, and aide-mémoire. Candida Moss, "Fashioning Mark: Early Christian Discussions about the Scribe and Status of the Second Gospel," *New Testament Studiers* 67, no. 2 (2021): 181–204. But emphasis on Mark's ability to remember Peter's teaching indicates that Papias is not envisioning dictation with contemporary transcription, but the student's recollection of a former teacher's words. Two readers who likely had access to the full text of Papias (not to mention greater familiarity with cultural norms), understand Papias in this way (Irenaeus, *Against Heresies* 3.1.1; Clement *apud* Eusebius, *Church History* 6.14.5-7). Papias's emphasis on accuracy is probably apologetic for Mark's lack of *taxis*. Larsen cites Papias's characterization of Mark as evidence that the gospels were viewed as *hypomnemata*—which he understands as referring to subliterary, unauthored, unfinished notes. Papias, however, never refers to any gospel as either ὑπομνήματα or ἀπομνημονεύματα. Rather, Papias uses the verbs μνημονεύω and ἀπομνημονεύω to describe Mark's recollection of Peter's teaching. For further critique of Larsen, see Keith, *The Gospel as Manuscript*, 51–55.

8. Diogenes Laertius, *Lives* 1.5.23; 8.1.6.

9. Aulus Gellius's use of *dictitare* to describe Arrian's behavior parallels Papias's description of Mark (*Attic Knights* 17.19).

teaching as compiled by Mark. Still, nothing about that description would seem especially complicated to second-century readers. In each of the well-known cases considered above, ancient commentators treated the student in question as author of the relevant text. Aulus Gellius, for example, refers to the Discourses of Epictetus "composed by Arrian" (*Attic Nights* 19.1). Plato and Xenophon, likewise, are consistently credited for their Socratic books. Just as ancient readers praised (and sometimes criticized) Plato for his representation of Socrates, so too Papias defends Mark's reputation (not Peter's) against an implied critique of the gospel. Authorship is a matter of attributed responsibility, and Papias holds Mark responsible for composing the gospel in question. In sum, Papias imagines this gospel as authored according to well-established conventions of Hellenistic literature.[10]

Papias defends Mark on several points. He wrote "accurately" (ακριβώς), did not err in producing a composition when Peter had not, and did not falsify (ψεύσασθαι) or omit (παραλιπεῖν) anything.[11] Papias concedes, however, that Mark did not record Jesus's words or deeds "in order" (τάξει). Why this concession?

Comparison with Papias's statement on Matthew might clarify this statement and the argument in which both fragments were embedded.

> Matthew, then, composed the *logia* in the Hebrew dialect, and each person translated these as he was able.

Probably, Papias is admitting a contrast between the gospels in his use of the verb "to compose" (συντάσσω) to describe Matthew's behavior

10. Notably, Papias does not follow the trend of authorship evident in most of the noncanonical texts considered in chapter 5. With the exception of the *Protevangelium*, each of these works followed the Johannine pattern of representing itself as authored by an actor in the narrative. But Papias, like the Lukan prologue, represents gospel literature as authored by someone connected to relevant authorities.

11. This line of reasoning suggests that Papias does not envision Mark writing his gospel while Peter was still active. The emphasis on memory only reinforces that point. See my comments on Moss in note 8 above.

and the related adjective "order" (τάξει) that Papias denies to Mark's gospel.[12] Matthew's gospel, according to Papias, is a life of Jesus with the appropriate order absent from Mark. And it is not difficult to see how Papias reached this conclusion: Mark describes much of Jesus's ministry as a series of decontextualized teachings and miracles, while Matthew incorporates the same material into larger stories and sermons.[13]

Papias's assertion that "Mark did not err" and the concession that Mark lacks proper "order" (in contrast to Matthew) suggests that this discussion of gospels is a response to a critical reader, real or imagined, who has compared Mark to another gospel and judged Mark deficient.[14] If we assume that each of Papias's claims corresponds to a complaint against Mark, then our critic has accused this gospel of omitting parts of Jesus's story, falsifying Jesus's teachings, and presenting the narrative out of order. Again, if we take any other gospel as a point of comparison, it easy to see what motivated these charges: Mark lacks Matthew's nativity, sermon on the mount, and resurrection scenes; Mark and Matthew present Jesus's evening healing in Capernaum (Mark 1:32–34 // Matt 8:16–17) and the healing of a leper (Mark 1:40–45 // Matt 8:1–4) in the opposite order; and, of course, there are important differences in the content of Jesus's teaching throughout

12. See, for instance, Francis Watson, *Gospel Writing: A Canonical Perspective* (Eerdmans, 2013), 122–130. The account of Jesus's life that Papias acknowledges Peter *did not* produce is called a σύνταξις. It is unclear whether Papias would have also applied the term to Mark's work.

13. It is important not to overstate the contrast. There is, in fact, continuity and progression between episodes in Mark (e.g., 6:52, 13:28). And the construction of a biography out of discrete episodes was not unliterary. See Helen K. Bond, *The First Biography of Jesus: Genre and Meaning in Mark's Gospel* (Eerdmans, 2020).

14. "Papias' statement that Mark did nothing wrong in writing things as he remembered them would indicate that some at least thought that he had." Alistair Stewart-Sykes, "*Τάξει* in Papias: Again," *Journal of Early Christian Studies* 3, no. 4 (1995): 488. Quite plausibly, Michael Goulder places this fragment into conversation with the Lukan prologue. Michael D. Goulder, *Luke: A New Paradigm*, Journal for the Study of the New Testament Supplement Series 20 (Sheffield Academic Press, 1989), 198–202.

the two gospels.[15] The contrast would be even more drastic if Mark were compared to Luke or John.

Papias, in response, does not deny differences between the gospels. And he does not attempt to harmonize them. Instead, Papias defends the pluriformity of this narrative tradition. Just as Dio Chrysostom invokes Euripides's authorial interests to explain disagreements with Aeschylus, so Papias invokes Mark's authorial situation to explain disagreements with other gospels. This gospel really is different, says Papias, but that is no reason to fault its author.

The fragment of Papias on the origin of Matthew may itself be a response to a related line of criticism. The final clause, "each translated as he was able," seems to acknowledge that there were different versions of the same gospel in circulation. Papias claims that these different versions are the result of multiple good-faith translations of an underlying Hebrew gospel. Of course, there never was such a gospel.[16] The different versions may refer to normal scribal variation in the gospel's text tradition. Another second-century author would criticize Christians for tampering with the text of their gospels (Origen, *Against Celsus* 2.27).[17] Or the different versions might reflect Papias's knowledge of a Greek Gospel of the Hebrews—a synoptic-type gospel sometimes treated as a variant version of Matthew.[18] In either case, Papias responds to an implied critique of pluriformity by providing an innocent explanation for that variety.

15. I presented an innocuous example in the introduction to this book, but a more theologically significant case study might be the assumption that Jesus's followers observed the sabbath introduced into Matthew's synoptic apocalypse (Mark 13:17 // Matt 24:19–20).

16. Matthew is dependent word-for-word on the Greek text of Mark.

17. On Celsus's argument, see Jeremiah Coogan, "Meddling with the Gospel: Celsus, Early Christian Textuality, and the Politics of Reading," *Novum Testamentum* 65, no. 3 (2023): 400–422.

18. In another testimony, Eusebius reports that Papias discussed a story known to Eusebius from the *Gospel of the Hebrews* (*Church History*, 3.39.16–17).

This critique of Matthew and Papias's response are both premised on the assumption that Matthew is the kind of book that ought to be copied in the form it was received. The same attitude toward copying gospel literature is found in other early second-century works, including the *Epistula Apostolorum* (29.1) and an epistle of Dionysius of Corinth (*apud* Eusebius, *Church History* 23.12).[19] At the beginning of the second century, then, gospels were regarded by their readers, like other Hellenistic literature, as texts to be preserved.[20]

Barely anything survives of Papias's account of the gospels, and these two fragments do not invoke a narrative *hypothesis*.[21] But Papias shows that Irenaeus's way of thinking about gospels as literature was not foreign to the readerly imagination in the early second century. Matthew and Mark, according to Papias, are distinct books with identifiable authors. For Papias, they are the kind of books that invite evaluation with the categories of Hellenistic literary criticism and ought to be preserved as written.[22] Finally, Papias acknowledges real differences between the gospels. But, unlike later harmonists, he does not attempt to reconcile their plots. Rather, like Dio Chrysostom and other Hellenistic literary critics, Papias explains that gospel authors tell the same story in different ways for their own legitimate reasons.

---

19. This passage from the *Epistle to the Apostles* is discussed at greater length in chapter 5.

20. On interest in authorial texts, see Katharina de la Durantaye, "The Origins of the Protection of Literary Authorship in Ancient Rome," *Boston University International Law Journal* 25, no. 37 (2008): 37–111.

21. There is a third reference to the gospels in Papias's declaration that he prefers to learn about the teachings of Jesus from "the living voice" of Jesus's followers rather than "books" (βιβλίων). Carlson, *Papias of Hierapolis Exposition of Dominical Oracles*, 118. This fragment only corroborates our interpretation that Papias imagines the gospels as distinct literary works (as opposed to notes or memory aides).

22. On the meaning of *taxis* (and other rhetorical vocabulary) for Papias in light of Hellenistic literary criticism, see Matthew Black, "The Use of Rhetorical Terminology in Papias On Mark and Matthew," *Journal for the Study of the New Testament* 12, no. 37 (1989): 31–41.

Justin Martyr

The Socrates of popular imagination is Plato's Socrates. For many readers today, the skeptical gadfly of Plato's dialogues simply *is* Socrates. But Plato's portrait has not always so predominated. Xenophon, another of Socrates's corrupted youths, wrote his own accounts of the philosopher's teachings, controversies, trial, and execution. Xenophon's Socrates was at least as well known in the Roman period as Plato's.

Xenophon's most famous Socratic work was the *Memoirs* (ἀπομνημονεύματα).[23] This work inspired a subgenre of philosophical biography in the Hellenistic and Roman periods. Works titled *Memoirs* can be found in every century between Xenophon and Irenaeus.[24] To select one example, Origen refers to an otherwise unknown *Memoirs of Apollonius of Tyana,* written sometime in the second century (*Against Celsus* 6.54). The subgenre was so well known that it was codified in the textbooks: Aelius Theon, writing in the late first century, describes *Memoirs* as a subclass of history writing, related to but distinct from biography (*Progymnasmata* 13).[25]

Writing in the middle of the second century, Justin Martyr repeatedly refers to the gospels as *Memoirs* (ἀπομνημονεύματα).[26]

---

23. Despite suggestions to the contrary, there is extensive evidence that ἀπομνημονεύματα was a conventional title for Xenophon's work in the first and second centuries. See the evidence adduced in Gabriella Aragione, "Justin 'Philosphe' Cretien et Les Memoires Des Apotre," *Apocrypha* (2004): 47–48.

24. See Aragione, "Justin 'Philosphe' Cretien et Les Memoires Des Apotre," 48–50. *Memoirs* were not used exclusively for philosophical figures (e.g., Plutarch, *Life of Brutus* 13.3; 27.3).

25. This passage is only extant in Classical Armenian. Kennedy, *Progymnasmata*, 68. Elsewhere, Theon reveals that he knows Xenophon's work by the title Ἀπομνημονεύματα (12.252).

26. *First Apology* 66.3; 67.3 and *Dialog with Trypho* 100.4; 101.3; 102.5; 103.6, 8; 104.1; 105.1, 5, 6; 106.1, 4; 107,1.

> For the apostles in the *Memoirs* composed by them—which are called gospels—hand down in this way what they were commanded (*First Apology* 66.3).[27]

In this introduction to a gospel quotation, Justin acknowledges that the "Memoirs" containing Jesus's teaching are otherwise known as "gospels." The use of the plural *gospels* here is significant as it reveals that Justin's typical reference to "Memoirs (of the Apostles)" does not pick out a single work but, rather, refers to several different books, each called a "gospel" by other readers.[28] Decades before Irenaeus, then, Justin speaks of gospels as multiple, discrete books.[29]

Although Justin several times refers to the gospels as simply *Memoirs*, he more often uses the fuller construction *Memoirs of the Apostles* (e.g., *First Apology* 33.5).[30] The phrase "of the apostles" does not, of course, refer to the subject of these *Memoirs*.[31] Rather, it designates Jesus's disciples as their authors. In another place, Justin states clearly that the *Memoirs* were "composed by [Jesus's] apostles and

---

27. Text from Denis Minns and Paul Parvis, eds., *Justin, Philosopher and Martyr: Apologies* (Oxford University Press, 2009), 256.

28. Justin can also refer to a singular "gospel" (*Dialogue* 10.2; 100.1). Philippe Bobichon, *Justin Martyr, Dialogue Avec Tryphon: Édition Critique: Introduction, Texte Grec, Traduction*, Paradosis: Études de Littérature et de Théologie Anciennes (Academic Press Fribourg, 2003), 452–454.

29. Apollinarius Claudius, whom Eusebius places before Irenaeus (*Church History* 4.21) uses "gospels" in the plural (*Chronicon Paschale*, Preface). Other early uses of the plural include *The Epistle to Diognetus* 11, Theophilus of Antioch, *To Autolycus* 3.12, and Clement, *Stromata* 1.21, 3.13.

30. The term *Memoirs* is used by itself at *1 Apology* 66.3, *Dialog* 103.8, 105.5, 6, 107.1.

31. This usage is an alleged disanalogy with Xenophon by Richard Heard, "The 'Apomnemoneumata' in Papias, Justin, and Irenaeus," *New Testament Studies* 1 (1954): 122–129; Radka Fialová, "'Scripture' and the 'Memoirs of the Apostles': Justin Martyr and His Bible," in *The Process of Authority: The Dynamics in Transmission and Reception of Canonical Texts*, ed. Jan Roskovec and Jan Dušek (De Gruyter, 2016), 165–178. See note 33 below.

their followers" (*Dialog* 103.8).[32] And the construction "Memoirs of [Author]" is perfectly in keeping with titling conventions for the genre: Xenophon's *Memoirs* about Socrates, for instance, were often referred to as *The Memoirs of Xenophon* by ancient readers.[33]

That Justin's use of the generic title "Memoirs" is meant to associate the gospels with the literary tradition inaugurated by Xenophon is further suggested by Justin's representation of Christianity as a philosophy. In his *First Apology*, Justin argues that the *logos* incarnate in Christ spoke also through Socrates (5). Even more persuasively, Justin's *Second Apology* compares Jesus's death to that of Socrates (10), immediately before quoting from Xenophon's *Memoirs* (11). The *Dialog with Trypho*, then, begins with Justin hailed as "philosopher" (1). Its first chapters compare Christianity favorably with various philosophical schools and then credit gospel literature with leading him to "the only sure and beneficial philosophy"—that is, Christianity (8.1).[34] Clearly, Justin wished to portray Jesus as a Socrates-type figure and his followers as philosophers. His ascription of the gospels to a subgenre of philosophical biography (i.e. *Memoirs*) fits Justin's apologetic program.

Justin's use of this literary genre to describe the gospels reveals other assumptions he held about gospel literature. For instance, the generic *Memoirs of the Apostles* reveals that Justin shared the assumption of other early- to mid-second-century readers that the gospels were conventionally authored books. In fact, Justin seems to share Papias's assumption that the gospels were authored by either *dramatis personae*

32. Text from Bobichon, *Justin Martyr, Dialogue Avec Tryphon*, 464.

33. Instances of the authorial genitive applied to *Memoirs* include Theon, *Progymnasmata* 2; Diogenes Laertius, *Lives* 7.2; Theodoret of Cyr, *Cure of Greek Maladies* 4.30; Stobaeus, *Extracts* 1.1.36. The epexegetical genitive, by way of contrast, is found in Diogenes Laertius, *Lives* 7.4 and the eighteenth Socratic letter (attributed to Xenophon) in R. Hercher, *Epistolographi Graeci* (Paris: Firmin Didot, 1873), 623. The most common title is simply "*Memoirs.*"

34. Justin does not use the term "gospel" here but clearly refers to them as books written by the "friends of Christ" (8.1) which contain the "words of the savior" (8.2). Bobichon, *Justin Martyr, Dialogue Avec Tryphon*, 204.

or persons connected to such relevant authorities. Just as Plato and Xenophon were well positioned to write accounts of Socrates's life, so too the disciples (the analogy suggests) were appropriate author-figures for *Memoirs* about Jesus.

The precise identity of these authors is somewhat less clear: Justin's reference to the composition of the gospels by "the apostles and their followers" (*Dialog* 103.8)—the plural nouns probably implying that more than one of Jesus's disciples and more than one of their followers were responsible for the (likewise plural) gospels—has suggested to some scholars that Justin used the same four gospels accepted by Irenaeus.[35] And historical parsimony suggests that Justin probably knew, at least, some of the same gospel etiologies known to other second-century Christians. But Justin's sole reference to a specific gospel makes it unlikely that Justin shared Irenaeus's four-fold collection of the gospels (*Dialog* 106.3).[36]

> And it is said that he changed one of the names of the apostles to Peter, and it is written in the *Memorabilia* of him that this happened . . ..[37]

Instead of the phrase "of the apostles," Justin here uses the singular "of him." The nearest antecedent is "Peter," and the genitive phrase with *Memoirs* in Justin always refers to their authors. Justin, it seems, cites the *Gospel of Peter*. This story about Peter's name was probably known to Justin from multiple gospels but he breaks from his usual practice of citing the *Memoirs* in general to cite a specific gospel because it is a story about Peter. Here and elsewhere, Justin's gospel citations suggest

35. Martin Hengel, *The Four Gospels and the One Gospel of Jesus Christ* (Trinity Press International, 2000), 20.

36. The use of *Memoirs* might itself suggest Justin thinks about gospels as having a different kind of authority from the Jewish Scriptures. See Charles H. Cosgrove, "Justin Martyr and the Emerging Christian Canon. Observations on the Purpose and Destination of the Dialogue with Trypho," *Vigilae Christianae* 36 (1982): 209–32.

37. Text from Bobichon, *Justin Martyr, Dialogue Avec Tryphon*, 470.

that he did not share Irenaeus's view of the fourfold gospel but, rather, used a variety of gospels, including some excluded by later Christians.[38]

By associating gospels with philosophical *Memoirs* Justin portrayed gospels as participants in a tradition of philosophical literature that began in Classical Athens. These *Memoirs* were classified as a subgenre of history by Justin's scholarly contemporaries (e.g., Theon, *Progymnasmata* 13). And like Papias before him, Justin thought of gospels as the records of a teacher composed by his students. As such, Justin clearly anticipated Irenaeus in imagining gospels as distinct, authored books at home in Hellenistic literary culture.

Unfortunately, Justin's surviving works contain no explicit reflection on the pluriformity of gospel literature. But Justin did assimilate the gospels to a notoriously pluriform narrative tradition. Both Athenaeus and Diogenes Laertius use the idea of a narrative *hypothesis* to describe the overlapping Socratic narratives written by Xenophon and Plato.[39] Indeed, Justin himself cites both Xenophon and Plato for their portrayals of Socrates. Given his background in contemporary forms of Platonism, Justin may have known yet other versions of the same Socratic stories.[40] It is more than plausible, therefore, that Justin thought about Socratic literature in the same way as his contemporaries and transferred those conceptual categories to the gospels. That is, Justin

---

38. Justin's paraphrases and harmonization are too consistent in details large and small across his corpus to be the product of memory or *ad hoc* paraphrase. See A. J. Bellinzoni, *The Sayings of Jesus in the Writings of Justin Martyr*, vol. 17 of *Supplements to Novum Testamentum*, ed. W. C. van Unnik (Brill, 1967), 30, 47–48, 95–100. The best explanation is Justin's use of one or more gospels that conservatively rework material from the synoptic gospels, such as P.Dura 24, P.Oxy. 4009, P.Oxy. 5575. Serapion's description of the *Gospel according to Peter* suggests that it too may have been this sort of gospel, especially with respect to the ministry/teaching of Jesus (see the next section of this chapter). Justin's use of gospel traditions beyond the now canonical four is also evident at *Dialog* 47.5 and 78.5.

39. Athenaeus, *Deipnosophists* 11.504d-e; Diogenes Laertius, *Lives* 3.34, 57. See chapters 2 and 6 for further discussion.

40. M. J. Edwards, "On the Platonic Schooling of Justin Martyr," *Journal of Theological Studies* 42, no. 1 (1991): 17–34.

probably thought about Christian *Memoirs* in the same way that he (and his contemporaries) thought about Socratic *Memoirs*—i.e., as distinct books written on a common *hypothesis*.

Justin's rare reference to the singular "gospel" supports this inference. In the opening chapters of the *Dialog*, Justin depicts his Jewish opponent Trypho praising Christian ethical teaching. These teachings are attributed to "the so-called gospel" (10.2).

> I know also that your precepts in the so-called gospel are so wonderful and great that I suppose no one is able to keep them—for I made a point to consult them myself.[41]

Given Justin's customary reference to *Memoirs* and use of "gospels" elsewhere in the plural, the singular "gospel" in this passage is striking. Trypho's insistence that he consulted the precepts for himself excludes the possibility that *gospel* here refers to Christian preaching (i.e., the *kerygmatic* sense). It can only refer to a book or books. And Justin, as other passages make clear, knows that more than one gospel contains the ethical precepts of Jesus. Justin's Trypho, then, appears to use the singular *gospel* to refer to the basic story or contents of a multiply instantiated narrative tradition—that is, the *hypothesis*.

Justin never reflects on the fact that there is more than one gospel. It is not surprising, therefore, that he never uses the term *hypothesis*. Nevertheless, decades before Irenaeus, Justin describes gospels as multiple distinct, authored books that belong to an established literary genre. Moreover, Justin's assimilation of the gospels to Socratic *Memoirs* and his use of the singular *gospel* to refer to an entire literary tradition suggest that Justin may have drawn on the same conceptual categories that his contemporaries used to think about overlapping accounts of Socrates. A combination of circumstantial and textual evidence suggests

41. Text from Bobichon, *Justin Martyr, Dialogue Avec Tryphon*, 208.

that Justin's thinking about gospels was shaped by this same "standard model" for pluriform narrative traditions—i.e., discrete authorial works on a common *hypothesis*.

Serapion of Antioch

Serapion was a junior contemporary of Irenaeus. He was bishop of Syrian Antioch at about the same time that Irenaeus published his *Against Heresies*. These two bishops lived, however, on opposite ends of the Mediterranean. While Serapion does not strictly antedate Irenaeus, then, his remarks provide a window onto the reception of gospel literature without the influence of Irenaeus's protocanonical argumentation.

In book six of his *Church History*, Eusebius quotes from a work of Serapion "on the so-called Gospel according to Peter" (6.12.2).[42] Serapion had traveled to nearby Rhosus where he learned of a dispute among the Christians in that city over which gospels ought to be read.

> When I was with you, I thought everyone adhered to the correct faith and, since I had not gone through the gospel which is put forward by them in the name of Peter, I said that if this alone seems to cause dissension among you, let it be read. (6.12.4)[43]

Serapion, he tells us himself, initially approved the reading of a gospel attributed to Peter. He accepted this gospel without studying it thoroughly (μὴ διελθὼν) in hopes of ending a local dispute. It is clear from this detail alone that Serapion and the church in Rhosus had multiple gospels but, like Justin before them, lacked anything like Irenaeus's notion of a rigidly fourfold collection.

42. Text from Gustave Bardy, *Eusèbe de Césarée. Histoire ecclésiastique. Livres V-VIII*, Sources Chrétiennes 41 (Les Éditions du Cerf, 1955), 102.

43. Text from Bardy, *Eusèbe de Césarée. Histoire ecclésiastique. Livres V-VIII*, 103.

Serapion then learned from unnamed informants that some Christians in Rhosus held heretical opinions and planned a return trip. While away from Rhosus, presumably back in Antioch, Serapion acquired a copy of *The Gospel according to Peter* for himself (6.12.6).

> For I was able to acquire this gospel from others who studied it—namely, from the successors of those who were the source of it (whom we call *Docetics*, since most of their opinions belong to this school). Since I was provided with this gospel by them, I was able to go through it and discover that most of it belonged to the true account of the savior, but some things were added which we append for you.[44]

Serapion discovered that a group of Christians with objectionable theology were using the gospel attributed to Peter. This prompted the bishop to write to the Christians in Rhosus to warn them against the gospel he had previously approved. Even still, Serapion does not simply condemn the Gospel of Peter.[45] Instead he provides a brief but nuanced description of the gospel's content. According to Serapion, "most of [the gospel attributed to Peter] belonged to the true account of the savior, but some things were added."

Serapion's assertion that "some things were added" is what we might expect from such polemics.[46] What stands out is Serapion's claim that much in this gospel agreed with the "true account" (ὁ ὀρθὸς λόγος). This clause appears to be a concession against Serapion's rhetorical interests. It might be understood as Serapion's self-justification for having previously approved the use of this gospel. The verb (διελθὼν) used by

44. Text from Bardy, *Eusèbe de Césarée. Histoire ecclésiastique. Livres V-VIII*, 103.

45. Serapion's earlier statement that he rejects works falsely attributed to Peter suggests that he condemned the gospel because it was a forgery.

46. Compare Dionysius of Corinth's accusation of "tampering with the writings of the Lord" *apud* Eusebius, *Church History* 4.23.12.

Serapion to describe the kind of reading that he was initially unable to perform in Rhosus and then, subsequently did perform when later given his own copy of the gospel suggests that Serapion did, in fact, briefly consult the gospel on his visit to Rhosus, but did not study it thoroughly. On this interpretation, Serapion's self-justifying logic is that if "most" of the gospel agreed with the true account of the Lord, Serapion cannot be faulted for approving it after only a quick perusal. Alternatively, the clause might be a concession to Christians in Rhosus who had grown accustomed to using this gospel as a source for Jesus's teachings. On this interpretation, Serapion conceded that most of what these Christians appreciate in this gospel agrees with the true account of the Lord (presumably, as found in other gospels).[47] On either interpretation, then, the purpose of the clause seems to be an acknowledgment that most of the gospel was, in fact, worthy of being read.

Serapion's assessment of the gospel involves an appeal to an imagined external standard. The disputed gospel of Peter is not compared to any particular gospel or creed, but to a notional "true account" of Jesus's life. Serapion is not the first author to use the term "account" (λόγος) this way. The author of the *Gospel according to Luke* states that authors before himself had composed their own "narrative" (διήγησις) of "the account (λόγος) handed down to us" (1:1).[48] The Lukan prologue uses the term descriptively, while Serapion uses it to evaluate a particular gospel. In both instances, however, the term refers to the story about Jesus underlying but distinct from any of its many written instantiations.

The Greek term translated as "account" (λόγος) is notoriously flexible in meaning. It is not a term of art, like *hypothesis*. In the

47. The initial line quoted by Eusebius (*Church History* 6.12.2) implies that Serapion knew other gospels attributed to the apostles. Given Serapion's prominent position at the end of the second century, it would be exceptional if he did not use, at least, Matthew.

48. The Lukan prologue is discussed at greater length in the following chapter.

gospels alone, it refers to statements (e.g., Mark 5:36), teachings (Mark 4:14–20), explanations (Matt 12:36), and stories (Matt 28:15). The Lukan prologue and Serapion, however, use the term as a near synonym for *hypothesis*.[49] That is, both authors use *account* to refer to an imagined basic story that constitutes a narrative tradition, instantiated in several distinct works. The sense of these two passages would be little changed by substituting *hypothesis* for *account*.[50] Although Serapion does not use the term *hypothesis*, this passage suggests that he thought about the gospels with the same conceptual model that Hellenistic literary critics used to evaluate their own narrative traditions. Each version of a story could be assessed with reference to a basic narrative (i.e., *hypothesis*) abstracted away from any particular version.

A papyrus fragment from Oxyrhynchus gives a plausible glimpse of what Serapion described as belonging to "the true account of the savior." The fragment is identifiable as a witness to the Gospel according to Peter because of a quotation in a second-century sermon, known to us as *Second Clement*. This sermon is replete with scriptural quotations, including an explicit citation of "the gospel" (8.5) and the attribution of Jesus's teaching to "scripture" (2.4).[51] This second-century preacher knows *at least* one book as a "gospel." And among the gospel quotations in *Second Clement* is a brief dialogue between Jesus and Peter not found in John or the synoptics but resembling the gospel text on one side of P.Oxy. 4009.

---

49. The literary use of *hypothesis* often connotes a certain schematism or lack of detail not necessarily implied by λόγος. Likewise, the prefix υπο- marks the contrast between instantiations and the story imagined to underly them.

50. The terms are not, of course, generally interchangeable. Λόγος is the more flexible term, here being used to refer to something like a narrative *hypothesis* (see the discussion of the Lukan prologue in chapter 5).

51. Text from Michael W. Holmes, *The Apostolic Fathers: Greek Texts and English Translations*, Apostolic Fathers (Early Christian Collection). English & Greek. (Baker Academic, 2007), 140, 148.

P.Oxy. 4009	***Second Clement* 5**
"...the harvest... ...be in]nocent as the [doves a]nd wis[e as the snakes.]	For the Lord says,
You will be like [sheep am]ong wolves."	"You will be like sheep among wolves."
[And I said to hi]m, "What then if we are [torn apart]?"	And Peter answered him, saying "What then if the wolves tear apart the sheep?"
[And Jesus] says to me, "The [wolves having to]rn apart the [sheep can] do no[thing any]longer to it.	Jesus said to Peter, "The lambs, after they have died, should not fear the wolves.
There[fore, I say to y]ou, do [n]ot fe[ar th]ose who ki[ll yo]u and [after having killed you] no long[er ca]n [do anything to you..."[52]	And do not fear those who, having killed you, can do nothing to you.
	But fear the one who after you have died has authority to throw body and soul into Gehenna fire."

In both P.Oxy. 4009 and *Second Clement*, an interlocutor asks Jesus to consider the threat against the lives of Jesus's followers.[53] In both passages, Jesus responds that physical death is less consequential than what comes after. These are self-evidently two witnesses to the same story.

---

52. Translated from the reconstructed text in Dieter Lührmann, "P.Oxy. 4009: Ein Neues Fragment Des Petrusevangeliums?," *Novum Testamentum* 35, no. 4 (1993): 390–410; Dieter Lührmann and P. J. Parsons, "4009. Gospel of Peter?," in *The Oxyrhynchus Papyri* (Egypt Exploration Fund, 1994), 1–5. See also Lincoln H. Blumell and Thomas A. Wayment, eds., *Christian Oxyrhynchus: Texts, Documents, and Sources* (Baylor University Press, 2015), 201–205. I address criticisms of Lührmann's reconstruction in notes 53 to 56.

53. Paul Foster expresses skepticism that P.Oxy. 4009 can be identified as a version of this same dialogue, describing the agreements between the two texts as "not significant." Paul Foster, "Are There Any Early Fragments of the So-Called Gospel of Peter?," *New Testament Studies* 52, no. 1 (2005): 19. But there is considerably more shared vocabulary than Foster acknowledges (as, indeed, Blumell and Wayment subtly noted). The conversation in P.Oxy. 4009 begins with Jesus's statement that his hearers "will be like [something] among wolves," including a distinctive verb form (ἔσεσθε) in agreement with *Second Clement* (without parallel in the canonical gospels). In the conversation that follows, both texts share the same verbs of speaking (λέγει), fearing (φοβεῖσθε), and killing (ἀποκτενόντων). The even more distinctive verb of "tearing apart" (σπαράξαντες) is suggested by the ending -ξαντες with sheep as the direct object (see discussion in the next paragraph). Lastly, both sources introduce the interlocutor's question with the same phrase, ἐὰν οὖν. Given the citation habits of the preacher (discussed later in this section), the agreements between P.Oxy. 4009 and *Second Clement* justify Luhrmann's identification.

The relationship between these two texts is not just a matter of conceptual parallels, however. Jesus's initial statement, "You will be like sheep among wolves," is nearly verbatim in both witnesses.[54] Both P.Oxy. 4009 and *Second Clement* use the future tense verb "you will be" (ἔσεσθε), not found in the canonical parallels.[55] Peter's question then begins with the same phrase in both texts, "what then" (ἐὰν οὖν). This interrogative construction is fine Greek and occasionally appears in the gospels, but it is neither the only nor the obvious way to pose such a question. It appears also that P.Oxy. 4009 and *Second Clement* both use the verb "to tear apart" (σπαράσσω) to describe the action of wolves.[56] Other gospels use this verb to describe the violent shaking of demoniacs (Mark 1:26 and 9:26) and the waking of the disciples (Luke 9:29), but never for killing.

It is important to remember that P.Oxy. 4009 and *Second Clement* are not the same kind of source. The papyrus fragment is a copy of the text itself. But *Second Clement* is a sermon that is prone to free adaptation of scripture.[57] The preacher liberally paraphrases Jewish scripture, even where he cites written sources by name (e.g., Isa 29:13 at 5.2). And gospel references in the sermon often appear to be allusions or loose adaptations (e.g., Matt 24:45 and parallels at 8.5).[58] It is not surprising, then, to discover that the

54. The only difference is the reconstructed ἀνὰ μέσον instead of the attested ἐν μέσῳ. Even if we grant the reconstruction, the minor difference is easily attributable to paraphrase by the preacher (discussed in the next paragraph).

55. The closest parallel is the use of the imperative γίνεσθε in Matthew 10:16. The verb ἔσεσθε is used in the distinct but related passage at Matthew 10:22.

56. Not enough of the verb is attested on line 10 to identify it without using the parallel in *Second Clement* (which would beg the question). In line 13, however, the ending . . . ξαντες makes the identification more likely. Other verbs one might use to describe the wolves killing the sheep (e.g., ἀποκτείνω, ἀποθνήσκω) would not form their aorist with a ξ.

57. Oxford Society of Historical Theology, *The New Testament in the Apostolic Fathers* (Clarendon Press, 1905), 130–34.

58. This inference is necessarily less certain since we do not know exactly which gospels the preacher used.

second half of the dialogue between Peter and Jesus does not reproduce the precise wording of P.Oxy. 4009. In fact, the preacher is confronted with the special problem of how best to quote the interlocutor's first-person speech. And that, in a passage where the interlocutor is never explicitly named. It is precisely where a first-person verb would have first appeared (off the edge of line 9 on the recto of P.Oxy. 4009) that the reference deviates from the wording of the fragment. Instead of quoting the words of the interlocutor in the first person, the author presents the dialogue in the third person—naming Peter as the speaker. Presumably, the preacher of *Second Clement* knew that the author of the gospel had identified themself as Peter based on a self-disclosure in another passage, like that at the end of P.Cairo 10759.[59] The fragment appears, therefore, to be a piece of a gospel attributed to Peter.[60]

If this is, indeed, a fragment of the gospel known to Serapion, a comparison with other gospels will shed light on Serapion's appeal to the "true account of the savior."[61]

---

59. Peter reporting a gospel narrative in the first person and the use of the vocative κ(υρι)ε are characteristic of the Gospel of Peter as found in the Akhmim codex but not found in other gospel books. The first-person speech in the Petrine epistles, acts, and apocalypses—cited by Kraus and Nicklas (63)—do not enervate this parallel because first person speech is conventional in these other genres, but exceptional in gospel literature. Even many of the gospels where the author discloses themself as a participant in the drama (e.g., John, Thomas, Protoevangelium of James), narrative is given in the third person. Thomas J. Kraus and Thomas Nicklas, *Das Petrusevangelium und die Petrusapokalypse: Die griechischen Fragmente mit deutscher und englischer Übersetzung (Neutestamentliche Apokryphen I)* (De Gruyter, 2011).

60. For a reconstruction of the other side of the papyrus, see Matti Myllykoski, "The Sinful Woman in the Gospel of Peter: Reconstructing the Other Side of P.Oxy. 4009," *New Testament Studies* 55, no. 1 (2009): 104–115; Matti Myllykoski, "Tears of Repentance or Tears of Gratitude? P.Oxy. 4009, the Gospel of Peter and the Western Text of Luke 7.45–49," *New Testament Studies* 55, no. 3 (2009): 380–389.

61. See note 48 above on Serapion's knowledge of other gospels. I provide the Lukan parallel for the sake of completeness, but nothing in my argument requires that Serapion knew the third gospel. If the fragment of the Gospel of Peter from the Akhmim Codex/P.Cairo 10759 (discussed in chapter 5) were used instead, these gospels would appear to relate more like John relates to the Synoptics. This difference would not affect my argument.

Matthew 10:16	P.Oxy. 4009	Luke 10:2–3
"Look, I am sending you like sheep among wolves. Therefore, be wise as the snakes and innocent as the doves."	". . .the harvest. . . . . .be in]nocent as the [doves a]nd wis[e as the snakes.] You will be like [sheep am]ong wolves." [And I said to hi]m, "What then if we are [torn apart]?" [And Jesus] says to me, "The [wolves having to]rn apart the [sheep can] do no[thing any]longer to it. There[fore, I say to y]ou, do [n]ot fe[ar th]ose who ki[ll yo]u and [after having killed you] no long[er ca]n [do anything to you . . ."[62]	And he said to them, "The harvest is great but workers are few. Therefore, ask the Lord of the harvest to send out workers into his harvest. Get going! Look, I am sending you like sheep among wolves."

The author of the gospel attributed to Peter has rewritten the story. Where the texts overlap, the gospel attributed to Peter subtly reworks synoptic language. And just as the author of Matthew added the interaction with Peter (14:28–32) to Mark's episode of Jesus walking on the water (Mark 6:45–52), so too this evangelist has expanded Jesus's warning to his disciples.

The gospel preserved in P.Oxy. 4009 is clearly distinct from either Matthew or Luke. And yet, it is easy to imagine Serapion reading such a passage from a *Gospel according to Peter*, recognizing the episode from its synoptic parallel, and approving its content for the Christians at Rhosus. In the idiom of Hellensitic literary criticism, the author of this gospel has "prepared" or "worked out" the story in their own way but maintained the gospel *hypothesis.* And this is more or less what Serapion claims by describing most of this gospel as belonging to "the true account."

Serapion's initial approval of the *Gospel according to Peter* makes it clear that this Syrian bishop did not share Irenaeus's protocanonical notion of a fourfold gospel. And yet, like Irenaeus, Serapion sought both

62. Adapted from the reconstruction in Lührmann and Parsons, "4009. Gospel of Peter?"

to legitimize and limit narrative pluriformity in the gospel tradition. The idea of a *hypothesis*—described as "the true account"—furnished Serapion with a notional rubric for evaluating books in the pluriform gospel tradition.

Conclusion

These three second-century gospel readers did not share Irenaeus's conviction that the gospel must exist in four specific versions. There is no trace of later notions of canonicity in their treatment of gospel literature. And yet, they describe gospels with the categories of Hellenistic literature. Papias, Justin, and Serapion imagined gospels as distinct books with identifiable authors. Papias and Justin even associate gospels with well-known literary genres. These early readers of the gospels undermine any attempt to couple the invention of the canon with bookish thinking about gospel literature. The imagination of gospels as Hellenistic literature predates Irenaeus.

Conventions for thinking about pluriform narratives in Hellenistic literature were well established in the first and second centuries. It is hard to imagine that a reader like Justin would be unfamiliar with this way of thinking about the overlapping versions of Socrates's life. And while none of these readers uses the term *hypothesis* in their brief or fragmentary discussions of gospel literature, they describe gospels as multiple instantiations of a common narrative substrate. This notional substrate serves both descriptive and evaluative functions for these readers, allowing them to organize and regulate the pluriform narrative of Jesus's life. Irenaeus may be the earliest surviving author to use the word *hypothesis* to describe the gospels, but this way of thinking about gospel literature predates him as well.

CHAPTER FIVE

The Gospels According to the Gospels

> "Since many have attempted to arrange a narrative about the things that happened among us. . ."
>
> —Luke 1:1

Introduction

THE EARLIEST READERS of the gospels known to us are themselves authors of later gospels.[1] Histories of reception often begin with named, postcanonical figures, like Papias and Justin. But the gospels themselves and several gospel-type books provide important information about how gospel literature was understood in the century before Irenaeus. None of these texts provides an extended reflection on their own literary tradition. Collectively, however, they paint a picture of how the first generation of gospel readers thought about these books.

Justin, Irenaeus, and Serapion thought about gospels as authored, published, and distinct works of Hellenistic literature on a common

1. I use "author" language for the gospels in opposition to certain alternative models for their composition. Hellenistic and Roman literature was not imagined in its cultural contexts as the product of communities or collectives. See Robyn Faith Walsh, *The Origins of Early Christian Literature: Contextualizing the New Testament Within Greco-Roman Literary Culture* (Cambridge University Press, 2021); de la Durantaye, "The Origins of the Protection of Literary Authorship in Ancient Rome." Additionally, the idea of the gospels as gradually evolving into their preserved forms is not supported by the manuscript evidence. At the same time, my use of "author" language in characterizing the reception of the gospels does not deny the labor of enslaved persons in the production of many such books. See especially Moss, *God's Ghostwriters*. For the purposes of reconstructing how these books were imagined by their users, however, it is important to remember that enslaved labor in the production of books was not acknowledged as impinging on authorial responsibility for the work. Of course, we need not (and, often, ought not) agree with these ancient readers.

narrative *hypothesis*. The gospels themselves, I argue, furnished these readers with the building blocks of this conceptual model. Of course, not every gospel-type book gives evidence of every one of these elements. But these readers-turned-authors attest all the bookish aspects of Irenaeus's description of the gospels without any hint of his protocanonical, fourfold gospel.

Matthew

On the consensus view of gospel relations, the author of Matthew was a reader of Mark.[2] This evangelist not only drew upon Mark as a source for traditions but closely modeled his new composition on Mark's gospel. There is nothing necessary about writing a book of this kind. The author of Matthew might have written a commentary, a community rule, a *chreia* collection, an epistle, or an apocalypse. But the author of Matthew imitated Mark, producing a life of Jesus that resembles both ancient biographies and the narratives of Jewish scripture.[3]

The Gospel according to Matthew tells us very little about how its author understood Mark. The clearest indication appears in the opening line of the gospel.

Mark 1:1	**Matthew 1:1**
The beginning of the gospel of Jesus Christ, son of God.[4]	The book of the beginning of Jesus Christ, son of David, son of Abraham.

2. For an accessible introduction to the synoptic problem, there is nothing better than Mark Goodacre, *The Synoptic Problem: A Way Through the Maze* (Bloomsbury T&T Clark, 2004).

3. On the identification of the gospels as ancient biographies, see Richard A. Burridge, *What Are the Gospels? A Comparison with Graeco-Roman Biography*, Society for New Testament Studies Monograph Series 70 (Cambridge University Press, 1992). For a powerful critique of Burridge, see Adela Yarbro Collins, "Genre and the Gospels," *Journal of Religion* 75, no. 2 (1995): 239–246.

4. The twenty-eighth edition of the Nestle-Aland critical text omits "son of God." The editorial committee of the United Bible Societies assigned this decision a "C" confidence rating. Metzger, *A Textual Commentary on the Greek New Testament*, 73. The

The first lines of these two gospels are strikingly similar. But Matthew writes "book" where Mark had written "gospel."[5]

These verses raise several interpretive issues. First, the word *beginning* in the opening line of Matthew has sometimes been understood to refer only to the genealogy or nativity of Jesus.[6] On this interpretation, the author of Matthew understood this new gospel as consisting of more than one "book," only the first of which is introduced explicitly. The term translated as "beginning" in Matthew is literally "Genesis" (γένεσις)—the title of the first book of the Pentateuch. Given Matthew's presentation of Jesus as a new Moses, it is possible that the author of Matthew thought about the gospel as a new Pentateuch.[7] On this interpretation, the first verse of Matthew identifies the nativity story as this gospel's equivalent of Genesis.[8]

The parallel with the opening of Mark, on the other hand, suggests that the "book" in the first verse of Matthew might refer to the gospel as a whole. On this interpretation, the author of Matthew considered the "The Book of Genesis of Jesus Christ" to be an appropriate title for

---

manuscript evidence, however, strongly favors the longer reading, and transcriptional probabilities are balanced. Furthermore, the parallel between the sonship language used to introduce Jesus in Matthew and Mark is suggestive.

5. My argument is indebted to several recent treatments of the same interpretive questions, especially Keith, *The Gospel as Manuscript*, 115–123; Elder, *Gospel Media*, 91–102.

6. For a summary of interpretive options, see W. D. Davies and Dale C. Allison Jr, *Matthew 1-7*, vol. 1 (T&T Clark, 2004), 149–154. For a full argument in favor of the interpretation advocated here, see Theodor Zahn, *Das Evangelium des Matthäus* (Deichert, 1922), 39–44.

7. Dale C. Allison Jr., *The New Moses: A Matthean Typology* (Fortress Press, 1993).

8. The use of γένεσις at Matthew 1:18 to introduce the ensuing narrative makes it particularly unlikely that the term in Matthew 1:1 refers only to the genealogy. See Keith, *The Gospel as Manuscript*, 116.

the entire life of Jesus.[9] At least some early commentators understood the verse this way.[10]

On either interpretation, the author of Mathew compares this new gospel to the Jewish scriptures. It is either a "book" comparable to Genesis or a grander work composed of several such books. This self-representation has clear implications for understanding how this author thought about gospel literature. The books of Moses were the pinnacle of high literature for Hellenistic Jews. In *Against Apion*, Josephus claims his scriptures are superior to Plato and Homer. Likewise, Philo begins the *Life of Moses* by asserting the Pentateuch's superiority to Greek literature. Probably we should *not* assume that the author of Matthew would claim for themself every accolade Philo and Josephus ascribe to Moses, but the opening line of Matthew invites the comparison. The evangelist, at the very least, aspired to write something recognizable as *literature*—a published (i.e., made public) book in an established literary tradition.[11]

---

9. By way of analogy, the author of Acts refers to the entire gospel of Luke as "what Jesus *began* to teach and do" (1:1). Perhaps the author of Matthew considered the gospel an origin story for the church (i.e., similar to Genesis for Israel). Davies and Allison point to widespread Christian parallelism between Jesus and Adam. Davies and Allison, *Matthew 1-7*, 150–151.

10. John Chrysostom, *Homily on Matthew* 2.5. The title *Genesis of Mary* for the *Protevangelium* also suggests that its author understood the first verse of Matthew this way. See note 36 below.

11. Publication is a less well-defined phenomenon in antiquity than today. Nevertheless, ancient readers and writers worked with a distinction between private and public texts. They treat this distinction as *typically* determined by authorial choices. Exceptions to that model—though notorious—are usually marked as atypical and raised precisely in order to maintain conventional distinctions (e.g., Cicero, *To Atticus* 13, Galen, *On My Own Books* 10–11). For a simplistic but still serviceable account of conventional publication in Roman antiquity see, Raymond J. Starr, "The Circulation of Literary Texts in the Roman World," *Classical Quarterly* 37, no. 1 (1987): 213–223. For a more nuanced account, see Elder, *Gospel Media,* 211–235; though Elder is, perhaps, too credulous toward claims of unpublished and stolen work (and, following Matthew Larsen, fails to account for the consistent censure toward publishing the work of others). Mathew Larsen, "Accidental Publication, Unfinished

Both Matthew's gospel and the Books of Moses are formally anonymous. But the author of Matthew did not see the Pentateuch this way. The author of Matthew believed that Moses had written the first five books of Jewish scripture (e.g., Matt 8:14). Indeed, readers frequently assumed that formally anonymous narratives were written by *dramatis personae.*[12] Irrespective of the author's intentions, the gospel's self-representation as a new Genesis (or Pentateuch) could have invited similar assumptions about its authorship.[13] Given first- and second-century attitudes about the authorship of the Pentateuch, it is easy to see how the first verse of Matthew might have provided early readers with impetus to infer that the gospel was written by a character in its narrative.

Another interpretive question is raised by Matthew's substitution of *book* for Mark's use of *gospel.* It might be that the author understood "book . . . of Jesus Christ" as roughly synonymous with "gospel." In this case, the author of Matthew seems to have understood both Mark and their own book as a "gospel." Alternatively, the author might have attempted to contrast their "book of Genesis" with Mark's "good news." In that case, the author of Matthew rejected the appellation "gospel" for their new work. In either case, however, Matthew's substitution of *book* for *gospel* suggests that the author of Matthew read "gospel" at the beginning of Mark's gospel as self-referential in its Markan context. Whatever the author of Mark meant by "gospel," its earliest known reader apparently understood the term to refer to the text in front of them (i.e., the

---

Texts and the Traditional Goals of New Testament Textual Criticism" *Journal for the Study of the New Testament* 39, no. 4 (2017), 362–387.

12. To select one example, Clement of Alexandria assigns Esther to Mordecai (*Stromata* 1.21). The *Bava Batra* 14b–15a assigns most works to *dramatis personae*, though it is more often cited for exceptions to that rule (e.g., Job and Daniel).

13. If (reasoning by analogy) we read Matthew in light of the same literary conventions of authorship and audience reflected in the Lukan prologue, the gospel's formal anonymity probably reflects circulation in a setting (characteristic of so-called technical literature) where the audience was expected to know (of) the author. See Alexander, *The Preface to Luke's Gospel*, 188–190.

Gospel according to Mark).[14] The *bibliographic* or *titular* interpretation of "gospel" is, therefore, at least as old as Matthew's gospel.

No matter how one answers the interpretive questions above, the opening verse of Matthew provides a few basic insights. First, the author of Matthew presents this new work as a book (or a work composed of several books) belonging to the same genre as Jewish scripture. This observation does not tell us much about the place of gospels in Hellenistic book culture, but it does reveal that gospels were imagined by at least one reader as a recognized kind of literature almost a century before Irenaeus. Second, the anonymity of Matthew and the parallel with the books of Moses (irrespective of the author's intention) might have suggested to readers that the author was a character in the gospel's narrative. Third, at least one reader at the end of the first century understood Mark's use of the term *gospel* to refer to a book about Jesus's life (i.e., the titular or *bibliographic* sense of the term). Given these features in the very earliest evidence for a readerly encounter with gospel literature, it should be unremarkable that the century between the composition of Matthew and Irenaeus's *Against Heresies* is filled with references to gospels as public and authored works of literature.

Luke

The author of Luke is the first reader to comment explicitly—though briefly—on the multiplicity of gospels.[15] Luke's first four verses constitute an authorial preface, which according to the conventions of similar prefaces, identify the work's subject matter, intended readership, and literary predecessors.[16]

---

14. Andrew J. Byers, "The Genre of Mark's Gospel Is 'Gospel': Reconsidering Literary Innovation in the Markan Incipit," *Journal for the Study of the New Testament* 46, no. 2 (2023): 168–192.

15. For recent and largely corroborative treatments of the same interpretive issues, see Keith, *The Gospel as Manuscript*, 123–129; Elder, *Gospel Media*, 102–113.

16. I remain convinced by the thesis of Loveday Alexander that the Lukan preface is a highly conventional introduction to technical literature. Alexander, *The Preface*

> Since many have attempted to arrange a narrative about the things that happened among us, just as those who were eyewitnesses from the beginning and ministers of the account handed down to us, it seems right to me also, having followed everything thoroughly and accurately to write for you, most excellent Theophilus, in order that you might know with certainty about the accounts of which you have been informed.[17]

Before discussing the content of these four verses, it is worth remarking on the fact *that* the third gospel begins with a highly conventional preface. The author speaks of himself as an author, the gospel is described as a literary work, and its dedicatee is addressed by name.[18] This story of Jesus's life—also drawn from and modeled upon the *Gospel according to Mark*—is introduced as part of the same Hellenistic literary culture that produced many similarly prefaced works.[19]

The third evangelist is perfectly explicit about his participation in a narrative tradition. The author does not refer to his work as a message, sermon, or notes. It is, rather, a "narrative" (διήγησις). But this gospel narrative is only one of "many" (πολλοὶ) attempts to pass down "the account" (ὁ λόγος) of Jesus.[20] The same language (i.e., "the true account") is used by Serapion to refer to a notional standard for

---

to Luke's Gospel. For a response to her critics, see Mills, "Rewriting the Gospel," 137–148.

17. Here and throughout, the New Testament text is taken from Eberhard Nestle et al., *Novum Testamentum Graece*, 28th ed. (Deutsche Bibelgesellschaft, 2012).

18. The use of the masculine participle in verse 3 suggests that the author was male. Analogous prefaces suggest that "Theophilus" was a historical person and that dedication to one person does not imply exclusive readership. Alexander, *The Preface to Luke's Gospel*, 188–190.

19. An especially close *comparandum* is the preface to Hero's *Pneumatics*. See Wilhelm Schmidt, *Herons von Alexandria Druckwerke und Automatentheater* (Leipzig: Teubner, 1899), 2.

20. The competitive implications of ἐπεχείρησαν will be discussed at greater length in chapter 6.

evaluating different versions of the gospel tradition. The "account" is, for Serapion, the story of Jesus existing independent of any particular instantiation that can be used to judge the acceptability of the *Gospel according to Peter.* Likewise, the third evangelist introduces his own book as just one version of a story that already existed in multiple forms.[21] These two uses of "account" (λόγος) correspond neatly to the descriptive and evaluative uses of *hypothesis* language in the dramatic and Homeric scholia. Both terms pick out a notional story, abstracted away from the multiple media in which it was found.

The author of Luke does not use *hypothesis* language. The preface dedicates only a single sentence to the tradition of gospel writing. But the third evangelist clearly describes this new gospel as an authored piece of Hellenistic literature instantiating a traditional narrative with multiple extant versions. Even without the word *hypothesis*, the "standard model" for imagining pluriform narratives can be recognized in the Lukan preface. Irenaeus needed little imagination to move from this account of gospel literature to his description of the gospels as several books written on a shared *hypothesis*.

John

The differences between John and the Synoptics are manifold and significant. But these differences consist in the use of sources, style of expression, and the characterization of Jesus. In terms of genre—and on the landscape of Hellenistic literature—John and the Synoptics are much more similar than they are different. In all likelihood, the fourth evangelist knew one or more of the Synoptic Gospels.[22] Whatever else it may be, the fourth gospel is certainly a gospel.

21. The reference to several tradents (οἱ ἀπ' ἀρχῆς αὐτόπται καὶ ὑπηρέται γενόμενοι τοῦ λόγου) suggests also that the narrative tradition existed in multiple media.

22. There is a growing body of recent scholarship that argues in favor of the fourth evangelist's use of the synoptic gospels as literary models and sources for traditions about Jesus. See especially the contributions to Eve-Marie Becker, Helen K. Bond, and Catrin H. Williams, eds., *John's Transformation of Mark* (Bloomsbury Publishing, 2021).

John reflects on its own literary character in the gospel's closing chapters. After narrating Jesus's resurrection appearances, a colophon states the purpose of the fourth gospel (20:30–31).

> Jesus also did many other signs for his disciples which are not written in this book. These signs have been written in order that you might believe that Jesus is the Messiah, the Son of God—and believing you might have eternal life in his name.

Whereas Matthew 1:1 refers to the gospel as a "book" (βίβλος), the fourth evangelist identifies their own work as a "booklet" (βιβλίον). While the term used by Matthew typically refers to literary texts (e.g., Mark 12:26), John's term is applied to both literary (e.g., Luke 4:17) and subliterary texts (e.g., Matt 19:7) in the gospels.[23] Considered in a vacuum, this term leaves open the possibility that the fourth gospel represents itself as something less than a work of published literature. But is it plausible that the fourth gospel, in particular, was understood as a kind of subliterary record, collection of notes, or aide-mémoire?[24]

The fourth gospel's self-presentation is clarified by the subsequent address to the gospel's reader. Namely, the author states their purpose for writing the gospel: "that y'all might believe." The verb, here, is in the second person plural. Without any named or otherwise specified addressee in the gospel, this "y'all" probably refers to a general

Important individual contributions include Wendy E. S. North, *What John Knew and What John Wrote: A Study in John and the Synoptics* (Rowman & Littlefield, 2020); James W. Barker, *Writing and Rewriting the Gospels: John and the Synoptics* (Eerdmans, 2025).

23. This wider range of uses seems best explained by the supposition that βιβλίον draws attention to the physical instantiation of the text.

24. In its own way, the Johannine prologue assimilates the gospel to Jewish Scripture and, so, accomplishes the same purpose as Matthew 1:1. It seems unlikely that the fourth evangelist could emulate the first chapters of Genesis *and* imagine their own work as subliterary.

or indefinite readership. There is a textual variant that implies the envisioned readers are either unbelievers (πιστεύσητε) or already converted (πιστεύητε).[25] In either case, however, the evangelist addresses an unspecified audience for whom the gospel will promote belief. The second person plural suggests an expectation that this book will be read by indeterminate others. If this is correct, the gospel describes itself as a book to be "published" (i.e., made public).[26]

The epilogue to the fourth gospel further clarifies its literary charter. After an apparent conclusion at John 20:30–31, the final chapter of John describes a fourth appearance of the resurrected Jesus. This twenty-first chapter includes a discussion of the respective fates of Peter and the Beloved Disciple. Many scholars have identified this epilogue as a kind of addendum, perhaps appended to an already circulating twenty-chapter gospel by some subsequent author(s).[27] If this reconstruction is accepted, the subsequent characterization of the fourth gospel should be attributed to an early reader of John, rather than the author of the rest of the gospel.[28] In either case, the Johannine epilogue is a witness to the imagination of gospel books from the first generation of their readers.

---

25. Metzger considers the support for the alternative readings evenly balanced and so place the distinguishing *sigma* in brackets. Metzger, *A Textual Commentary on the Greek New Testament*, 256.

26. See note 11 above on publication in antiquity.

27. For contrasting perspectives, see Richard Bauckham, *The Testimony of the Beloved Disciple: Narrative, History, and Theology in the Gospel of John*, Illustrated edition (Baker Academic, 2007), 271–284; Armin D. Baum, "The Original Epilogue (John 20:30–31), the Secondary Appendix (21:1–23), and the Editorial Epilogues (21:24–25) of John's Gospel: Observations Against the Background of Ancient Literary Conventions," in *Earliest Christian History: History, Literature, and Theology. Essays from the Tyndale Fellowship in Honor of Martin Hengel*, ed. Michael F. Bird and Jason Matson, WUNT 2/320 (Mohr Siebeck, 2011), 231–271. For purposes of reconstructing the reception of the gospels in the early to mid-second century, it is unnecessary to adopt either position.

28. The earliest evidence for the Johannine epilogue is Tatian's *Diatessaron*, composed in the second half of the second century—probably before Irenaeus's *Against Heresies*.

After discussing the fate of the Beloved Disciple, the author clarifies the relationship of the fourth gospel to this enigmatic figure. The statement is an unambiguous allusion to an earlier description of the disciple as a witness to the crucifixion.

John 19:35	**John 21:24**
And the [Beloved Disciple] who saw has testified, and his testimony is true; and that one knows that he speaks truth in order that you too might believe.	This is the [Beloved Disciple] who testified to these things and wrote them—and we know that his testimony is true.

In chapter 19, the author of the fourth gospel claims that the Beloved Disciple was the gospel's source for traditions about Jesus.[29] It might be a case of (pseudo-)authorial *illeism*—a common historiographical practice of referring to oneself in the third person in the course of the narrative.[30] On this interpretation, the passage in chapter 19 is identifying the Beloved Disciple as the author of the fourth gospel and, so, is the first explicit attribution of a gospel to an apostolic figure.[31] The language in chapter 19, however, does not require this interpretation. It is also possible to read the passage as identifying the Beloved Disciple as merely an eyewitness whose testimony is presented in the fourth gospel.[32]

In either case, the author of the Johannine epilogue understood this earlier passage as an authorial self-identification. In a recapitulation

29. The language, "in order that you too might believe," anticipates the purpose statement in chapter 20 (discussed above). There is a parallel textual variation in the tense of the verb.

30. Howard M. Jackson, "Ancient Self-Referential Conventions and Their Implications for the Authorship and Integrity of the Gospel of John," *Journal of Theological Studies* 50, no. 1 (1999): 1–34.

31. Richard Bauckham makes a compelling argument that the Beloved Disciple is characterized throughout the fourth gospel as an ideal author. Richard Bauckham, "The Beloved Disciple as Ideal Author," *Journal for the Study of the New Testament* 49 (1993): 21–44.

32. Raymond E. Brown, *The Gospel According to John (I-XII)*, 29 (Doubleday, 1966), xcviii–cii; Raymond E. Brown, *The Gospel According to John (XIII-XXI)*, vol. 29A of *The Anchor Bible* (Doubleday, 1970), 936–937.

of John 19:35, the epilogue clarifies that the Beloved Disciple not only "testified" to the works of Jesus but "wrote them." Probably the author of the epilogue read the reference in chapter 19 as *illeism* and now explicitly asserts that the fourth gospel was written by the Beloved Disciple—a relevant authority from the apostolic age. The fourth gospel was, therefore, imagined as an authored book by its earliest known reader.

Through their self-presentations, the fourth gospel and its epilogue reflect then-current assumptions about the character of gospel-type books. Like the authors of Matthew and Luke, these readers imagine gospels as public. And the ascription of the fourth gospel to the Beloved Disciple suggests that gospel readers already assumed that gospels were written by relevant authorities. It is unclear whether Papias and Justin knew or used the fourth gospel, but these second-century readers shared the same assumptions about the literary character of these books.

New Testament Apocrypha

The so-called New Testament apocrypha are less often discussed as part of the reception history of the gospels.[33] Through imitation of preexistent gospel books and explicit commentary, these early and diverse Christian texts reflect then-current assumptions about the character of gospel literature. Their authors do not, of course, dwell on the place of gospels in the milieu of Hellenistic book culture or reflect on the pluriformity of their narrative tradition. There is no explicit use of *hypothesis* language. Nevertheless, like the authors of Matthew, Luke, and John, these second-century authors are themselves early readers of gospel literature.

As a rule, these extracanonical texts are difficult to date. Given Irenaeus's polemic against the textual profligacy of his opponents,

33. The category New Testament apocrypha is hopelessly anachronistic. It is, nevertheless, a convenient rubric for organizing a group of second-century pseudepigrapha that reflect their author's conception of gospel literature. The categorization itself is irrelevant to my argument.

however, many such books must have preexisted his *Against Heresies* (e.g., 1.20.1; 3.11.9). Some such works—like the *Protevangelium of James* and *Epistula Apostolorum*—can be dated to the early or mid-second century. But even where a late second- or early third-century date cannot be excluded, the ideological diversity of these texts provides an additional control (to borrow a metaphor from the experimental sciences) for reconstructing how the first generations of readers imagined gospel literature.

These so-called apocrypha make it clear that a broad spectrum of second-century readers were conditioned to think about gospels as authored and published works of Hellenistic literature. Some of these gospel-like texts, moreover, further specify the place of gospel literature in contemporary book culture. Irenaeus's fourfold gospel is unknown to these authors, but his literary and bookish conception of gospels is well attested throughout the second century.

The Protevangelium of James

The *Protevangelium of James* is transparently an imitation of the gospels. It is a life of Mary, the mother of Jesus, up through Jesus's nativity. In the course of its narrative, the author of the *Protevangelium* draws language from the very text of the gospels, harmonizes differences between the nativities in Matthew and Luke, and answers interpretive questions raised by conflicting versions of Jesus's story.[34] Though it is a life of Mary rather than Jesus, the *Protevangelium* is modeled on the gospels.[35]

34. Thomas O'Loughlin, "The Protevangelium Iacobi: A Case of Gospel Harmonization," ed. Markus Vinzent, *Studia Patristica* 55 (2014): 165–173; Mark Goodacre, "The Protoevangelium of James and the Creative Rewriting of Matthew and Luke," in *Connecting Gospels: Beyond the Canonical/Non-Canonical Divide*, ed. Francis Watson and Sarah Parkhouse (Oxford University Press, 2018), 57–76.

35. The manuscript tradition reflects several different titles. Many of the earliest manuscripts use γέννησις (Genesis) modified by Mary. This closely resembles the *incipit* of Matthew. Other manuscripts use ἱστορία, λόγος, or and/or διήγησις. The first reflects the author's generic self-identification (see further discussion in this section). The

At the end of the narrative, the *Protevangelium* reveals its author's conception of its own literary character.

> And I, James, who wrote this history when a commotion arose in Jerusalem at Herod's death, withdrew into the desert until the commotion in Jerusalem stopped. I glorify the Lord God who has given me the wisdom to write this history.[36]

The author of the *Protevangelium* ascribes their book to a figure of the apostolic age—James, the brother of Jesus. Though the author was themself some unknown, Greek-speaking Christian of the early or middle second century, they evidently felt it appropriate that a book of this kind should be written by a relevant authority of the apostolic age. Probably the interpretive conventions surrounding the gospels (as suggested by Matthew, evinced in John, and explicit in Papias) prompted this gospel reader-turned-author to present themself in this way.

Even more revealing is the author's own understanding of the work's genre. Twice the author identifies the *Protevangelium* as a "history" (ἱστορία).[37] The term "history" was well established as a genre of literature in the late Hellenistic period.[38] Indeed, the *Protevangelium*

---

latter two mirror the language used in Luke (1:4) and Acts (1:1) to refer to the third gospel. George T. Zervos and James H. Charlesworth, *The Protevangelium of James: Greek Text, English Translation, Critical Introduction: Volume 1*, Bilingual edition (T&T Clark, 2019), 95–99.

36. Text from Bart D. Ehrman, and Zlatko Pleše, eds., *The Apocryphal Gospels: Texts and Translations* (Oxford University Press, 2011), 70. I am influenced by punctuation in Ronald F. Hock, *The Infancy Gospels of James and Thomas: With Introduction, Notes, and Original Text Featuring the New Scholars Version Translation* (Polebridge Press, 1996), 77.

37. Hock identifies the Protevangelium as a history in the Hellenistic tradition influenced by encomiastic literature. Hock, *The Infancy Gospels of James and Thomas*, 17–18.

38. Gerald A. Press, "History as Literary Genre: The Hellenistic Age," in *The Development of the Idea of History in Antiquity*, McGill-Queen's Studies in the History of Ideas 2 (McGill-Queen's University Press, 1982), 35–60.

begins with a reference to other "histories of the twelve tribes of Israel" (1.1).[39] That is, the author opens a life of Mary by referring to other Jewish "histories" (ἱστορίαι) with the same term the author uses to identify their own work. Modern scholarship often speaks of the gospels as biographies, but the ancient biography was not clearly distinguished from the genre of history in the first and second centuries.[40] Likewise, the genre of philosophical *Memoirs* used by Justin to describe the gospels (and plausibly assumed by Papias's description of Mark) was considered a subgenre of historical literature (see Theon, *Progymnasmata* 13). In sum, this imitator of the gospels understood their work as belonging to a well-known category of Hellenistic literature. The *Protevangelium* is only one more data point for the reception of the gospels, but this early to mid-second-century reader thought of gospel-type books as histories authored by a relevant authority.[41]

The Epistle of the Apostles

The *Epistle of the Apostles* is not an attempt to write another gospel.[42] It purports, rather to be a letter written by the eleven apostles sometime

39. Ehrman and Pleše, *The Apocryphal Gospels*, 40. I have capitalized and italicized the phrase following Lilly C. Vuong's suggestion that the author is imitating references to unknown historical works in Jewish Scripture (e.g., 2 Chron 16:11). Lily C. Vuong, *The Protevangelium of James*, Annotated edition. (Cascade Books, 2019), 49.

40. Guido Schepens, "Zum Verhältnis von Biographie und Geschichtsschreibung in hellenistischer Zeit," in *Die griechische Biographie in hellenistischer Zeit* (De Gruyter, 2012), 335–362. Burridge, *What Are the Gospels? A Comparison with Graeco-Roman Biography*, 60–67.

41. George Themelis Zervos, "Dating the 'Protevangelium of James': The Justin Martyr Connection," *Society of Biblical Literature 1994 Seminar Papers* 33 (1994): 415–434.

42. Although the synopsis of Jesus's life (4–6, 9–12) does depend on the gospels, the *Epistula* is written in a meaningfully different mode. For an argument that the *Epistula* owes more to gospel literature, see Francis Watson, "A Gospel of the Eleven: The Epistula Apostolorum and the Johannine Tradition," in *Connecting Gospels:*

after the resurrection. Much of the *Epistle* recounts an appearance of the resurrected Jesus to his disciples. Jesus explains his death and resurrection, instructs his disciples concerning eschatology, and warns against heresy. Amidst this wide-ranging resurrection dialogue, Jesus gives a specific timeline for the end of the world. He promises his return to judge the world after one-hundred and twenty years (17.2).[43] On the assumption that the author did not attribute an already-falsified prophecy to Jesus, the *Epistle* must belong to the first half of the second century.

The *Epistle* begins with an explanation of why the apostles are writing a letter to their churches.

> This [epistle] has been written . . . so that you may be strong and not waver or be disturbed or depart from what you have heard—the word of the gospel. As we have heard, kept, and have written [the word of the gospel] for the whole world, so we entrust [it] to you, our sons and daughters.[44]

The pseudo-apostolic authors of the *Epistle* claim responsibility for writing "the word of the gospel." This portion of the text survives only in Ethiopic, but the underlying Greek for "the word" is likely the same word translated "account" (ὁ λόγος) in the Lukan prologue (1:2) and

Beyond the Canonical/Non-Canonical Divide, ed. Francis Watson (Oxford University Press, 2018), 189–215.

43. For a discussion of the three versions of this passage, see Francis Watson, *An Apostolic Gospel: The "Epistula Apostolorum" in Literary Context* (Cambridge University Press, 2020), 240–242.

44. For the Ethiopic text and French translation, see Louis Guerrier and Sylvain Grébaut, *Le Testament en Galilée de Notre-Seigneur Jésus-Christ: Texte éthiopien, édité et traduit en français*, Patrologia Orientalis 9, ed. René Graffin and François Nau (Firmin-Didot, 1913), 118. My translation is adapted from Watson, *An Apostolic Gospel*, 44, see also 219. I follow the interpretation advocated in Charles E. Hill, *The Johannine Corpus in the Early Church* (Oxford University Press, 2006), 370.

Serapion's letter concerning the Gospel of Peter. This term was used in these contexts to describe something like the basic story of the gospels. Given the author's knowledge of the third gospel and this prologue's description of "the account of the gospel" as something *written*, the author of the *Epistle* is almost certainly referring to gospel books. This interpretation of the *Epistle* is confirmed later in the text, when Jesus refers to sayings from the Gospel of John as "[words] that I have spoken to you and that you write about me" (31.11).[45] Here, Jesus describes his own words as texts written by the apostles. Throughout the *Epistle*, then, this reader from the early second century attributes written gospels to apostolic authors.[46]

The same opening paragraph attests the author's imagination of how gospel literature was published and circulated. According to the *Epistle*, the apostles wrote "for the whole world." This early second-century author, then, does not imagine gospel texts as an intramural text, like a community charter, or as a subliterary collection of notes, or memory aids. Rather, the author of the *Epistle* imagined gospels as books intentionally released by their authors to an indefinite audience—that is, *published*.[47] The final phrase "so we entrust [it] to you, our sons and daughters" even suggests the process by which gospels were imagined to have been published. The author of the *Epistle* describes the circulation of gospels through the social networks of churches established by the

45. Watson, *An Apostolic Gospel*, 64. Hannah, "The Four-Gospel 'Canon' in the Epistula Apostolorum," 608–610.

46. Julia D. Lindenlaub, "The Gospel of John as Model for Literate Authors and Their Texts in Epistula Apostolorum and Apocryphon of James (NHC I,2)," *Journal for the Study of the New Testament* 43, no. 1 (2020): 3–27.

47. See Richard Bauckham, "For Whom Were Gospels Written?," *HTS Teologiese Studies / Theological Studies* 55, no. 4 (1999): 865–882. Along with others, I have suggested that early readers imagined an even more expansive audience for the gospels. Ian N. Mills, "Pagan Readers of Christian Scripture: The Role of Books in Early Autobiographical Conversion Narratives," *Vigiliae Christianae* 73, no. 5 (2019): 481–506.

disciples of Jesus. The apostles, it is supposed, released gospels to their disciples with the expectation that those books would be copied and distributed "for the whole world." The early-second-century author of the *Epistle* imagines the gospels following a more or less conventional course of publication for Hellenistic and Roman literature.

After summarizing the life, death, and resurrection of Jesus, the *Epistle* depicts Jesus warning his followers against tampering with the written record of his teachings (29.1).

> But those who transgress my commandments and teach teachings other [than] what is written, and who add to them and establish their own glory, teaching with different words those who believe in me rightly—if they fall away through such people, they will receive an eternal punishment.[48]

As in the *Epistle*'s prologue, Jesus's teachings are here discussed as something "written." Given the earlier references to a published "account of the gospel" containing the words of Jesus, it is safe to assume that the author is here again speaking of gospel books. It is notable, then, that the *Epistle* condemns any modification of these written works. Notebooks, memory aids, and other sub-literary texts are, by design, mutable. Texts of this sort are meant to be revised, redacted, and expanded. In contrast, powerful and widespread social conventions obliged readers and copyists to transmit literary texts in the form they were received.[49] Of course, these texts still changed in transmission—motivating the kind of injunctions found in the *Epistle*—but that behavior was widely condemned. The *Epistle* clearly imagines the gospels as belonging to

48. Text and translation adapted from Watson, *An Apostolic Gospel*, 61–62.

49. de la Durantaye, "The Origins of the Protection of Literary Authorship in Ancient Rome." See an extended treatment of this social pressure in Ian Mills, "Marcion as Textual Critic? Heresiological Rhetoric and the Conventions of Roman Scholarship" *Journal of Early Christian Studies* 33, no. 1 (2025): 27–54, esp 42–47.

the kind of literary texts that readers and copyists were expected to preserve as written.[50]

The author of the *Epistle of the Apostles* was a reader of the gospels several decades before Irenaeus. The author evidently knows nothing of Irenaeus's fourfold collection, citing at least one Jesus tradition known only from the noncanonical *Infancy Gospel of Thomas* alongside John and the synoptics (*Epistle of the Apostles* 4.1). But the author imagines gospel literature as authored books, published and transmitted according to the conventions of Hellenistic and Roman literature.

The Gospel according to Thomas

The only complete copy of the *Gospel according to Thomas* contains 114 sayings of Jesus with only a few narrative details.[51] As such, *Thomas* closely resembles a genre of literature known as *chreiai* or a *chreia* collection.[52] These works were collections of short anecdotes and sayings attributed to well-known personalities. The surviving examples of such collections appear to be pedagogical exercises, but second- and third-century sources make frequent reference to the production and

50. The same conventions are applied to the gospels by the roughly contemporary Dionysius of Corinth (*apud* Eusebius, *Church History* 23.12) and Papias (discussed in chapter 4).

51. See, for example, the introductory narrative element in Saying 60.

52. Simon Gathercole proposes the closely related genre of *gnomai*. Simon James Gathercole, *The Gospel of Thomas: Introduction and Commentary* (Brill, 2014), 141–142. Sean Adams, likewise, associates *Thomas* with *gnomai*, proposing the sentence collection of pseudo-Phocylides. Adams, *Greek Genres and Jewish Authors*, 86–88. Christopher Skinner and Nicholas Perrin criticize earlier scholarship (especially that of Vernon Robbins) for treating the influence of the *progymnasmatic* tradition as grounds for identifying *Thomas* as a *chreia* collection. Nicholas Perrin and Christopher Skinner, "Recent Trends in Gospel of Thomas Research (1989–2011). Part II: Genre, Theology and Relationship to the Gospel of John," *Currents in Biblical Research* 11, no. 1 (2012): 65–86. This critique, however, overlooks the formal characteristics *Thomas* shares with surviving evidence for *chreiai*.

use of collections as a kind of literature, written by famous authors or the disciples of famous philosophers.[53]

Authors in antiquity drew *chreia* from other books.[54] In fact, Menander of Laodicea singles out biographies as particularly useful sources for these short anecdotes (2.3.17).[55] Given the evidence that other authors used biographies in this way, it is not surprising that the content of *Thomas* betrays a literary dependence on the Synoptic Gospels (and, probably, other sources).[56] The author of *Thomas* used the narrative gospels in the same way that contemporaries used the biographies of Plutarch, excerpting and adapting sayings and anecdotes into a novel composition in a different literary genre.

Ancient rhetorical handbooks indicate that *chreiai* presuppose the reader's familiarity with the life and character of those persons to whom sayings or anecdotes were attributed.[57] Jesus, the disciples, Mary Magdalene, and James the Just all appear in *Thomas* without any introduction, contextualization, or characterization.[58] In fact, some of *Thomas*'s sayings are premised on the reader's knowledge of an implicit narrative context. In Saying 55, for instance, Jesus says that his followers will imitate him in taking up their own crosses. But Jesus's crucifixion is never described in *Thomas*. This excerpted saying apparently assumes the reader's familiarity with the basic story of Jesus's life. Likewise, the entirety of Saying

53. Ronald F. Hock, *The Chreia in Ancient Rhetoric*, vol. 1, *The Progymnasmata* (Sanderson Books, 1986), 1–22.

54. See Hock, *The Chreia in Ancient Rhetoric*, 8–9.

55. Text from William H. Race, *Menander Rhetor. Dionysius of Halicarnassus, Ars Rhetorica*, LCL 539, ed. Jeffrey Henderson (Harvard University Press, 2019), 206–207.

56. Mark Goodacre, *Thomas and the Gospels: The Case for Thomas's Familiarity with the Synoptics* (Eerdmans, 2012); Simon Gathercole, *The Composition of the Gospel of Thomas: Original Language and Influences*, Society for New Testament Studies Monograph Series 151 (Cambridge University Press, 2012).

57. See Hock, *The Chreia in Ancient Rhetoric*, 24–25.

58. By way of contrast, the authors of narrative gospels generally (though not invariably) provide an introduction for new characters.

42 is "Be passers-by." This pithy aphorism is probably a subversive allusion to the Parable of the Good Samaritan.[59] Jesus, according to this gospel, instructs his followers to behave like the priest and the Levite, passing by the injured man from Jerusalem. This saying can only be understood by someone already familiar with the teaching of Jesus from other gospels.

The indebtedness of *Thomas* to other gospel books is suggested not only by its literary genre and content but, in fact, acknowledged in the gospel's very first line.

> These are the hidden words which Jesus spoke while living.
> And Judas Thomas wrote them.[60]

The author of *Thomas* thus introduces this gospel as a kind of second-order text. The reference to "hidden teachings" implies an awareness of other, public teachings. Probably, this refers to narrative gospels from which the author excerpted so many sayings of Jesus. This contrast of secret versus public, along with *Thomas*'s genre as a second-order text, suggests that the author of *Thomas* thought of the synoptic gospels as published (i.e., made public) books.[61]

Additionally, this opening line identifies Thomas, the disciple of Jesus, as its author. There is no evidence that the author of *Thomas* knew the Johannine epilogue, *Protevangelium,* or *Epistle of the Apostles*. And yet, like these early second-century works, the author of *Thomas* takes for granted that a gospel-like book ought to be attributed to a relevant authority of the apostolic age. Probably, *Thomas* provides a glimpse of what this second-century author expected their readers to believe about the authorship of other public gospel books.

---

59. Note the repeated use of ἀντιπαρῆλθεν in Luke 10. This interpretation of *Thomas* 42 is consonant with the condemnation of almsgiving in Saying 6 and 14. For a review of other interpretive options, see Gathercole, *The Gospel of Thomas*, 379–382.

60. I follow the text of P.Oxy. 654. The Coptic does not differ in any relevant respect. Text from Uwe-karsten Plisch, *The Gospel of Thomas: Original Text with Commentary*, trans. Gesine Schenke Robinson, Bilingual edition, (Hendrickson, 2009), 37.

61. On the notion of publication in antiquity, see note 11 above.

This interpretation is corroborated by Saying 13, which represents the disciple-turned-author Thomas as someone who understood Jesus better than the other disciples.

> Jesus said to his disciples, "Compare me, and tell me what I am like." Simon Peter said to him, "You are like a righteous angel." Matthew said to him, "You are like a wise philosopher." Thomas said to him, "Master, my mouth is entirely unable to say what you are like." Jesus said, "I am no longer your master because you drank and became drunk from the bubbling spring that I issued." And he took him, withdrew, and spoke three words to him. But when Thomas returned to his disciples, they asked him, "What did Jesus tell you?" Thomas said to them, "If I tell you one of the words he spoke to me, you will pick up stones and throw them at me. And fire will come out from the stone and burn you."[62]

Given that the preface explicitly represents Thomas as this gospel's author (not merely an authority or tradent) and acknowledges other, public gospels, it is difficult to read this elevation of Thomas over Peter, Matthew, and the other disciples as anything other than a claim of superiority for this collection of sayings over other accounts of Jesus.[63] If that reading is correct, the contrast between Thomas and other disciples provides further evidence that gospel literature was already imagined as authored by the followers of Jesus.

The *Gospel according to Thomas* provides more indirect evidence for the reception of gospel books. Its genre, opening lines, and the contrast of Thomas with other apostolic author-figures suggest that this reader thought of the synoptic gospels as public literature, authored by relevant authorities. The author of *Thomas* is only one more witness to the

62. Text from Plisch, *The Gospel of Thomas*, 62–63.

63. Gathercole, *The Composition of the Gospel of Thomas*, 169–174. The reference to Peter might be a reference to the Gospel of Peter or the Gospel of Mark which (as discussed in chapter 4) is often associated with Peter.

imagination of gospels in the second century but, considered alongside contemporary sources, there is a clear pattern of evidence for the reception of gospels as Hellenistic literature.

The Gospel According to Peter

More clearly than any other New Testament apocryphon, the *Gospel according to Peter* (as preserved in the Akhmim Codex) is modeled on the gospels. This gospel apparently contained a life of Jesus, closely resembling the canonical gospels.[64] *Peter* even reproduces some of the wording of its sources.[65] The author of this gospel emulated, at least, some of the now-canonical gospels.

The most extensive witness to the *Gospel according to Peter*, the Akhmîm Codex (P.Cair. 10759), contains the passion and resurrection of Jesus. The fragment concludes with the self-disclosure of the gospel's fictional author.[66]

> But I, Simon Peter, and my brother Andrew—taking our nets, we went away to the sea.[67]

The author identifies themself as Simon Peter, the disciple of Jesus. While emulating the other gospels, this author represents their work as attributable to an eyewitness and participant in the narrative. This gospel attributed to Peter is, again, only a single datum and difficult to place chronologically. But this emulation of earlier gospels

64. The similarity between Peter and the canonical gospels is suggested by Serapion's description (Eusebius, *Church History* 6.12) and the surviving fragments. See the discussion of P.Oxy. 4009 in chapter 4.

65. The longest parallel in the Akhmîm fragment is eight words at Peter 8:30 // Matthew 27:64. See the discussion at Timothy P. Henderson, *The Gospel of Peter and Early Christian Apologetics: Rewriting the Story of Jesus' Death, Burial, and Resurrection* (Mohr Siebeck, 2011), 128.

66. The author speaks in the first person earlier in the same fragment as well as in P.Oxy. 4009. Likely, the author introduced themself as Peter early in the narrative.

67. Text from Ehrman and Pleše, *The Apocryphal Gospels*, 386.

provides another glimpse of what early readers expected of gospel literature.

Conclusion

Individual gospels do not tell us enough about themselves (or their predecessors) to reconstruct anything approaching a robust account of how gospel books were understood by their first generation of readers. But the authors of Matthew, Luke, and John were all imitators of Mark. Likewise, the authors of the *Protevangelium*, *Epistle of the Apostles*, *Gospel of Thomas*, and *Gospel of Peter* were readers of earlier gospel literature. In their self-presentation, many of these works offer a glimpse of how their authors thought about gospel books.[68] And taken together, these sources provide evidence that Papias, Justin, and Irenaeus were inheritors of an early and widespread tradition of reading gospels as Hellenistic literature.

Each individual gospel does not describe itself as a public and authored work of a particular subgenre, composed on a shared narrative *hypothesis*. But the gospels collectively supplied subsequent readers with each of these elements. A reader of these gospels at any point in the second century would have been prompted by the texts themselves to think about gospel literature in ways that Irenaeus would recognize.

The authors of these texts were not who they claimed to be. The disciple Thomas did not compile the collection of Jesus's sayings, and

68. Nick Elder argues throughout *Gospel Media* that "the gospels were not all read, written, and circulated the same way." Elder, *Gospel Media*, 275. And that is certainly possible. But Elder draws distinctions between the gospels based on the same minutia and interpretive ambiguities outlined above. Since the gospels tell us almost nothing about how they were written and cannot tell us how they themselves were read and circulated, all such arguments (including Elder's) must be analogical. In all surviving Greek literature, Luke is the closest analogy to Matthew by some measure—and so too with each of the others. In response to a similar argument from Rudolf Bultmann, Charles Talbert once wrote, "If two so similar writings as Mark and Luke do not belong to the same genre, then genre distinctions seem devoid of any meaning." Charles Talbert, *What Is a Gospel? The Genre of the Canonical Gospels* (Fortress Press, 1977), 6.

the eleven apostles did not pen the *Epistle* predicting Jesus's return in the early second century. Likewise, there is no good reason to suppose that the son of Zebedee had anything to do with composing the *Gospel according to John*. The present argument that the gospels were understood by their earliest readers as authored texts is not a defense of traditional authorial ascriptions. It is, rather, a way of identifying what kind of books the gospels were understood to be. Early readers expected the gospels to be the kind of books that were authored by relevant authorities, published to an indefinite audience, and preserved as written. These aspects of Irenaeus's conception of gospel literature were anticipated by readers and writers of gospel literature throughout the second century.

None of these texts suggests anything approaching a canon. Matthew recapitulates almost all of Mark without any acknowledgement that the earlier gospel existed. The Lukan prologue criticizes those who had already "attempted" to compose a life of Jesus.[69] The *Epistle of the Apostles* incorporates elements of the *Infancy Gospel of Thomas* alongside John and the Synoptics. And the *Gospel of Thomas*, on one interpretation, critiques *Matthew* and *Mark* in order to elevate the status of its own putative author. These first- and second-century authors know nothing of a fourfold gospel. The gospels, instead, reflect a certain competitiveness inherent in writing on an established *hypothesis*.

69. See the extended discussion of Luke's competitiveness in chapter 6.

CHAPTER SIX

Competition and Gospel Etiology

"And so also the doctors from Cnidos published the second *Cnidian Opinions* in the place of the former—some things being entirely the same, some things added, some things removed, even as also things were changed."

—Galen, *On Hippocrates' Regimen in Acute Diseases*

Introduction

SOCRATES STOOD ALONE before the court. The philosopher was accused of impiety, the invention of new deities, and corrupting the youth. Five hundred Athenians had gathered to determine his fate. The prosecution gave the first speech—entirely lost to history. Then Socrates delivered his defense. To explain the charges against him, said Socrates, he would need to tell a story: Chaerephon, another companion of Socrates, had visited the temple of Apollo at Delphi. This temple was famous for its oracle, a priestess who could speak for the god. Chaerephon petitioned the oracle for a judgment about Socrates. And the god answered. It was this answer, according to Socrates, that was the root of all his troubles.

What did the oracle say? According to Plato's *Apology*, the oracle proclaimed that no man was wiser than Socrates. It was his failed quest to disprove the oracle, claimed Socrates, that kindled the ire of certain Athenians against him. But Xenophon tells the story differently. According to Xenophon's *Apology*, the Delphic oracle declared that no man was freer, more just, or more prudent than Socrates. It was the quality of his life, claimed Socrates, that attracted the youth of Athens.

What Apollo *really* told Chaerephon lies beyond the scope of our inquiry. And scholars debate the literary relationship between Plato and Xenophon.[1] But ancient readers were not particularly perplexed. It was clear to Hellenistic and Roman readers what gave rise to these two overlapping accounts of Socrates. Namely, books written on the same *hypothesis* were self-evidently products of literary, ideological, or interpersonal rivalries.

The readers and writers of gospel literature brought the same assumptions to overlapping accounts of Jesus's life. It was obvious to some readers that the gospels differed because their authors disagreed. At the same time, however, Hellenistic reading culture provided early Christians with resources for resisting the agonistic implications of this model. Gospel etiologies—stories about where, when, and how the gospels were written—reflect early resistance to interpreting gospel authors as competitors.

The Lives of Socrates

Athenaeus of Naucratis flourished in the reign of Marcus Aurelius, making him an exact contemporary of Justin.[2] Athenaeus wrote a fifteen-volume work titled *The Dinner Experts* (or *Deipnosophistoi*). This work is a kind of miscellany, framed as a series of dinner conversations and, for present purposes, rich with insight into contemporary reading cultures.

Athenaeus's eleventh volume is an extended discussion of drinking vessels. Near the end of this conversation, Potianus (one of Athenaeus's experts) cites the advice of Socrates against excessive drinking as found in Xenophon's *Symposium*. The contrasting picture of a bibulous

1. See Holger Thesleff, "The Interrelation and Date of the 'Symposia' of Plato and Xenophon," *Bulletin of the Institute of Classical Studies* 25 (1978): 157–170; Gabriel Danzig, "Intra-Socratic Polemics: The Symposia of Plato and Xenophon," *Greek, Roman, and Byzantine Studies* 45 (2005): 331–357.

2. Suda A731.

Socrates in Plato's *Symposium*, then, gives rise to an extended critique of Plato himself.

> If one considers these words of the noble Xenophon, they will be able to recognize the jealousy which the most brilliant Plato had toward him. Or, possibly, these men were contentious from the beginning since they perceived each other's unique virtue and, probably, they competed to be first in rank as we can perceive not only from what they said about Cyrus but also from [what they wrote] on the same *hypothesis*. For, indeed, both men wrote *Symposia*. And in them, [Plato] expels the flute girls, while [Xenophon] brings them in. And [Xenophon's Socrates], as mentioned above, refuses to drink with big cups, while [Plato] depicts Socrates drinking with the wine-cooler until dawn (11.504d–e).[3]

The rivalry between Plato and Xenophon is evident, according to Potianus, not only from their different opinions on specific subjects but from their compositions on the same *hypothesis*. To illustrate, Athenaeus's Potianus cites Socrates's treatment of flute-girls and drinking vessels in each author's *Symposium*. Plato depicts Socrates expelling the girls and drinking until dawn. Xenophon, by way of contrast, depicts Socrates welcoming the flautists and rejecting large vessels. Athenaeus interprets the combination of differences in detail and a shared narrative framework (i.e., a common *hypothesis*) as evidence of a rivalry between the two authors.

Athenaeus offers several explanations for the competition between Plato and Xenophon. He suggests, first, that Plato was jealous of Xenophon—probably due to his literary reputation. Then he suggests that Xenophon and Plato may have had a longstanding interpersonal conflict. Finally, Athenaeus proposes good-natured rivalry. That is,

3. Text from S. Douglas Olson, *Athenaeus: The Learned Banqueters*, vol. 5, *Books 10.420e-11*, Loeb Classical Library 274 (Harvard University Press, 2009), 466–469.

Xenophon and Plato were simply both striving to be the best. In any case, Athenaeus takes it for granted that writing on the same *hypothesis* was evidence of a literary rivalry.

Diogenes Laertius wrote his *Lives of the Philosophers* at roughly the same time as Athenaeus's *Deipnosophists.* In his biography of Plato, Diogenes provides a parallel—but importantly, different—account of Plato's and Xenophon's Socratic compositions.

> And it appears that Xenophon was not well-disposed toward [Plato] since they have written similar things in rivalry: a Symposium, a Socratic Apology, and ethical Memorabilia—as well the Republic and the Education of Cyrus.

Diogenes, like Athenaeus, cites the overlapping accounts of Socrates as evidence of competition between the two authors. Diogenes, however, assumes that Plato wrote first and Xenophon composed his Socratic works in response. While Athenaeus cites only details from the Socratic Symposia, Diogenes lists several overlapping accounts of Socrates (as well as two very different books on education).[4] Diogenes, however, does not refer to any specific differences between, for instance, the two *Apologies.* The mere act of writing on the same *hypothesis* is, for Diogenes, sufficient evidence of the rivalry between the two authors.

Aulus Gellius, a contemporary of Irenaeus in Rome, provides a third data point for the reception of Socratic literature. His *Attic Nights*, like Athenaeus's *Dinner Experts* is a miscellany, collecting, summarizing, and editorializing on anecdotes, factoids, and trivia. It is, likewise, a rich store of evidence for popular reading culture.

In his fourteenth volume, Gellius acknowledges that most commentators believe Plato and Xenophon were rivals. "[These readers] have presented," says Gellius, "some conjectural arguments of this [rivalry] from their writings" (14.3)—that is, the writings of Plato and

4. As discussed at length in chapter 2, Diogenes uses the titles of these works as a shorthand for their *hypothesis.*

Xenophon.[5] It is crucial to Gellius's argument that the rivalry between these two authors was derived from their writings and not any other source of biographical information since Gellius will go on to argue against this inference based on the character of these philosophers. For our purposes, however, it is important to note that Gellius acknowledges that the books themselves suggest a rivalry to second-century readers.

Gellius refuses to believe that such great men really could have enmity between them or would have competed over the legacy of their teacher. "Such considerations," he says, "are wholly alien to the character of philosophers." The "appearance of rivalry," according to Gellius, is a result of "the very equality and parity of similar talents."[6] Their striving for excellence gives only "the appearance of a competitive rivalry (*contentionis aemulae*)."[7] But Gellius concludes that this cannot be. The moral qualities of a philosopher, reasons Gellius, are incompatible with the rivalry these writings suggest. As we will see, early Christians confronted with lives of Jesus written on the same *hypothesis* felt the need to make the same kind of arguments for the gospels.

These rough contemporaries of Justin, Irenaeus, and Clement report the same basic reading of Plato and Xenophon. Overlapping accounts of Socrates, they agree, are evidence of literary rivalry between their authors. Someone like Gellius might resist this conclusion on other grounds, but these readers all share the assumption that writing a book on an established *hypothesis* is a conventionally competitive act.

Competing over a *Hypothesis*

The reception of Socratic literature may be an especially useful analog for the gospels but the assumptions that shaped Athenaeus's understanding

5. Text from J. C. Rolfe, trans., *Gellius: Attic Nights*, vol. 3, *Books 14–20*. Loeb Classical Libary 212 (Harvard University Press, 1927), 32.

6. Text from Rolfe, *Gellius, Attic Nights*, vol. 3, 34.

7. Text from Rolfe, *Gellius, Attic Nights*, vol. 3, 36. Earlier in the same passage, Gellius refers to an apparent *aemulatio* between the two authors (3.14.8).

of books written on the same *hypothesis* were not unique to accounts of Socrates. The same set of literary conventions can be found in history, drama, and other genres. Readers in the first and second centuries consistently interpreted writing on an established *hypothesis* as a competitive act.

In his (mostly) lost treatise *On Imitation*, Dionysius of Halicarnassus discussed the relationship between the classical historians (*Letter to Gnaeus Pompeius* 3.1).[8] Herodotus of Halicarnassus, according to Dionysius, wrote "on the same *hypothesis*" as two earlier historians, Hellanicus and Charon. But Herodotus "did not give up and turn away" from the challenge, says Dionysius. Instead, he "trusted in himself to produce something better—which is what he did." Dionysius, thus, infers that historians write on an established *hypothesis* to improve on the work of their predecessors.

Dionysius was not only a commentator on earlier histories but also a historian himself. His *Roman Antiquities* shows that this description of Herodotus's motives also reflects the motives of working historians. Dionysius says that he wrote his history "to remove erroneous opinions" espoused by earlier historians (1.5.1). His predecessors, according to Dionysius, had not yet produced a worthy account of this *hypothesis* (1.2.1).[9] Just as readers of Plato and Xenophon understood contradictory accounts of Socrates as evidence of rivalry, so historians in the late Hellenistic and Roman period contradicted their predecessors in order to correct them.

The same conventions appear in discussions of drama. When Dio Chrysostom selected three versions of *Philoctetes* to read side-by-side-by-side, he imagined himself first as "*choregus*" (i.e., the sponsor of a performance) and then as judge.[10] The three playwrights were

8. The passage is discussed at length in chapter 1. Text from Usher, *Dionysius of Halicarnassus*, 374.

9. Dionysius later names these predecessors as Hieronymus of Cardia, Timaeus of Sicily, Antigonus, Polybius of Megalopolis, and Silenus (1.6–7).

10. Text from H. Lamar Crosby, *Dio Chrysostom. Discourses 37–60*, Loeb Classical Library 376 (Harvard University Press, 1946), 340.

"competing" (ἀνταγωνίζομαι), says Dio, for him and him alone. After reading all three plays, Dio decides that he cannot declare a victor, since each *Philoctetes* is excellent in its own way. Like Gellius, then, Dio refuses to hold any one of these versions above another. Nevertheless, the scenario described by Dio is premised on the assumption that there is something inherently competitive about books written on the same *hypothesis*.

Galen invokes the same conventions of dramatic criticism in order to explain the relationship between closely related works of medical literature.

> A second book written in the place of an older book is said to be "re-prepared" (ἐπιδιεσκευάσθαι) when they have the same *hypothesis* and most of the words—some of these [words] removed from the former composition, some added, and some subtly changed. But, for the sake of clarity, if you want an example of this, you have the second *Autolycus* of Eupolis composed (διεσκευασμένον) from the first. And so also the doctors from Cnidos published the second *Cnidian Opinions* in the place of the former—some things being entirely the same, some things added, some things removed, even as also things were changed. This, therefore, is the second book, which Hippocrates, having compared, says is more medical than the former. (*HVA* 1.4)[11]

To explain the multiple versions of the *Cnidian Opinions* in circulation, Galen draws an analogy from Athenian theatre.[12] Eupolis was a comedic playwright, exactly contemporary with Sophocles and Euripides. His

11. Text from Galien. Œuvres. Tome IX, 1re partie : Commentaire au régime des maladies aiguës d'Hippocrate. Livre I. (Les Belles Lettres, 2019), 8. Kühn 15.424.

12. The *Cnidian Opinions* were not understood as an unauthored, evolving text but, rather, attributed to a specific Cnidian doctor, Euryphon. Text from Johannes Ilberg, "Die Arzteschule von Knidos," *Berichte über die Verhandlungen der Sächsischen*

Autolycus was a traditional story about one of the argonauts, a shape-shifting thief and the grandfather of Odysseus. Eupolis had written and staged two plays on the same *hypothesis*, both titled *Autolycus*. The purpose of such rewriting, according to Galen, is for the latter work to take "the place of the former." This kind of competition over an established *hypothesis* is widespread in technical literature, but Galen appeals to his reader's knowledge of the same convention in narrative literature.[13]

Across the generic landscape of the late Hellenistic and Roman Principate period, authors and readers assumed that narratives written on an established *hypothesis* were intended to supersede their predecessors. Whatever was intended by Plato or Herodotus or Sophocles or Eupolis, these antagonistic assumptions were how overlapping narratives were understood in the first centuries on either side of the millennium. It was into this world of books and readers that the gospels emerged.

Calling the First Disciples

Jesus's public ministry began with baptism. In the *Gospel according to Mark*, Jesus comes up from the water (1:10), hears the voice from heaven (1:11), and then "immediately" enters the wilderness to remain for forty days (1:12–13). After this period of temptation, John the Baptist is arrested and Jesus begins preaching in Galilee (1:14–15). It is there, along the Sea of Galilee, that Jesus meets his first disciples, Simon and Andrew (1:16–20).

Simon and Andrew are also among the first disciples called by Jesus in the *Gospel according to John*, but the narrative proceeds differently.

Akademie der Wissenschaften zu Leipzig. Philologisch-Historische Klasse 76 (1924): 3–4.

13. Thessalus, *De Virtutibus Herbarum* 1; Hero of Alexandria, *Automata* 2.12, 20.5; Aelius Tactica, *Ars Tactica* Preface. Vitruvius tries to distinguish his work from technical literature by denying participation in this conventional practice (*On Architecture* 7.Preface.10).

Jesus's baptism is only referenced indirectly (1:31–34). Then, "on the next day," Jesus recruits two disciples from John's entourage with the Baptist's blessing (1:35–39). One of these is Andrew, who brings along his brother Simon (1:40–42). It is only "on the next day," after the call of Simon and Andrew, that Jesus travels to Galilee (1:43). The arrest of John the Baptist is not even mentioned until chapters later (3:24).

Differences between the gospels are clear from their first chapters. Were Simon and Peter recruited after John's arrest or at John's behest? Did Jesus meet them on the banks of the Jordan or along the sea of Galilee? Did Jesus "immediately" enter the wilderness for forty days of fasting or did he meet with John "on the next day"? These differences are at least as significant as Socrates's treatment of flute-players.

There must have been many readers already acquainted with Mark (or another synoptic gospel) when they encountered John for the first time. Perhaps some were Papias's parishioners in Hierapolis or Justin's pupils in Rome.[14] As literate, Greek-speaking inhabitants of the Roman Empire, the gospels could not have been their first exposure to a narrative tradition. How did their familiarity with pluriform biographies, histories, or dramas condition their reading of John's first chapter?

There is no need to speculate. The differences surrounding the call of Jesus's first disciples were cited already in antiquity as evidence of a conflict between the gospels. Epiphanius reports the arguments used by a group of Christians whom he calls "the stupid-people" (*Alogoi*)—a pun on the discussion of the *logos* that is unique to the Gospel of John (*Panarion* 4.51, see esp. 4.51.3.1). Probably this group was associated with a third-century Roman teacher, named Gaius.[15] But since Irenaeus

14. There is no good reason to believe that either of these authors used the fourth gospel, though this point (based on an argument from meaningful silence) is unimportant for the present argument. But Tatian, one of Justin's pupils, wrestled with this very contradiction between John and the synoptics. See Ian N Mills, "John's Jesus in Tatian's Diatessaron and the Muratorian Fragment," in *John, Jesus, and History*, vol. 4, *Jesus Remembered in the Johannine Situation*, ed. Paul Anderson (Society of Biblical Literature, 2024), 335–352.

15. Eduard Schwartz and James Rendel Harris make the case for this identification based on parallels between Epiphanius's *Alogoi* and the fragments of Hippolytus's

already knew of Christians who rejected the fourth gospel in the late second century (*Against Heresies* 3.11.9), Gaius may have simply been a prominent representative of a more widespread perspective. Atop the list of objections reported by Epiphanius is the disagreement between the different accounts of Jesus's baptism, temptation, and the call of the disciples. These readers observed that the Fourth Gospel specifies that Jesus called his disciples on the days immediately following an encounter with the Baptist, while "the other evangelists say that [Jesus] spent forty days in the desert being tempted by the devil" (*Panarion* 51.4.10).[16] "The books of [John]," they conclude, "do not agree with the rest of the apostles" (51.4.5).

These early readers noticed differences between John and the other gospels and, on that basis, rejected John. Probably these Roman Christians at the end of the second century already knew multiple synoptic gospels. They were tolerant, therefore, of a certain amount of variation. But, it seems, the complete rewriting of Jesus's life in the *Gospel according to John* was received differently. Perhaps Gaius argued that the differences between the synoptics belonged to every author's "authority to make each part happen as they wish," while the omission

treatise against Gaius. J. Rendel Harris, "Presbyter Gaius and the Fourth Gospel," in *Hermas in Arcadia, and Other Essays* (Cambridge University Press, 1896), 43–59; Eduard Schwartz, "Über den Tod der Söhne Zebedaei. Ein Beitrag zur Geschichte des Johannesevangeliums," in *Zum Neuen Testament und zum frühen Christentum* (De Gruyter, 1963), 48–123. The identification has been criticized in Allen Brent, *Hippolytus and the Roman Church in the Third Century: Communities in Tension Before the Emergence of a Monarch-Bishop* (Brill, 1995); Charles E. Hill, "The Johannine Corpus in the Early Church," in *Gaius of Rome and the Johannine Controversy* (Oxford University Press, 2004), 175–204; T. Scott Manor, *Epiphanius' Alogi and the Johannine Controversy: A Reassessment of Early Ecclesial Opposition to the Johannine Corpus* (Brill, 2016). But newly recovered fragments of Hippolytus from Syriac sources have vindicated Harris and Schwartz. See Thomas Schmidt, *The Book of Revelation and Its Eastern Commentators: Making the New Testament in the Early Christian World* (Cambridge University Press, 2021), 165 fn. 37; see also the critique of Manor's reading of Bar Salibi at 47 fn. 48. On Hippolytus's work against Gaius, see T.C. Schmidt, "Canon of Hippolytus," *Brill Encylcopedia of Early Christianity Online*.

16. Text from Holl and Dummer, *Epiphanius II Panarion haer. 34-64*, 252.

of Jesus's temptation or the new version of Simon's and Andrew's call would "harm the *hypothesis*."[17] His own reasoning does not survive. What seems anyways certain is that these early Roman readers were not inclined to ignore the differences between John and the Synoptics, interpret them as complementary, or otherwise harmonize them. Instead, like so many other readers of books written on the same *hypothesis*, these Christians saw a rivalry between these different versions of Jesus's life.

The Lukan Preface

The author of Luke is the first gospel reader (known to us) to comment on the multiplicity of gospels.[18] The evangelist describes the work as one "narrative" (διήγησις) of many, passing down "the account" (ὁ λόγος) of Jesus's life. This single sentence description of gospel literature does not use *hypothesis* language, but the third evangelist imagines these books according to the same basic paradigm. Predictably, then, the third evangelist reflects the same competitive assumptions attested for other first- and second-century narrative traditions.

The language used in the Lukan preface to describe previous gospel books contains an implicit critique. It begins, "Since many have attempted to arrange a narrative about the things that happened among us. . ." (1:1). The verb translated as "attempted" (ἐπιχειρέω) usually implies a lack of success—especially in similar contexts.[19] Josephus, for instance, twice uses the term to describe an earlier history of the Jewish War written by Justus of Tiberius. Justus, says Josephus, "was

---

17. Sch. Soph. *El.* 446. Text from Xenis, *Scholia Vetera in Sophoclis "Electram,"* 175.

18. The Lukan prologue's place in Hellenistic literature is treated in chapter 5.

19. Alexander argues persuasively that the Lukan preface closely follows the conventions of technical writing. Citing more than a dozen parallels, Alexander identifies the use of this verb in the third person as "derogatory." Nevertheless, she dismisses the competitive implications by suggesting that the third evangelist was merely following convention. Alexander, *The Preface to Luke's Gospel*, 109–110, 115–116. If technical literature is the appropriate intertext for understanding the Lukan preface, then the derogatory use of ἐπιχειρέω in the preface to the Hippocratic *On Ancient Medicine* is instructive.

unacquainted with the education of the Greeks and, emboldened by this [ignorance], attempted (ἐπεχείρησεν) to write a history of these events so as to exceed the truth in this account" (*Life* 9/40).[20] Then, at the beginning of a sustained critique of Justus's history, Josephus says "Justus, attempting (ἐπιχειρήσας) to write about these things—the events of the war—in order to seem industrious, lied about me and did not tell the truth about his own country" (65/338).[21] In both instances, Josephus chooses the language of "attempting" to slight his predecessor.[22]

An author's own use of a term in other contexts is often the best guide to its sense. While this verb never appears again in the third gospel, it is used twice in its sequel, *The Acts of the Apostles*. Here, the verb describes a failed attempt to kill Saul/Paul (9:29) and a botched exorcism (19:13). The rhetorical contexts are, of course, less close in these examples from Acts than the parallels in Josephus. Still, both instances of the verb in Acts are unmistakably derogatory. The third evangelist only ever used the verb "to attempt" to describe failed efforts.[23]

Finally, early readers acquainted with the conventions of Hellenistic literature understood Luke's statement as a criticism of his predecessors. In his homily on the first verses of Luke, Origen writes that the word *attempted* is "an accusation against those who came to write gospels without grace" (1.4).[24] The canonical evangelists, Origen goes on to insist, did not "attempt" to write gospels, since they wrote "from the

20. Text from H. St. J. Thackeray, trans., *Josephus, The Life; Against Apion*, Loeb Classical Library 186 (Harvard University, 1926), 16.

21. Text from Thackeray, *Josephus, The Life; Against Apion*, 124. The attention to "the order" of the events is a striking parallel to the concerns of the Lukan prologue (καθεξῆς) and the fragments of Papias (τάξει).

22. Josephus is broadly critical of his historiographic predecessors in the preface to his *War of the Jews* (1.1).

23. The derogatory sense of ἐπιχειρέω is specific to its use in the third person. In the first person, the same verb is a conventional expression of modesty. Alexander, *The Preface to Luke's Gospel*, 109–110, 115–116.

24. Text from M. Rauer, *Origenes Werke*, 2nd ed., vol. 9 of *Die Griechischen Christlichen Schriftsteller* 49 (35) (Leipzig: J. C. Hinrichs, 1899), 3.

Holy Spirit." Likewise, Epiphanius in his response to the aforementioned critics of the Fourth Gospel cites the Lukan phrase, "since many have attempted" as evidence that heretics also wrote gospels—naming Cerinthus and Merinthus as examples (*Panarion* 51.7.4).[25] Origen and Epiphanius understood the third evangelist to be using the term in the same derogatory sense as Josephus.

Like Dionysius of Halicarnassus, the third evangelist was both a reader of books written on the same *hypothesis* and a contributor to an already established narrative tradition. The Lukan preface provides evidence from the first generation of gospel readers and writers that gospel literature was understood according to the same competitive conventions that Dionysius used to describe overlapping historical works. Those conventions evidently included the implicit (and, sometimes, explicit) claim to supersede earlier instantiations of a narrative *hypothesis*.

Other Gospel Writers

The competitiveness inherent in writing on an established *hypothesis* is reflected also in several second-century gospels. Marcion was a teacher in Rome sometime in the middle of the second century.[26]

25. Text from Holl and Dummer, *Epiphanius II Panarion haer. 34–64*, 257. The idea that Cerinthus wrote a gospel seems to be based on a misreading of Irenaeus's *Against Heresies* 1.26. On Epiphanius's conflation of Cerinthus with the Ebionites, see A. F. J. Klijn and G. J. Reinink, *Patristic Evidence for Jewish-Christian Sects* (Brill, 1973), 8–12; Charles E. Hill, "Cerinthus, Gnostic or Chiliast? A New Solution to an Old Problem," *Journal of Early Christian Studies* 8, no. 2 (2000): 146–147. That Epiphanius misread Irenaeus this way is further suggested by his insertion of Cerinthus into other discussions of the Ebionite gospel (*Pan* 30.3.7; 30.14.2).

26. Justin's καὶ νῦν makes him the apologist's elder contemporary (*First Apology* 58). Irenaeus says Marcion flourished during the bishopric of Anicetus, tenth from Peter (*Against Heresies* 1.27). The Marcionites, according to Tertullian, put *anni fere centum quindecim et dimidium anni cum dimidio mensis* between Jesus and Marcion (*Against Marcion* 1.19) whereas Tertullian himself dates Marcion's advent to the bishopric of Eleutherius (*Prescription* 30.2) and his ascendency to the rule of Antoninus Pious (*Against Marcion* 5.19).

His opponents attributed to him the preparation of a new gospel, derived from Luke.[27] If this attribution can be credited, Marcion's behavior offers a glimpse of how another gospel writer positioned his work relative to his predecessors.[28] Marcion, according to Tertullian, prefaced his gospel with another text, the *Antitheses*. Tertullian says this lost prefatory work was designed "to patronize belief" in Marcion's gospel (*Against Marcion* 4.1.1) and contained criticism of other gospels (4.4.4).[29] Irenaeus, likewise, reports that Marcion recognized only his own gospel (*Against Heresies* 3.12). Based on these reports, Marcion shared the author of Luke's perspective on competitive gospel writing.

Tatian, a disciple of Justin Martyr, also composed a gospel based on the work of his predecessors.[30] But the earliest references to Tatian's

---

27. The earliest testimony to this gospel appears in Irenaeus, *Against Heresies* (1.17.2). The primary sources for its content, however, are the fourth book of Tertullian's *Against Marcion* and the forty-second book of Epiphanius's *Panarion*. For a scholarly reconstruction, see Dieter T. Roth, *The Text of Marcion's Gospel*, New Testament Tools, Studies and Documents 49, ed. Bart D Ehrman and Eldon J Epp (Brill, 2015).

28. For recent critiques of Marcion's use of Luke, see Jason BeDuhn, *The First New Testament: Marcion's Scriptural Canon* (Polebridge Press, 2013); Markus Vinzent, *Marcion and the Dating of the Synoptic Gospels* (Peeters Publishers, 2014); Matthias Klinghardt, *Das älteste Evangelium und die Entstehung der kanonischen Evangelien Band I: Untersuchung* (Francke A. Verlag, 2015). For defenses of Marcionite posteriority, see Leland Edward Wilshire, "Was Canonical Luke Written in the Second Century?—A Continuing Discussion," *New Testament Studies* 20, no. 3 (1974): 246–253; Christopher M. Hays, "Marcion vs. Luke: A Response to the Plädoyer of Matthias Klinghardt," *Z. Für Neutestamentliche Wissenchaft Kunde Älteren Kirche Berl* 99, no. 2 (2008): 213–232; Dieter Roth, "Review of Marcion and the Dating of the Synoptic Gospels. By Markus Vinzent," *Studia Patristica* Supplement 2 (2014): 800–803.

29. Text from Claudio Moreschini and René Braun, eds., *Tertullien Contre Marcion Tome IV*, Sources Chrétiennes 456 (Éditions du Cerf, 2001), 56–58, 78.

30. Matthew Crawford argues compellingly that the title "Diatessaron" mischaracterizes this work. Matthew R. Crawford, "Diatessaron, a Misnomer? The Evidence from Ephrem's Commentary," *Early Christianity* 4, no. 3 (2013): 362–385.

gospel say nothing about his intentions.[31] Descriptions of its circulation, however, reveal a striking parallel with Marcion's gospel. Just as the followers of Marcion used only this gospel, so too many early Christians who used Tatian's gospel used it alone.[32] The most explicit evidence is supplied by Theodoret, the bishop of Cyrrhus in the mid-fifth century.

> [Tatian's gospel] was used not only by members of his group but also by those who follow apostolic doctrines, who were not aware of the wickedness of its composition, but were simply using it as a concise book. I myself found more than two hundred such books being revered in the churches among us. I collected and removed all of them and I introduced in their place the gospels of the four evangelists.[33]

Theodoret says he discovered more than two hundred copies of this gospel in churches without the four-gospel collection. In the centuries between Tatian and Theodoret, the Christians who used Tatian's gospel had no need for the others. Indeed, *The Doctrine of Addai* describes the practices of those Christians in the intervening centuries. According to this legendary account of how Christianity came to Syria, the first generation of Christians (i.e., the disciples of Addai) used Tatian's gospel, the letters of Paul, and the Acts of the Apostles alongside the Jewish scriptures.[34]

---

31. The earliest explicit references to Tatian's gospel are Eusebius, *Church History* 4.29.6 and Epiphanius, *Panarion* 1.46.1.6–9.

32. The *Dialogue of Adamantius* indicates that the use of only one gospel continued among Marcion's followers (4–8).

33. Text from PG 83 372.

34. This list is a combination of two separate passages. For text and translation, see George Howard, *The Teaching of Addai* (Society of Biblical Literature, 1981), 72–73, 93.

Probably Tatian himself wrote his gospel to supersede its predecessors.[35] But irrespective of Tatian's intentions, his gospel was propagated by readers without its predecessors. For many Christians, it was simply "the gospel." Given the assortment of gospels known already to Tatian's teacher, Justin, it is likely that this exclusive use of one gospel reflects the same competitive assumptions about gospel literature attested by Marcion, Gaius, and the author of Luke.

There is, at least, one other example of a new gospel displacing its predecessors.[36] Epiphanius reports that the Ebionites used only a gospel "according to the Hebrews."[37] From Epiphanius's quotations (e.g., 30.13.7-8), it appears this gospel was yet another creative rewriting of the synoptics.[38] It is, however, impossible to date this gospel or the reading practices described by Epiphanius with any amount of confidence.

Irenaeus was a critic of Marcion, Tatian, and the Ebionites. The circulation of gospels among their followers, therefore, reflects the expectations and norms for the treatment of such literature in early

35. This is the conclusion of Nicholas Zola, "Evangelizing Tatian: The Diatessaron's Place in the Emergence of the Fourfold Gospel Canon," *Perspectives in Religious Studies* 43 (2016): 399–414; Francis Watson, "Harmony or Gospel? On the Genre of the (So-Called) Diatessaron," in *The Gospel of Tatian: Exploring the Nature and Text of the Diatessaron*, ed. Matthew Crawford and Nicholas Zola (T&T Clark, 2019), 69–92. For an alternative perspective, see James Barker, "Tatian's Diatessaron and the Proliferation of Gospels," in *The Gospel of Tatian: Exploring the Nature and Text of the Diatessaron*, ed. Matthew Crawford and Nicholas Zola (T&T Clark, 2019), 111–142. Barker fails to account for how often one work was able to displace its rivals for reading communities.

36. We have no external testimony to the reception of the *Gospel According to Peter*, Egerton Gospel, Dura Fragment, or P.Oxy. 5575. If my argument holds, probably some of these were also put forward as superseding their predecessors.

37. Text from Holl, *Epiphanius I Ancoratus und Panarion haer. 1–33*, 337–38. On the so-called Jewish-Christian gospels, see Andrew Gregory, *The Gospel According to the Hebrews and the Gospel of the Ebionites*, Oxford Early Christian Gospel Texts (Oxford University Press, 2017).

38. On the use of the synoptics in this gospel, see especially Daniel A. Bertrand, "L'*Evangile des Ebionites*: Une Harmonie Evangelique Anterieure au Diatessaron." *New Testament Studies* 26, no. 4 (1980): 548–563; Michael Kok, "The Gospel of the Ebionites and the Synoptic Problem," *Catholic Biblical Quarterly* 86, no. 2 (2024): 300–325.

Christian networks *not* influenced by Irenaeus and his proto-canonical gospel collection. Presumably most of these gospel readers knew that other gospels had been written. But in their promulgation of only one gospel, these Christians participated in the same competitive book culture reflected in Dionysius's critiques of his predecessors or Gaius's rejection of John.

Resisting Competition with Gospel Etiologies

There is a tension evident in the way that readers talk about books written on the same *hypothesis*. On one hand, writing on an established *hypothesis* was understood as a competitive act. At the same time, however, the idea of a narrative *hypothesis* was used to legitimize variation in the retelling of a story. Readers saw a rivalry between works written on the same *hypothesis* but, at least sometimes, insisted on their ability to appreciate more than one version at the same time.

This perspective is evident in Dio Chrysostom's meditation on the three *Philoctetes* and Aulus Gellius's reflection on Socratic literature. Even as these readers acknowledged an apparent competitiveness between the works that make up these narrative traditions, they argued against a preference for any one version over the others. Dio explained each of the differences between the versions as emerging from the author's admirable literary agenda. Gellius argued that the virtues of the authors were incompatible with literary rivalry. Early Christians used these same arguments in their gospel etiologies to resist the uncomfortable implications that the evangelists wrote on the same *hypothesis* out of rivalry.

Stories about the apostolic origins of the canonical gospels go back to sometime in the second century. Papias already knows stories about the origin of Matthew and Mark (Eusebius, *Church History* 3.39.14–16). Likewise, Clement of Alexandria is reported to have said something about the origin of gospels with genealogies, presumably including Luke (Eusebius, *Church History* 6.14.5).[39] And early works

39. On the evangelists traditions in Clement, see Stevens, "The Evangelists in Clement's Hypotyposes."

like the *Protevangelium of James* and *The Epistula Apostolorum* suggest that apostolic attributions for the gospels were already widespread in the second century.[40] Although etiologies for all four gospels are not extant until Irenaeus's third book of *Against Heresies*, stories of this kind clearly predate the establishment of a four-gospel canon. And while these stories are preserved primarily in authors who propound this protocanonical collection, they reflect earlier strategies for legitimizing the pluriform gospel tradition.

The Muratorian fragment provides a particularly stark illustration. The origins of this canon list are disputed, but it is probably a Latin translation of a late second- or third-century Greek text.[41] The list originally contained origin stories for all four gospels but the first line on the first surviving page is the very conclusion of a gospel etiology—probably Mark. It then introduces "the third book of the gospel according to Luke" and "the fourth of the gospels of John from among the disciples," each followed by an account of that gospel's composition.[42] The etiology for John runs as follows:

40. See the extended argument in chapter 5.

41. The fragment describes *en passant* the mid-second-century Shepherd of Hermas as a "very recent" composition. It seems implausible that a work primarily concerned with the New Testament canon would purposefully place itself in the late second century while dating the canonical writings to the mid-first century. Advocates of a second-century date include Philippe Henne, "La Datation Du 'Canon' De Muratori," *Revue Biblique* 100, no. 1 (1993): 54–75; Joseph Verheyden, "The Canon Muratori: A Matter of Dispute," in *The Biblical Canons*, ed. J.-M. Auwers and H. J. de Jonge, Bibliotheca Ephemeridum Theologicarum Lovaniensium 163 (Leuven University Press, 2003), 487–556. For arguments in favor of a fourth-century date, see Albert C. Sundberg, "Canon Muratori: A Fourth-Century List," *Harvard Theological Review* 66, no. 1 (1973): 1–41; Geoffrey Mark Hahneman, *The Muratorian Fragment and the Development of the Canon* (Clarendon Press, 1992). Claire Rothschild has argued for an even later date in Claire K. Rothschild, "The Muratorian Fragment as Roman Fake," *Novum Testamentum* 60, no. 1 (2018): 55–82; Claire K. Rothschild, *The Muratorian Fragment: Text, Translation, Commentary* (Mohr Siebrek Ek, 2022). But see Christophe Guignard, "The Muratorian Fragment as a Late Antique Fake?" *Revue des Sciences Religieuses* 93, no. 1–2 (2019): 73–90. In favor of its composition in Greek, see Christophe Guignard, "The Original Language of the Muratorian Fragment," *Journal of Theological Studies* 66, no. 2 (2015): 596–624.

42. Since the diplomatic edition is untranslatable, I use the emended text at Rothschild, *The Muratorian Fragment*, 33.

> When his fellow-disciples and overseers urged him, he said: "Fast with me today for three days and whatever shall be revealed to each, let us explain to each other." That same night it was revealed to Andrew of the apostles that, after they all approved [it], John, under his own name, should describe everything. And, for that reason, it is permissible that different beginnings should be taught by each of the evangelists. Nothing, however, differs with respect to the faith of believers since everything in all [the gospels] has been declared by one ruling spirit—about his passion, his resurrection, his interactions with his disciples, and his double advent: first, in humility when he was looked down upon and later second, in his glorious reign which is to be.[43]

According to the Muratorian fragment, John did not simply decide to write a new gospel. Instead, God revealed to Andrew that the disciples should confer together, and John should publish under his own name what they all approve.

This story, according to the fragment, proves a particular point. Divine sanction and the collaboration of the apostles demonstrates that "it is permissible" (*licet*) for the gospels to have "different beginnings" (*varia principia*). There is some question about the meaning of "beginnings" in this sentence, but the logic of this argument is clear even without interrogating that term.[44] The argument assumes that a reader might infer that there is something wrong about differences between the gospels. The fact that the fragment presents the collaboration of the disciples with John as an answer to that concern suggests that the anticipated inference is a rivalry between the disciples. The point of the

---

43. My own translation of the emended text at Rothschild, *The Muratorian Fragment*, 32–34.

44. On different interpretations of this term in the fragment, see Ian N. Mills, "John's Jesus in Tatian's Diatessaron and the Muratorian Fragment," in *John, Jesus, and History*, vol. 4, *Jesus Remembered in the Johannine Situation*, by Paul Anderson, Felix Just, SJ, and Tom Thatcher, Early Christianity and Its Literature 34 (Society of Biblical Literature, 2024), 335–352.

story, according to the fragment, is to show that despite the differences between the gospels there was no competition among the apostolic evangelists. The author of the fragment anticipates the gospels being read the same way that contemporaries were reading other books written on the same *hypothesis*.

The author of the Muratorian fragment does not merely anticipate others reading the gospels as books written on the same *hypothesis* but, like Dio Chrysostom and the Sophoclean scholiast, uses the concept of a narrative *hypothesis* to legitimize pluriformity. The fragment does not deny the existence of differences between the gospels or attempt to harmonize them. Instead, the fragment states that "nothing differs (*differt*) with respect to the faith of believers." The content of what does not vary between the gospels is then identified as "his passion, his resurrection, his interactions with his disciples, and his double advent." In other words, the fragment acknowledges differences between the gospels but asserts that that basic story of Jesus's life (i.e., the *hypothesis* of the gospels) is the same. The differences between the gospels, according to this reader, do not destroy the *hypothesis*.

At the same time, the fragment does not direct the reader to ignore the differences between gospels. Just as Dio Chrysostom sought to show how the differences between the three *Philoctetes* reflected the authorial agenda of each playwright, so too the Muratorian fragment states that "everything in all [the gospels] has been declared by one ruling spirit." Even the differences, according to the Muratorian fragment, are the product of a divine authorial agenda.

The author of the Muratorian fragment simultaneously draws on the idea of a narrative *hypothesis* underlying the gospels and resists some of its conventional implications. The fragment asserts that the gospels do not differ with respect to the gospel *hypothesis*. At the same time, the etiology of John shows that the differences between the gospels are not evidence of a rivalry between their authors. In both respects, the Muratorian fragment is drawing on highly conventional ways of reading narrative traditions in the late Hellenistic period.[45]

45. Eusebius reports that a similar sounding story was present in Clement's *Hypotyposes*, suggesting that the etiology for John goes back to the second century

Conclusion

Readers in the first and second centuries inferred that differences between books written on the same *hypothesis* were evidence of a rivalry between their authors. Indeed, ancient authors claim to surpass or even replace earlier books written on the same *hypothesis* as their own work. At the same time, however, some readers used the idea of a *hypothesis* to resist this inference. These readers insist that authors can tell the same story in different ways for equally good reasons. Even if the authors themselves were striving to outdo each other, a reader need not choose one version of a story over another.

All the same attitudes, assumptions, and expectations are evidenced among early readers of the gospels. Evangelists like Luke—not to mention Marcion, Tatian, and the author of *Thomas*—evidently sought to outdo their predecessors. Readers like Gaius understood contradictions between the gospels as evidence of competition. At the same time, however, readers like the author of the Muratorian fragment used the idea of a narrative *hypothesis* to defend variety among the gospels.

(*Church History* 6.14.5–7). See the possibilities raised in Hill, "What Papias Said about John (and Luke)" and Manor, "Papias, Origen, and Eusebius."

Conclusion

AUGUSTINE KNEW THERE were only four gospels. And he was certain that these gospels agreed. But Augustine could read with his own eyes that Jesus in Mark allowed his disciples a walking staff and Jesus in Matthew prohibited it (*On the Harmony of the Gospels* 2.30/71–74). Augustine saw that it was the same story, in the same context, with the same words. Augustine could not attribute this kind of contradiction to the creative freedom of authors "making each part happen as they wished."[1] Instead, he harmonized the gospels: Jesus told his disciples to bring "a staff and not a staff." And to make sense of this confusing instruction, Augustine reasoned that the word *staff* had a figurative meaning in one of its two uses. The conflation of these different stories and the figurative interpretation are premised on Augustine's conviction that all four gospels had one divine author.

Augustine also knew that his way of understanding such differences between the gospels would not be obvious to everyone. Another reader of the same passage, says Augustine, considered the gospels "opposed" (*contrarius*).[2] No doubt, this is how Athenaeus or Diogenes Laertius would have read the gospels. Gaius of Rome evidently understood the differences between John and the Synoptics this way. And probably the author of Luke, Marcion, and Tatian saw these kinds of differences

---

1. Sch. Soph. *El.* 446. Text from Xenis, *Scholia Vetera in Sophoclis "Electram,"* 175. This scholion is discussed in chapter 1.

2. Text from PL 34 1114.

between the gospels as a problem to be fixed.[3] But Augustine warns his reader, "let this not be thought."[4]

In setting up these two interpretive options, Augustine ignored another way to read the gospels. Other interpreters had acknowledged real differences between the gospels because, it was understood, authors were at liberty to tell the story as they saw fit so long as the basic story (i.e., the *hypothesis*) was unharmed. This approach to gospel literature is reflected in Irenaeus's insistence that each of the gospels equally preserves the *hypothesis,* Serapion's approval of a *Gospel according to Peter* as mostly agreeing with the "true account," and the Muratorian fragment's assertion that the gospels, despite their differences, do not differ concerning the basic details of Jesus's life. There are glimpses of this way of thinking about gospels also in later interpreters, like Clement, Origen, and Epiphanius. And it makes sense of *ad hoc* gospel collections, like that reflected in the writings of Justin and the *Epistle of the Apostles.*

This other approach to the gospels did not emerge from any special set of assumptions about gospel literature. Rather, early readers were treating the gospels like other well-known narrative traditions when they described and evaluated them with reference to a notional *hypothesis.* The idea of a basic story underlying a literary tradition was just part of how Hellenistic and Roman readers thought about pluriform narratives. Even as some readers looking through the lens of Hellenistic literary culture could see a rivalry between the gospels, so too other readers could draw on conventional lines of interpretation to argue that certain differences between certain gospels did not matter.

---

3. In fact, Tatian seems to have rewritten this very passage in order to resolve the contradiction. Tjitze Baarda, "A Staff Only, Not A Stick: Disharmony of the Gospels and the Harmony of Tatian (Matthew 10:9f.; Mark 6:8f.; Luke 9:3 and 10:4)," in *The New Testament in Early Christianity*, ed. Jean-Marie Sevrin and Barbara Aland, Bibliotheca Ephemeridum Theologicarum Lovaniensium 86 (Uitgeverij Peeters, 1989). The author of Luke adopted Matthew's prohibition on walking staffs (9:3). Marcion's text is unknown. Roth, *The Text of Marcion's Gospel*, 418.

4. Text from PL 34 1114.

What They Thought They Were Doing

No amount of evidence can close the gap between the intention of an author and the conventions, expectations, and norms of the culture in which they wrote. All claims about how an author understood their own behavior involve inferences from circumstantial evidence. And that remains true even when authors explicitly state their own purposes.[5] Nevertheless, such inferences toward intention are inescapable, and readers cannot be faulted for wondering why authors behaved the way they did.[6]

Writing on an established *hypothesis* was understood as an inherently competitive act. It is difficult to imagine that the author of Matthew would not have expected readers to understand a rewriting of Mark accordingly. And nothing in the gospel suggests otherwise.[7] This author could have written a sequel, a supplement, or something else. Instead, this reader of Mark composed (what was understood by readers as) a new work on the same *hypothesis.*

The critical description of earlier gospel writers in the Lukan prolog gives the same impression. The author of Mark was one of those who "attempted" to arrange a narrative of the same "account" (λόγος) about Jesus. The third evangelist's claims to accuracy (ἀκριβῶς) and order (καθεξῆς) can be mapped onto differences between the third gospel

5. Even a living author can only claim to describe their own motivations and must use conventional language to do so. A reader's conclusions about those intentions are still only inferences from text and convention.

6. On intention and interpretation, see Toril Moi, *Revolution of the Ordinary: Literary Studies After Wittgenstein, Austin, and Cavell* (The University of Chicago Press, 2018). On the inescapability of intentional language, see John Farrell, *The Varieties of Authorial Intention: Literary Theory Beyond the Intentional Fallacy* (Palgrave Macmillan, 2017), 21–100.

7. Such an agonistic attitude is not, however, incompatible with the kind of respect evinced by the evangelist's reproduction of so much of Mark. See J. Andrew Doole, *What Was Mark for Matthew?: An Examination of Matthew's Relationship and Attitude to His Primary Source* (Mohr Siebeck, 2013).

and its sources. Probably the author of Luke sought to supersede his now-canonical predecessors.

But did these gospel writers think their predecessors had "harmed" or even "destroyed" the *hypothesis*? Or did they accept that their predecessors also had an "authority to make each part happen" according to their own designs? Perhaps these authors were simply trying to exercise that same "authority" better than those who came before. Gellius urged his readers to entertain both possibilities for Plato and Xenophon.

The answer is probably different for different gospels. It is much easier to imagine that the author of John thought that Mark had preserved the *hypothesis* than to think that Marcion approved of Luke. And the history of interpretation suggests that even the first generation of readers reached different conclusions about some of the same gospels. Maybe our historical distance makes us better able to discern the motives of these ancient authors. Or maybe not.

BIBLIOGRAPHY

Adams, Sean A. *Greek Genres and Jewish Authors: Negotiating Literary Culture in the Greco-Roman Era*. Baylor University Press, 2020.

Alexander, Loveday. *The Preface to Luke's Gospel: Literary Convention and Social Context in Luke 1.1-4 and Acts 1.1*. Society for New Testament Studies 78. Cambridge University Press, 1993.

Allison, Dale C., Jr. *The New Moses: A Matthean Typology*. Fortress Press, 1993.

Aragione, Gabriella. "Justin 'Philosphe' Cretien et Les Memoires Des Apotre." *Apocrypha*, 2004.

Ayres, Lewis. "Irenaeus vs. the Valentinians: Toward a Rethinking of Patristic Exegetical Origins." *Journal of Early Christian Studies* 23, no. 2 (2015): 153–187.

Baarda, Tjitze. "A Staff Only, Not A Stick: Disharmony of the Gospels and the Harmony of Tatian (Matthew 10:9f.; Mark 6:8f.; Luke 9:3 and 10:4)." In *The New Testament in Early Christianity*, edited by Jean-Marie Sevrin and Barbara Aland. Bibliotheca Ephemeridum Theologicarum Lovaniensium 86. Uitgeverij Peeters, 1989.

Bal, Mieke. *Narratology: Introduction to the Theory of Narrative*. University of Toronto Press, 2009.

Bardy, Gustave. *Eusèbe de Césarée. Histoire ecclésiastique. Livres V-VIII*. Sources Chrétiennes 41. Les Éditions du Cerf, 1955.

Barker, James. "Tatian's Diatessaron and the Proliferation of Gospels." In *The Gospel of Tatian: Exploring the Nature and Text of the Diatessaron*, edited by Matthew Crawford and Nicholas Zola. T&T Clark, 2019.

Barker, James W. *Writing and Rewriting the Gospels: John and the Synoptics*. Eerdmans, 2025.

Bauckham, Richard. "The Beloved Disciple as Ideal Author." *Journal for the Study of the New Testament* 49 (1993): 21–44.

Bauckham, Richard. "For Whom Were Gospels Written?" *HTS Teologiese Studies/Theological Studies* 55, no. 4 (1999): 865–882.

Bauckham, Richard. *The Testimony of the Beloved Disciple: Narrative, History, and Theology in the Gospel of John*. Illustrated edition. Baker Academic, 2007.

Baum, Armin D. "The Original Epilogue (John 20:30–31), the Secondary Appendix (21:1–23), and the Editorial Epilogues (21:24–25) of John's Gospel: Observations Against the Background of Ancient Literary Conventions." In *Earliest Christian History: History, Literature, and Theology. Essays from the Tyndale Fellowship in Honor of Martin Hengel*, by Michael F. Bird and Jason Matson. WUNT 2/320. Mohr Siebeck, 2011.

Becker, Eve-Marie, Helen K. Bond, and Catrin H. Williams, eds. *John's Transformation of Mark*. Bloomsbury Publishing, 2021.

BeDuhn, Jason. *The First New Testament: Marcion's Scriptural Canon*. Polebridge Press, 2013.

Behr, John. *Origen: On First Principles*. Oxford University Press, 2017.

Bellinzoni, A. J. *The Sayings of Jesus in the Writings of Justin Martyr*. Vol. 17 of *Supplements to Novum Testamentum*. Edited by W. C. van Unnik. Brill, 1967.

Benoit, Andre. "Ecriture et Tradition chez saint Irenee." *Revue d'Histoire et de Philosophie Religieuses* 40, no. 1 (1960): 32–43.

Bertrand, Daniel A. "L'*Evangile des Ebionites*: Une Harmonie Evangelique Anterieure au Diatessaron." *New Testament Studies* 26, no. 4 (1980): 548–563.

Beschorner, Andreas. *Untersuchungen Zu Dares Phrygius*. Classica Monacensia 4. Gunter Narr, 1992.

Bingham, D. Jeffrey. "Paideia and Polemic in Second-Century Lyons: Irenaeus on Education." In *Pedagogy in Ancient Judaism and Early Christianity*, edited by Karina Martin Hogan, Matthew Goff, and Emma Wasserman. SBL Press, 2017.

Black, Matthew. "The Use of Rhetorical Terminology in Papias On Mark and Matthew." *Journal for the Study of the New Testament* 12, no. 37 (1989): 31–41.

Blowers, Paul M. "The Regula Fidei and the Narrative Character of Early Christian Faith." *Ecclesiology: The Journal for Catholic and Evangelical Theology* 6, no. 2 (1997): 199–228.

Blumell, Lincoln. "A Jew in Celsus' True Doctrine? An Examination of Jewish Anti-Christian Polemic in the Second Century C.E." *Studies in Religion/Sciences Religieuses* 36, no. 2 (2007): 297–315.

Blumell, Lincoln H., and Thomas A. Wayment, eds. *Christian Oxyrhynchus: Texts, Documents, and Sources*. Baylor University Press, 2015.

Bobichon, Philippe. *Justin Martyr, Dialogue Avec Tryphon: Édition Critique: Introduction, Texte Grec, Traduction*. Paradosis: Études de Littérature et de Théologie Anciennes. Academic Press Fribourg, 2003.

Bond, Helen K. *The First Biography of Jesus: Genre and Meaning in Mark's Gospel*. Eerdmans, 2020.

Brent, Allen. *Hippolytus and the Roman Church in the Third Century: Communities in Tension before the Emergence of a Monarch-Bishop*. Brill, 1995.

Briggman, Anthony. "Literary and Rhetorical Theory in Irenaeus, Part 1." *Vigiliae Christianae* 69, no. 5 (2015): 500–527.

Briggman, Anthony. "Literary and Rhetorical Theory in Irenaeus, Part 2." *Vigiliae Christianae* 70, no. 1 (2016): 31–50.

Brisson, Luc. *How Philosophers Saved Myths: Allegorical Interpretation and Classical Mythology*. University of Chicago Press, 2008.

Brooke, A. E. *The Fragments of Heracleon*. Gorgias Press, 2004.

Brown, Raymond E. *The Gospel According to John (I-XII)*. Vol. 29 of *The Anchor Bible*. Doubleday, 1966.

Brown, Raymond E. *The Gospel According to John (XIII-XXI)*. Vol. 29A of *The Anchor Bible*. Doubleday, 1970.

Bucur, Bogdan G. "The Place of the Hypotyposeis in the Clementine Corpus: An Apology for 'The Other Clement of Alexandria.'" *Journal of Early Christian Studies* 17, no. 3 (2009): 313–335. https://doi.org/10.1353/earl.0.0265.

Burridge, Richard A. *What Are the Gospels? A Comparison with Graeco-Roman Biography*. Society for New Testament Studies Monograph Series 70. Cambridge University Press, 1992.

Bury, R. G. *Sextus Empiricus: Against the Professors*. Loeb Classical Library 382. Harvard University Press, 1949.

Byers, Andrew J. "The Genre of Mark's Gospel Is 'Gospel': Reconsidering Literary Innovation in the Markan Incipit." *Journal for the Study of the New Testament* 46, no. 2 (2023): 168–192.

Calder III, William M. "Aeschylus' 'Philoctetes.'" *Greek, Roman, and Byzantine Studies* 11, no. 3 (1970): 171–179.

Carlson, Stephen C., ed. *Papias of Hierapolis Exposition of Dominical Oracles: The Fragments, Testimonia, and Reception of a Second-Century Commentator*. Oxford Early Christian Texts. Oxford University Press, 2021.

Clay, Diskin. "Framing the Margins of Philodemus and Poetry." In *Philodemus and Poetry: Poetic Theory and Practice in Lucretius, Philodemus, and Horace*. Oxford University Press, 1995.

Cohn, Leopold, and Paul Wendland. *Philonis Alexandrini Opera quae supersunt. Ediderunt Leopoldus Cohn et Paulus Wendland.* Vol. 4. Georg Reimer, 1902.

Collins, Adela Yarbro. "Genre and the Gospels." *Journal of Religion* 75, no. 2 (1995): 239–246.

Coogan, Jeremiah. *Eusebius the Evangelist: Rewriting the Fourfold Gospel in Late Antiquity.* Cultures of Reading in the Ancient Mediterranean. Oxford University Press, 2022.

Coogan, Jeremiah. "Meddling with the Gospel: Celsus, Early Christian Textuality, and the Politics of Reading." *Novum Testamentum* 65, no. 3 (2023): 400–422.

Coogan, Jeremiah. "Reading (in) a Quadriform Cosmos: Gospel Books in the Early Christian Bibliographic Imagination." *Journal of Early Christian Studies* 31, no. 1 (2023): 85–103.

Cosgrove, Charles H. "Justin Martyr and the Emerging Christian Canon. Observations on the Purpose and Destination of the Dialogue with Trypho." *Vigiliae Christianae* 36 (1982): 209–232.

Crawford, Matthew R. "Diatessaron, a Misnomer? The Evidence from Ephrem's Commentary." *Early Christianity* 4, no. 3 (2013): 362–385.

Crawford, Matthew R. *The Eusebian Canon Tables: Ordering Textual Knowledge in Late Antiquity.* Oxford University Press, 2019.

Cribiore, Raffaella. *Gymnastics of the Mind: Greek Education in Hellenistic and Roman Egypt.* Princeton University Press, 2005.

Crosby, H. Lamar. *Dio Chrysostom. Discourses 37–60.* Loeb Classical Library 376. Edited by Jeffrey Henderson. Harvard University Press, 1946.

Currie, Bruno. *Herodotus as Homeric Critic.* Histos, 2021.

D'Ales, A. "Le Mot Oikonomia Dans La Langue Théologique de Saint Irénée." *Revue des Études Grecques* 32 (1919): 1–9.

D'Angour, Armand. *The Greeks and the New: Novelty in Ancient Greek Imagination and Experience.* Cambridge University Press, 2011.

Danzig, Gabriel. "Intra-Socratic Polemics: The Symposia of Plato and Xenophon." *Greek, Roman, and Byzantine Studies* 45 (2005): 331–357.

Davidson, John. "Homer and Sophocles' Philoctetes." *Bulletin of the Institute of Classical Studies* 40, supplement 66 (1995): 25–35.

Davies, W. D., and Dale C. Allison Jr. *Matthew 1–7.* Vol. 1. T&T Clark, 2004.

Dawson, David. *Allegorical Readers and Cultural Revision in Ancient Alexandria.* University of California Press, 1991.

Dickey, Eleanor. *Ancient Greek Scholarship: A Guide to Finding, Reading, and Understanding Scholia, Commentaries, Lexica, and Grammatical*

Treatises, from Their Beginnings to the Byzantine Period. Annotated edition. Oxford University Press, 2007.

Dindorf, Wilhelm. *Scholia Graeca in Euripidis tragoedias.* Vol. 1. Oxford: Typ. Acad., 1863.

Dindorf, Wilhelm. *Scholia Graeca in Euripidis tragoedias.* Vol. 2. Oxford: Typ. Acad., 1863.

Domaradzki, Mikolaj. "Stoic Allegoresis: The Problem of Definition and Influence," *Classical Philology* 117, no. 1 (2022): 139–162.

Doole, J. Andrew. *What Was Mark for Matthew? An Examination of Matthew's Relationship and Attitude to His Primary Source.* Mohr Siebeck, 2013.

Dorandi, Tiziano, ed. *Diogenes Laertius: Lives of Eminent Philosophers.* Cambridge Classical Texts and Commentaries. Cambridge University Press, 2013.

Durantaye, Katharina de la. "The Origins of the Protection of Literary Authorship in Ancient Rome." *Boston University International Law Journal* 25, no. 37 (2008): 37–111.

Edwards, M. J. "On the Platonic Schooling of Justin Martyr." *Journal of Theological Studies* 42, no. 1 (1991): 17–34.

Ehrman, Bart D., and Zlatko Pleše, eds. *The Apocryphal Gospels: Texts and Translations.* Oxford University Press, 2011.

Elder, Nicholas A. *Gospel Media: Reading, Writing, and Circulating Jesus Traditions.* Eerdmans, 2024.

Erbse, Hartmut. *Scholia Graeca in Homeri Iliadem (Scholia vetera).* Vol. 1: *Praefationem et scholia ad libros A—D continens.* De Gruyter, 1969.

Erbse, Hartmut. *Scholia Graeca in Homeri Iliadem (Scholia vetera).* Vol. 2: *Scholia ad libros E—I continens.* De Gruyter, 1971.

Erbse, Hartmut. *Scholia Graeca in Homeri Iliadem (Scholia vetera).* Vol. 3: *Scholia ad libros K—Z continens.* De Gruyter, 1974.

Erbse, Hartmut. *Scholia Graeca in Homeri Iliadem (Scholia vetera).* Vol. 5: *Scholia ad libros Y—O continens.* De Gruyter, 1977.

Farrell, John. *The Varieties of Authorial Intention: Literary Theory Beyond the Intentional Fallacy.* Palgrave Macmillan, 2017.

Ferguson, Everett. "Functions of the Rule of Faith." In *The Rule of Faith: A Guide.* Cascade Books, 2015.

Fialová, Radka. "'Scripture' and the 'Memoirs of the Apostles': Justin Martyr and His Bible." In *The Process of Authority: The Dynamics in Transmission and Reception of Canonical Texts,* edited by Jan Roskovec and Jan Dušek. De Gruyter, 2016.

Foster, Paul. "Are There Any Early Fragments of the So-Called Gospel of Peter?" *New Testament Studies* 52, no. 1 (2005): 1.

Furlong, Dean. "Theodore of Mopsuestia: New Evidence for the Proposed Papian Fragment in Hist. Eccl. 3.24.5–13." *Journal for the Study of the New Testament* 39, no. 2 (2016): 209–229.

Gaines, Robert N. "Cicero, Philodemus, and the Development of Late Hellenistic Rhetorical Theory." In *Philodemus and the New Testament World*, edited by John T. Fitzgerald, Dirk Obbink, and Glenn Stanfield Holland. Brill, 2004.

Gaki, Maria. "Euphony in Theory and Practice: Sweet Sound in Composition." PhD diss., University of Cincinnati, 2022.

Gathercole, Simon. *The Composition of the Gospel of Thomas: Original Language and Influences.* Society for New Testament Studies Monograph Series 151. Cambridge University Press, 2012.

Gathercole, Simon James. *The Gospel of Thomas: Introduction and Commentary.* Brill, 2014.

Geiger, Joseph. *Cornelius Nepos and Ancient Political Biography.* Steiner, 1985.

Gifford, Edwin Hamilton. *Eusebius, Evangelicae Praeparationis Libri XV Ad Codices Manuscriptos.* Vol. 1. Academic Press, 1903.

Goodacre, Mark. *The Synoptic Problem: A Way Through the Maze.* Bloomsbury T&T Clark, 2004.

Goodacre, Mark. *Thomas and the Gospels: The Case for Thomas's Familiarity with the Synoptics.* Eerdmans, 2012.

Goodacre, Mark. "The Protoevangelium of James and the Creative Rewriting of Matthew and Luke." In *Connecting Gospels: Beyond the Canonical/Non-Canonical Divide*, edited by Francis Watson and Sarah Parkhouse. Oxford University Press, 2018.

Goulder, Michael D. *Luke: A New Paradigm.* Journal for the Study of the New Testament Supplement Series 20. Sheffield Academic Press, 1989.

Grady, Constance. "Why The Once and Future King Is Still the Best King Arthur Story Out There." *Vox*, May 18, 2017. https://www.vox.com/culture/2017/5/18/15649214/once-and-future-king-th-white-king-arthur.

Grafton, Anthony. *Christianity and the Transformation of the Book: Origen, Eusebius, and the Library of Caesarea.* Illustrated edition. Belknap Press of Harvard University Press, 2008.

Grant, Robert M. "Irenaeus and Hellenistic Culture." *Harvard Theological Review* 42, no. 1 (1949): 41–51.

Grant, Robert M. *Irenaeus of Lyons.* Routledge, 1997.

Gregory, Andrew. *The Gospel According to the Hebrews and the Gospel of the Ebionites.* Oxford Early Christian Gospel Texts. Oxford University Press, 2017.

Guerrier, Louis, and Sylvain Grébaut. *Le Testament en Galilée de Notre-Seigneur Jésus-Christ: Texte éthiopien, édité et traduit en français.* Patrologia Orientalis 9. Edited by René Graffin and François Nau. Firmin-Didot, 1913.

Guignard, Christophe. "The Original Language of the Muratorian Fragment." *Journal of Theological Studies* 66, no. 2 (2015): 596–624.

Guignard, Christophe. "The Muratorian Fragment as a Late Antique Fake?" *Revue des Sciences Religieuses* 93, no. 1–2 (2019): 73–90.

Hahneman, Geoffrey Mark. *The Muratorian Fragment and the Development of the Canon.* Clarendon Press, 1992.

Halliwell, Stephen, W. Hamilton Fyfe, Doreen C. Innes, W. Rhys Roberts, and Donald A. Russell, trans. *Aristotle: Poetics. Longinus: On the Sublime. Demetrius: On Style.* Loeb Classical Library 199. Harvard University Press, 1995.

Hankinson, R. J. *The Sceptics.* Psychology Press, 1998.

Harris, Brendan. "Irenaeus's Engagement with Rhetorical Theory in His Exegesis of the Johannine Prologue in *Adversus Haereses* 1.8.5–1.9.3." *Vigiliae Christianae* 72, no. 4 (2018): 405–420.

Harris, J. Rendel (James Rendel). "Presbyter Gaius and the Fourth Gospel." In *Hermas in Arcadia, and Other Essays.* Cambridge, UK: Cambridge University Press, 1896.

Hays, Christopher M. "Marcion vs. Luke: A Response to the Plädoyer of Matthias Klinghardt." *Zeitschrift für die Neutestamentliche Wissenschaft und die Kunde der älteren Kirche* 99, no. 2 (2008): 213–232.

Heard, Richard. "The 'Apomnemoneumata' in Papias, Justin, and Irenaeus." *New Testament Studies* 1 (1954): 122–129.

Heath, J. M. F. *Clement of Alexandria and the Shaping of Christian Literary Practice: Miscellany and the Transformation of Greco-Roman Writing.* Cambridge University Press, 2020.

Heath, Malcolm. "Dionysius of Halicarnassus *On Imitation.*" *Hermes* 117 (1989): 370–373.

Heikel, Ivar A. *Die Demonstratio Evangelica.* Vol. 6. Die griechischen christlichen Schriftsteller der ersten Jahrhunderte 23. De Gruyter, 1913.

Henderson, Timothy P. *The Gospel of Peter and Early Christian Apologetics: Rewriting the Story of Jesus' Death, Burial, and Resurrection.* Mohr Siebeck, 2011.

Hengel, Martin. *The Four Gospels and the One Gospel of Jesus Christ.* Trinity Press International, 2000.

Henne, Philippe. "La Datation Du 'Canon' De Muratori." *Revue Biblique* 100, no. 1 (1993): 54–75.

Henry, René. *Photius Bibliothèque Tome III (Codices 186–222).* Société Les Belles Lettres, 1962.

Hill, Charles E. "What Papias Said About John (and Luke): A 'New' Papian Fragment." *Journal of Theological Studies* 49, no. 2 (1998): 582–629.

Hill, Charles E. *Gaius of Rome and the Johannine Controversy.* Oxford University Press, 2004.

Hill, Charles E. *The Johannine Corpus in the Early Church.* Oxford University Press, 2006.

Hill, Charles E. "Cerinthus, Gnostic or Chiliast? A New Solution to an Old Problem." *Journal of Early Christian Studies* 8, no. 2 (2000): 135–172.

Hock, Ronald F. *The Chreia in Ancient Rhetoric.* Vol. 1: *The Progymnasmata.* Sanderson Books, 1986.

Hock, Ronald F. *The Infancy Gospels of James and Thomas: With Introduction, Notes, and Original Text Featuring the New Scholars Version Translation.* Polebridge Press, 1996.

Holl, Karl. *Epiphanius III Panarion Haer. 65–80 De Fide.* Akademie-Verlag, 1985.

Holl, Karl. *Epiphanius I Ancoratus und Panarion haer. 1–33.* De Gruyter, 2013.

Holl, Karl, and Jurgen Dummer. *Epiphanius II Panarion haer. 34–64.* Vol. 2. Die griechischen christlichen Schriftsteller der ersten drei Jahrhunderte 8. Akademie-Verlag, 1980.

Holmes, Michael W. *The Apostolic Fathers: Greek Texts and English Translations.* Apostolic Fathers (Early Christian Collection). Baker Academic, 2007.

Holwerda, D. "Zur szenisch-technischen Bedeutung des Wortes 'υποθεσις.'" In *Miscellanea Tragica in Honorem J.C. Kamerbeek.* Hakkert, 1976.

Howard, George. *The Teaching of Addai.* Society of Biblical Literature, 1981.

Jackson, Howard M. "Ancient Self-Referential Conventions and Their Implications for the Authorship and Integrity of the Gospel of John." *Journal of Theological Studies* 50, no. 1 (1999): 1–34.

Jacobs, Andrew. *Epiphanius of Cyprus: A Cultural Biography of Late Antiquity.* Christianity in Late Antiquity 2. University of California Press, 2016.

Jacobs, Andrew S. "Epiphanius of Salamis and the Antiquarian's Bible." *Journal of Early Christian Studies* 21, no. 3 (2013): 437–464. https://doi.org/10.1353/earl.2013.0026.

Janko, Richard. *Philodemus: On Poems, Book 1.* Oxford University Press, 2003.

Janko, Richard. *Philodemus: On Poems, Book 2: With the Fragments of Heracleodorus and Pausimachus.* Philodemus Translation Series. Oxford University Press, 2020.

Johnson, Aaron P. *Eusebius*. I. B. Tauris, 2014.

Jones, C. P. "Cicero's 'Cato.'" *Rheinisches Museum für Philologie* 113, no. 2/3 (1970): 188–196.

Kassel, R. "Hypothesis." In *ΣΧΟΛΙΑ: Studia Ad Criticam Interpretationemque Textuum Graecorum et Ad Historiam Iuris Graeco-Romani Pertinentia Viro Doctissimo D. Holwerda Oblata*. Edited by W. J. Aerts et al. E. Forsten, 1985.

Keith, Chris. *The Gospel as Manuscript: An Early History of the Jesus Tradition as Material Artifact*. Oxford University Press, 2020.

Kennedy, George Alexander. *Progymnasmata: Greek Textbooks of Prose Composition and Rhetoric*. Leiden, 2003.

Kingsbury, Jack Dean. *Matthew: Structure, Christology, Kingdom*. Augsburg Fortress Publishers, 1991.

Kinkade, Clinton Douglas. "Sophocles' Ancient Readers: The Role of Scholarship on the Reception of Greek Tragedy." PhD diss., Duke University, 2021.

Klijn, A. F. J., and G. J. Reinink. *Patristic Evidence for Jewish-Christian Sects*. Brill, 1973.

Klinghardt, Matthias. *Das älteste Evangelium und die Entstehung der kanonischen Evangelien Band I: Untersuchung*. Francke A. Verlag, 2015.

Kok, Michael. "The Gospel of the Ebionites and the Synoptic Problem." *Catholic Biblical Quarterly* 86, no. 2 (2024): 300–325.

Kraus, Thomas J., and Thomas Nicklas. *Das Petrusevangelium und die Petrusapokalypse: Die griechischen Fragmente mit deutscher und englischer Übersetzung (Neutestamentliche Apokryphen I)*. De Gruyter, 2011.

Kugel, James L. *The Bible As It Was*. Belknap Press of Harvard University Press, 1999.

Laing, Kenneth. *Irenaeus, the Scriptures, and the Apostolic Writings: Re-Evaluating the Status of the New Testament Writings at the End of the Second Century*. The Library of New Testament Studies 659. T&T Clark, 2022.

Larsen, Mathew. "Accidental Publication, Unfinished Texts and the Traditional Goals of New Testament Textual Criticism." *Journal for the Study of the New Testament* 39, no. 4 (2017), 362–387.

Larsen, Matthew. *Gospels Before the Book*. Oxford University Press, 2018.

Lefteratou, Anna. *The Homeric Centos: Homer and the Bible Interwoven*. Oxford Studies in Late Antiquity. Oxford University Press, 2023.

Lindenlaub, Julia D. "The Gospel of John as Model for Literate Authors and Their Texts in Epistula Apostolorum and Apocryphon of James (NHC I,2)." *Journal for the Study of the New Testament* 43, no. 1 (2020): 3–27.

Lührmann, Dieter. "P.Oxy. 4009: Ein Neues Fragment Des Petrusevangeliums?" *Novum Testamentum* 35, no. 4 (1993): 390–410.

Lührmann, Dieter, and P. J. Parsons. "4009. Gospel of Peter?" In *The Oxyrhynchus Papyri*. Egypt Exploration Fund, 1994.

Manor, T. Scott. "Papias, Origen, and Eusebius: The Criticisms and Defense of the Gospel of John." *Vigiliae Christianae* 67, no. 1 (2013): 1–21.

Manor, T. Scott. *Epiphanius' Alogi and the Johannine Controversy: A Reassessment of Early Ecclesial Opposition to the Johannine Corpus*. Brill, 2016.

Mansfield, Jaap. *Prolegomena: Questions to Be Settled Before the Study of an Author, or a Text*. Philosophia Antiqua 61. E.J. Brill, 1994.

Marcovich, Miroslav, ed. *Origenes Contra Celsum: Libri VIII*. Supplements to Vigiliae Christianae 54. Brill, 2001.

Marcus, Joel. *Mark 1–8: A New Translation with Introduction and Commentary*. Vol. 27 of *The Anchor Bible*. Doubleday, 1999.

Markschies, Christoph. *Valentinus Gnosticus?: Untersuchungen zur valentinianischen Gnosis; mit einem Kommentar zu den Fragmenten Valentins*. Wissenschaftliche Untersuchungen zum Neuen Testament 65. Mohr, 1992.

Mattila, Sharon Lea. "A Question Too Often Neglected." *New Testament Studies* 41, no. 2 (1995): 199–217.

McOsker, Michael. *The Good Poem According to Philodemus*. Oxford University Press, 2021.

Meijering, Roos. *Literary and Rhetorical Theories in Greek Scholia*. E. Forsten, 1987.

Mette, Hans Joachim. *Die Fragmente Der Tragödien Des Aischylos*. Akademie-Verlag, 1959.

Metzger, Bruce. *A Textual Commentary on the Greek New Testament*. 3rd ed. United Bible Societies, 1971.

Miller, Carolyn R. "Genre as Social Action." *Quarterly Journal of Speech* 70, no. 2 (1984): 151–167.

Mills, Ian N. "Pagan Readers of Christian Scripture: The Role of Books in Early Autobiographical Conversion Narratives." *Vigiliae Christianae* 73, no. 5 (2019): 481–506.

Mills, Ian N. "Rewriting the Gospel: The Synoptics Among Pluriform Literary Traditions." PhD diss., Duke University, 2021.

Mills, Ian N. "John's Jesus in Tatian's Diatessaron and the Muratorian Fragment." In *John, Jesus, and History*, vol. 4, *Jesus Remembered in the Johannine Situation*, edited by Paul Anderson, Felix Just, SJ, and Tom

Thatcher. Early Christianity and Its Literature 34. Society of Biblical Literature, 2024.

Minns, Denis, and Paul Parvis, eds. *Justin, Philosopher and Martyr: Apologies*. Oxford University Press, 2009.

Mirhady, D. C. "Dicaearchus of Messana. The Sources, Text and Translation." In *Dicaearchus of Messana. Text, Translation, and Discussion*, edited by W. W. Fortenbaugh and E. Schütrumpf. Rutgers University Studies in Classical Humanities 10. Routledge, 2018.

Moi, Toril. *Revolution of the Ordinary: Literary Studies after Wittgenstein, Austin, and Cavell*. University of Chicago Press, 2018.

Monfrinotti, Matteo, and Instituto Patristico Augustinianum. "Quis dives salvetur? Ricezione Ed Esegesi Di Mc. 10,17-31." *Augustinianum* 53, no. 2 (2013): 305–335.

Monier, Mina. "Mark's Endings in Context: Paratexts and Codicological Remarks." *Religions* 13, no. 6 (2022), 3–6.

Montanari, Franco. "Zenodotus, Aristarchus, and the Ekdosis of Homer." In *Editing Texts = Texte Edieren*, edited by Glenn W. Most. Aporemata 2. Vandenhoeck & Ruprecht, 1998.

Moreschini, Claudio, and René Braun, eds. *Tertullien Contre Marcion Tome IV*. Sources Chrétiennes 456. Éditions du Cerf, 2001.

Moss, Candida. "Fashioning Mark: Early Christian Discussions about the Scribe and Status of the Second Gospel." *New Testament Studies* 67, no. 2 (2021): 181–204.

Moss, Candida. *God's Ghostwriters: Enslaved Christians and the Making of the Bible*. Little, Brown, 2024.

Munck, Johannes. "Evangelium Veritatis and Greek Usages as to Book Titles." *Studia Theologica* 17, no. 2 (1963): 133–138.

Myllykoski, Matti. "Tears of Repentance or Tears of Gratitude? P.Oxy. 4009, the Gospel of Peter and the Western Text of Luke 7.45–49." *New Testament Studies* 55, no. 3 (2009): 380–389.

Myllykoski, Matti. "The Sinful Woman in the Gospel of Peter: Reconstructing the Other Side of P.Oxy. 4009." *New Testament Studies* 55, no. 1 (2009): 104–115.

Nestle, Eberhard, Erwin Nestle, Barbara Aland, et al. *Novum Testamentum Graece*. 28th ed. Deutsche Bibelgesellschaft, 2012.

Neuschäfer, Bernhardt. *Origenes Als Philologe* 2 vols. Friedrich Reinhardt, 1987.

Nickau, Klaus. *Untersuchungen zur textkritischen Methode des Zenodotos von Ephesos*. De Gruyter, 1977.

Niehoff, Maren. "Why Compare Homer's Readers to Biblical Readers?" In *Homer and the Bible in the Eyes of Ancient Interpreters*. Brill, 2012.

Niehoff, Maren R. "A Jewish Critique of Christianity from Second-Century Alexandria: Revisiting the Jew Mentioned in Contra Celsum." *Journal of Early Christian Studies* 21, no. 2 (2013): 151–175.

Norelli, E. *Papia Di Hierapolis: Esposizione Degli Oracoli Del Signore: I Fragmenti*. Paoline, 2005.

Norris, Richard A. "Theology and Language in Irenaeus of Lyon." *Anglican Theological Review* 76, no. 3 (1994): 285–295.

North, Wendy E. S. *What John Knew and What John Wrote: A Study in John and the Synoptics*. Rowman & Littlefield, 2020.

Nünlist, René. "Narratological Concepts in Greek Scholia." In *Narratology and Interpretation*, edited by Jonas Grethlein and Antonios Rengakos. De Gruyter, 2009.

Nünlist, René. *The Ancient Critic at Work: Terms and Concepts of Literary Criticism in Greek Scholia*. Cambridge University Press, 2009.

Nutton, Vivian. *Galen: A Thinking Doctor in Imperial Rome*. Routledge, 2020.

Oldfather, C. H., trans. *Diodorus Siculus, Library of History, Volume 1*. Loeb Classical Library 279. Harvard University Press, 1933.

O'Loughlin, Thomas. "The Protevangelium Iacobi: A Case of Gospel Harmonization." Edited by Markus Vinzent. *Studia Patristica* 55 (2014): 165–173.

Olson, S. Douglas. "Politics and the Lost Euripidean Philoctetes." *Hesperia: Journal of the American School of Classical Studies at Athens* 60, no. 2 (1991): 269–283.

Olson, S. Douglas. *Athenaeus. The Learned Banqueters*, vol. 5, *Books 10.420e-11*. Loeb Classical Library 274. Harvard University Press, 2009.

Olson, S. Douglas. *Fragementa Comica. Antiphanes Frr. 101–192*. Fragmenta Comica 19.2. Verlag Antike, 2022.

Osborn, Eric. *Clement of Alexandria*. Cambridge University Press, 2008.

Oxford Society of Historical Theology. *The New Testament in the Apostolic Fathers*. Clarendon Press, 1905.

Papageorgius, Petrus N. *Scholia in Sophoclis Tragoedias Vetera*. Leipzig: Teubner, 1888.

Parker, D. C. *The Living Text of the Gospels*. Cambridge University Press, 1997.

Perrin, Nicholas and Christopher Skinner. "Recent Trends in Gospel of Thomas Research (1989–2011). Part 2: Genre, Theology and Relationship to the Gospel of John." *Currents in Biblical Research* 11, no. 1 (2012), 65–86.

Perrin, Norman. *What Is Redaction Criticism?* Fortress Press, 1969.

Pfeiffer, Rudolf. *History of Classical Scholarship from the Beginnings to the End of the Hellenistic Age*. Clarendon Press, 1968.

Pietrobelli, Antoine, ed. *Galien, Oeuvres: Tome IX, 1re Partie: Commentaire Au Regime Des Maladies Aigues d'Hippocrate: Livre I*. Les Belles Lettres, 2019.

Plátová, Jana. "How Many Fragments of the Hypotyposes by Clement of Alexandria Do We Have?" *Studia Theologica* 18 (2016): 1–17.

Plátová, Jana. "The Text of Mark 10:29–30 in Quis Dives Salvetur? By Clement of Alexandria." In *The Process of Authority: The Dynamics in Transmission and Reception of Canonical Texts*, edited by Jan Dušek. Deuterocanonical and Cognate Literature Studies 27. De Gruyter, 2016.

Plátová, Jana. "Clement of Alexandria's Homily 'Quis Dives Salvetur?' And Its Pastoral Challenges for Alexandrian Christians." *Vox Patrum* 85 (2023): 7–22.

Plisch, Uwe-karsten. *The Gospel of Thomas: Original Text with Commentary*. Translated by Gesine Schenke Robinson. Bilingual edition. Hendrickson, 2009.

Pontani, Filippomaria. *Scholia Graeca in Odysseam*, vol. 2, *Scholia ad libros γ-δ*. Edizioni di Storia e Letteratura, 2010.

Press, Gerald A. "History as Literary Genre: The Hellenistic Age." In *The Development of the Idea of History in Antiquity*. McGill-Queen's Studies in the History of Ideas 2. McGill-Queen's University Press, 1982.

Race, William H. *Menander Rhetor. Dionysius of Halicarnassus, Ars Rhetorica*. LCL 539. Edited by Jeffrey Henderson. Harvard University Press, 2019.

Radt, Stefan. *Strabons Geographika Band 1*. Vandenhoeck & Ruprecht, 2002.

Rauer, M. *Origenes Werke*. 2nd ed. Vol. 9 of *Die Griechischen Christlichen Schriftsteller* 49 (35). Leipzig: J. C. Hinrichs, 1899.

Reed, Annette Y. "EUAGGELION: Orality, Textuality, and the Christian Truth in Irenaeus' Adversus Haereses." *Vigiliae Christianae* 56, no. 1 (2002): 11–46.

Reynders, D. B. "La polémique de saint Irénée Méthode et principes," *Recherches de théologie ancienne et médiévale* 7 (1935): 5–27.

Richardson, N. J. "Literary Criticism in the Exegetical Scholia to the Iliad: A Sketch." *Classical Quarterly* 30, no. 2 (1980): 265–287.

Robinson, Richard. *Definition*. Oxford University Press, 1963.

Rolfe, J. C., trans. *Gellius, Attic Nights*, vol. 3, *Books 14–20*. Loeb Classical Library 212. Harvard University Press, 1927.

Roth, Dieter. "Review of Marcion and the Dating of the Synoptic Gospels. By Markus Vinzent." *Studia Patristica* Supplement 2 (2014): 800–803.

Roth, Dieter T. *The Text of Marcion's Gospel.* New Testament Tools, Studies and Documents 49. Edited by Bart D. Ehrman and Eldon J. Epp. Brill, 2015.

Rothschild, Clare K. "The Muratorian Fragment as Roman Fake." *Novum Testamentum* 60, no. 1 (2018): 55–82.

Rothschild, Clare K. *The Muratorian Fragment: Text, Translation, Commentary.* Mohr Siebeck, 2022.

Rousseau, Adelin, and Louis Doutreleau, eds. *Irénée de Lyon: Contre les hérésies, Livre 1*, vol. 2. Sources chrétiennes 264. Éditions du Cerf, 1979.

Rousseau, Adelin, and Louis Doutreleau, eds. *Irénée de Lyon: Contre les hérésies, Livre 2*, vol. 2. Sources chrétiennes 294. Éditions du Cerf, 1982.

Rousseau, Adelin, and Louis Doutreleau, eds. *Irénée de Lyon: Contre les hérésies, Livre 3*, vol. 2. Sources chrétiennes 211. Éditions du Cerf, 1974.

Russell, D. A., and David Konstan. *Heraclitus: Homeric Problems.* Writings from the Greco-Roman World 14. Society of Biblical Literature, 2005.

Russell, Donald A. *Quintilian. The Orator's Education*, vol. 1, *Books 1–2.* Loeb Classical Library 124. Edited by Jeffrey Henderson. Harvard University Press, 2002.

Russell, Donald A. *Quintilian. The Orator's Education*, vol. 2, *Books 3–5.* Loeb Classical Library 125. Harvard University Press, 2002.

Santamaría, Marco Antonio. "Our Co(s)Mic Origins: Theogonies in Greek Comedy." *Archiv für Religionswissenschaft* 21–22, no. 1 (2020): 369–386.

Schepens, Guido. "Zum Verhältnis von Biographie und Geschichtsschreibung in hellenistischer Zeit." In *Die griechische Biographie in hellenistischer Zeit.* De Gruyter, 2012.

Schironi, Francesca. *The Best of the Grammarians: Aristarchus of Samothrace on the Iliad.* University of Michigan Press, 2018.

Schmidt, T. C. "Canon of Hippolytus." *Brill Encyclopedia of Early Christianity Online.*

Schmidt, Thomas. *The Book of Revelation and Its Eastern Commentators: Making the New Testament in the Early Christian World.* Cambridge University Press, 2021.

Schmidt, Wilhelm. *Herons von Alexandria Druckwerke und Automatentheater.* Leipzig: Teubner, 1899.

Schnebele, Andreas. "Die epischen Quellen des Sophokleischen Philoktet: die Postiliaca im frühgriechischen Epos" PhD diss., Universität Tübingen, 1988.

Schoedel, Tam R. "Philosophy and Rhetoric in the Adversus Haereses of Irenaeus." *Vigiliae Christianae* 13, no. 1 (1959): 22–32.

Schwartz, Eduard. *Scholia in Euripidem.* Vol. 2. Berolini: G. Reimer, 1887.

Schwartz, Eduard. "Über den Tod der Söhne Zebedaei. Ein Beitrag zur Geschichte des Johannesevangeliums." In *Zum Neuen Testament und zum frühen Christentum*. De Gruyter, 1963.

Scully, Stephen. *Hesiod's Theogony: From Near Eastern Creation Myths to Paradise Lost*. Oxford University Press, 2015.

Sellew, Melissa. "Achilles or Christ? Porphyry and Didymus in Debate over Allegorical Interpretation." *Harvard Theological Review* 82, no. 1 (1989): 79–100.

Shils, Edward. "Tradition." *Comparative Studies in Society and History* 13, no. 2 (1971): 122–159.

Skeat, T. C. "Irenaeus and the Four-Gospel Canon." *Novum Testamentum* 34, no. 2 (1992): 194–199.

Smith, Geoffrey S. *Guilt by Association*. Oxford University Press, 2015.

Smith, Geoffrey S. *Valentinian Christianity: Texts and Translations*. University of California Press, 2020.

Spengel, Leonhard von. *Rhetores Graeci*. Vol. 2. Lipsiae: B.G. Teubneri, 1854.

Squire, Daniel. "An Edition and Translation of the Scholia to Sophocles Antigone 1–581, with Commentary on the Scholia Vetera." PhD diss., University of California, Berkeley, 2022.

Stählin, O., L. Früchtel, Carlo Nardi, and Patrick Descourtieux. *Clément d'Alexandrie Quel riche sera sauvé?* Sources Chrétiennes 537. Les Éditions du Cerf, 2011.

Stanton, Graham. *Jesus and Gospel*. Cambridge University Press, 2004.

Starr, Raymond J. "The Circulation of Literary Texts in the Roman World." *Classical Quarterly* 37, no. 1 (1987): 213–223.

Stevens, Luke J. "The Evangelists in Clement's Hypotyposes." *Journal of Early Christian Studies* 26, no. 3 (2018): 353–379.

Stewart-Sykes, Alistair. "*Τάξει* in Papias: Again." *Journal of Early Christian Studies* 3, no. 4 (1995): 487–492.

Struck, Peter. *Birth of the Symbol: Ancient Readers at the Limits of Their Texts*. Princeton University Press, 2014.

Sundberg, Albert C. "Canon Muratori: A Fourth-Century List." *Harvard Theological Review* 66, no. 1 (1973): 1–41.

Talbert, Charles. *What Is a Gospel? The Genre of the Canonical Gospels*. Fortress Press, 1977.

Thackeray, H. St. J., trans. *Josephus, The Life; Against Apion*. Loeb Classical Library 186. Harvard University Press, 1926.

Thesleff, Holger. "The Interrelation and Date of the 'Symposia' of Plato and Xenophon." *Bulletin of the Institute of Classical Studies* 25 (1978): 157–170.

Thiel, Helmut van, ed. *Scholia D in Iliadem: secundum codices manu scriptos.* Elektronische Schriftenreihe der Universitäts- und Stadtbibliothek 7. Universitäts- und Stadtbibliothek Köln, 2006.

Thomassen, Einar. *The Spiritual Seed: The Church of the "Valentinians."* Brill, 2006.

Trimpi, Wesley. "The Ancient Hypothesis of Fiction: An Essay on the Origins of Literary Theory." *Traditio* 27 (1971): 1–78.

Usher, Stephen. *Dionysius of Halicarnassus. Critical Essays, Volume II: On Literary Composition. Dinarchus. Letters to Ammaeus and Pompeius.* Loeb Classical Library 466. Harvard University Press, 1985.

Verhasselt, Gertjan. "The Hypotheses of Euripides and Sophocles by Dicaearchus." *Greek, Roman, and Byzantine Studies* 55 (2015): 608–636.

Verheyden, Joseph. "The Canon Muratori: A Matter of Dispute." In *The Biblical Canons*, edited by J.-M. Auwers and H. J. de Jonge. Bibliotheca Ephemeridum Theologicarum Lovaniensium 163. Leuven University Press, 2003.

Vinzent, Markus. *Marcion and the Dating of the Synoptic Gospels.* Peeters Publishers, 2014.

Vuong, Lily C. *The Protevangelium of James.* Annotated edition. Cascade Books, 2019.

Walsh, Robyn Faith. *The Origins of Early Christian Literature: Contextualizing the New Testament Within Greco-Roman Literary Culture.* Cambridge University Press, 2021.

Ward, H. Clifton. *Clement and Scriptural Exegesis: The Making of a Commentarial Theologian.* Oxford University Press, 2022.

Watson, Francis. *Gospel Writing: A Canonical Perspective.* Eerdmans, 2013.

Watson, Francis. "How Did Mark Survive?" In *Matthew and Mark Across Perspectives*, edited by K. A. Bendoraitis and N. K. Gupta. Bloomsbury T&T Clark, 2016.

Watson, Francis. "A Gospel of the Eleven: The Epistula Apostolorum and the Johannine Tradition." In *Connecting Gospels: Beyond the Canonical/Non-Canonical Divide*, edited by Francis Watson. Oxford University Press, 2018.

Watson, Francis. "Harmony or Gospel? On the Genre of the (So-Called) Diatessaron." In *The Gospel of Tatian: Exploring the Nature and Text of the Diatessaron*, edited by Matthew Crawford and Nicholas Zola. T&T Clark, 2019.

Watson, Francis. *An Apostolic Gospel: The "Epistula Apostolorum" in Literary Context.* Cambridge University Press, 2020.

West, Martin L. "Zenodotus' Text." In *Studies in the Text and Transmission of the Iliad*. K.G. Saur, 2001.

Whitmarsh, Tim. "The Greek Novel: Titles and Genre." *American Journal of Philology* 126, no. 4 (2005): 587–611.

Wilken, R. L. "The Homeric Cento in Irenaeus, 'Adversus Haereses' I, 9,4." *Vigiliae Christianae* 21 (1967): 25–33.

Williams, Frank. *The Panarion of Epiphanius of Salamis: Book I*. SBL Press, 2016.

Williams, Michael Allen. *Rethinking "Gnosticism": An Argument for Dismantling a Dubious Category*. Princeton University Press, 1999.

Wilshire, Leland Edward. "Was Canonical Luke Written in the Second Century?—A Continuing Discussion." *New Testament Studies* 20, no. 3 (1974): 246–253.

Wilson, Nigel G. *Aelian. Historical Miscellany*. Loeb Classical Library 486. Harvard University Press, 1997.

Wolska-Conus, Wanda. *Cosma Indicopleusta Topographie Chretienne*. Vol. 2. Sources Chrétiennes 159. Les Éditions du Cerf, 1970.

Wright, Wilmer Cave France. *Philostratus and Eunapius: The Lives of the Sophists*. Putnam; 1922.

Wucherpfennig, Ansgar. *Heracleon Philologus: Gnostische Johannesexegese im zweiten Jahrhundert*. Mohr Siebeck, 2002.

Xenis, Georgios. *Scholia Vetera in Sophoclis "Electram."* De Gruyter, 2010.

Young, Frances. *Art of Performance: Towards a Theology of Holy Scripture*. Darton, Longman & Todd, 1990.

Young, Frances M. *Biblical Exegesis and the Formation of Christian Culture*. Baker Academic, 2002.

Zahn, Theodor. *Das Evangelium des Matthäus*. Deichert, 1922.

Zervos, George T. "Dating the 'Protevangelium of James': The Justin Martyr Connection." *Society of Biblical Literature 1994 Seminar Papers* 33 (1994): 415–434.

Zervos, George T., and James H. Charlesworth. *The Protevangelium of James: Greek Text, English Translation, Critical Introduction: Volume 1*. Bilingual edition. T&T Clark, 2019.

Zola, Nicholas. "Evangelizing Tatian: The Diatessaron's Place in the Emergence of the Fourfold Gospel Canon." *Perspectives in Religious Studies* 43 (2016): 399–414.

SUBJECT INDEX

INDEX OF MODERN AUTHORS

SCRIPTURE INDEX

INDEX OF ANCIENT SOURCES